THE TRAGIC FLAW

By dhtreichler

Chapter One

The explosion pierced the night-time quiet with a white-light ball of fire rising. It was followed after an all too brief silence with a clap of thunder. No one noticed the pencil thin trail of light. No one heard the sudden whoosh drop from the sky just before the Googlecar garage was destroyed in the ensuing fire. Why would anyone want to destroy an LA area repair facility for autonomous drive automobiles? Not a single media report I saw was able to lay blame, or even explain the event – credibly. All sorts of rumors circulated. As many opinions were expressed as there were expressers. Every authority needed their fifteen seconds of fame, even if they had nothing to add. The Hamartia, if indeed responsible, must have been happy that in a world of omnipresent information, and so many experts, no one spoke their name in relation to the events.

Who are the Hamartia? At that time no one I knew had heard of them. I certainly hadn't. Not sure even to this day that I know who they are or their real objectives. But we're getting ahead of ourselves. There's much to tell before you'll be able to judge for yourself about the Hamartia. I have to admit the first time I heard their name it meant nothing to me. But society has fractured into so many groups calling themselves one thing or another that I rarely pay any attention. After all, I'm only an actor with a weekly series. I'm no one who could or would affect world events. I'm just someone people watch to relieve their boredom. I hope my audience can vicariously live a different life, if only for a few minutes each week, just as I do when we produce the show's episodes.

And really, that's why I act, or at least why I became an actor. Growing up in a small town outside Dallas imbued me with the notion I could do most anything. I was a smart kid from a lower middle class family. That meant I had to do things on my own as my family had no money to do things together. If I wanted something I had to earn the money for it. If I wanted to learn something, I had to do it on my own because my parents were both working just to pay the bills. I was a voracious reader. I lived a life far beyond that small town; but only in my head. Acting gave me an opportunity to experience the worlds I created. They really didn't exist, as I saw them in my mind's eye. The same is true of the world I create by acting. It's a notion of a world, a conception, a conceit maybe. Who am I to change the world to a different one that matches the maps in my head? And since I'm an action hero in a mystery series, my world is all about clues that reveal the intentions of bad people. I'm also someone who brings them to justice, although the legal remedy is something my audience never sees. That's the subject of another series and another company of actors.

Why would someone blow up a Googlecar repair facility? I wondered, probably because I waited at the curb for one to pick me up and deliver me to the studio in Burbank. The driverless car stopped in front of my condo.

I memorized my lines for the day in the car, as always. The script was the second installment. We shot the set up the day before and now we would solve the mystery. As I worked the lines I realized there was a major disconnect between the words I was given and what was about to happen. Lots of times the writer wants to create such a disconnect, if he wants to show the character has misjudged the situation, or to reveal what the character really feels is different from what he says. But in this case, it was neither of those situations. The dialog just made no sense. It didn't add to the depth of the scene. I hoped Mimi would take care of it, but if not I had to discuss it with the writers when I got in.

I thought on the set I had the reputation as a professional, who came ready to deliver the lines and actions called for in the script. But every once in a while I had to push back. Now my costar, Mimi, had exactly the opposite reputation. She pushed back on nearly every line, always feeling the writers had completely missed the essential make up of her character. I loved Mimi, literally on more than one occasion, but she could be a real pain in the ass on the set. She usually delayed production while she worked things out with the writers and director. I came to expect and actually count of her delays to give me more time to work out the scene in my head. I always listen to her discussions and make changes on the fly that actually improve my performances. At least I think they improve them. I guess my director, John LiBretto, thought so too as he often complimented me on the nuances I brought to the scene after listening to those discussions.

Mimi was already in deep with John and Robert Anderson, the head writer. I spotted my chair with Desmond Jensen written across the back. I took my seat to listen in. The chair with Mimi Theroux on the back was next to mine, but she was on her feet in full animation expressing her displeasure with what she thought was the obtuse portrayal given her character in the lines they asked of her.

"You never get it right. Interpol is not just some bureaucratic organization that runs data bases. Our agents are key members of the law enforcement teams solving these crimes," she explained.

"And that's how I show you. As a member of the team, not the one who solves it by yourself. You advise, nothing more. That's you're role. Now get over it, Mimi and read your damn lines." Robert was getting testy having gone down this same road every day since we began shooting.

But Mimi was never predictable in her response. "Now Robert, I know you have to make all kinds of compromises in the writer's room." It was a conciliatory tact. She hadn't used that one in a while. "My god, with the egos you have to deal with every day it's no wonder you're short tempered when you finally get to me. But still, that's no reason to shut down and not listen to the person who has to deliver your lines. It not only has to sound authentic, but it has to feel authentic. Don't you agree?"

"Yes, I agree. But that's not Samantha's role."

"But it's Samantha's character. She's never been one to limit herself to her role. Why would she change now? She's always competed with every man who thinks he's superior. She's never submitted. Look back at all those scripts you've written. When did she ever limit herself?"

John stepped between them, apparently thinking they might actually come to blows. I, for one, was convinced that Mimi would throw the first punch. And knowing Mimi, she would be going for the knock-out. "Alright children. It's time for an adult to put you back in your places. Robert, you wrote a great script as usual. Mimi, you will interpret that script. And you'll do it professionally and brilliantly, as you always do. So now it's time for us to put our arguments aside and deliver the scenes our sponsors pay us for. So, Places everyone!"

Mimi came over and gave me my 'welcome to the set' morning kiss, which lingered a little longer than usual, which meant she was aroused. Given the lines she was going to deliver, I wondered about the cause of her arousal. It wasn't the lines and it wasn't the argument with Robert. I'd need to keep that in mind when we were finished as something to explore further.

Chapter Two

The day went as most days, with multiple takes, long breaks while the crew reset the stage and moved the cameras to get different angles. John was his usual patient self, even when Mimi went off the rails and changed the dialog, not a little bit, as she always did, but the whole scene. I ad-libbed as best I could to make the scene flow, but she changed it so she solved the mystery, not me. Robert came storming onto the set to chew her out once the take was done. Curious that he waited. He usually didn't.

Mimi argued with great animation about how the scene worked so much better the way she played it. Robert argued back that she'd missed the entire point of the scene and it couldn't be used. I noticed her taught nipples through her blouse. This argument was all just foreplay for her. I remembered those taught nipples. I wondered who the lucky guy was who would bed her after we were done. I was sorry it wasn't going to be me. Then it occurred to me that she was probably sleeping with Robert. He was probably getting as much out of all this as she was. Realizing who she was with put the loss of her intimacy right in my face. I felt the hollowness I'd come to expect, only now it was so much harder than usual. I'd have to watch them more carefully to see if I was right.

Mimi stormed off the set, "That's the only take you get, you'll just have to use it," she tossed over her shoulder without looking back.

Robert and John approached me, "Do you think you can do it as a monologue?"

"Not as effective. Half the audience is watching her nipples and not mine." I offered knowing it wasn't what they wanted to hear, but I knew I was right.

Robert looked after her, probably wondering how long she would stay aroused and how much time he had before he'd miss his window of opportunity. It occurred to me I should go console her, but things had cooled between us. We hadn't been together in over a year. I didn't think she was ready to forgive and forget my unfortunate night with the gorgeous Alison Andress.

Alison had made a guest appearance on our show. When we finished shooting I invited her and Mimi out to dinner. Mimi had a cold and took a rain check. Alison and I had a great discussion at dinner and I only intended to drop her at her place afterwards, but she invited me in. When I returned to my apartment in the morning, Mimi had already moved out. She kept her own place throughout our relationship. Nothing was ever said about that night either way. Mimi only reacted, in her personal life, to what someone did, never to what that person said. Maybe she behaved that way because as an actor she knew words seldom told the audience what it really wanted to know.

"You're right." Robert must have judged that he didn't have much time left. "I'll go see if I can get her back out here."

Attaboy, Robert.

"So, John." I asked. "Can we can do the close ups since I predict Mimi is finished for today?"

John examined the shooting script. After a half hour and no Mimi or Robert, we shot the close ups and a chase scene that Mimi wasn't in. When we were done and Mimi still hadn't returned, John shut things down for the night. Tomorrow would be a very long day to finish up, since we were now behind schedule, but we'd get through it somehow.

I checked my watch, noted that it was about 4:00 pm, which meant it was about 7:00 am in Guangzhou, China. So Xian Zhe, my friend and law enforcement mentor would be up and available to take a call. Xian and I became friends when I shot a movie in China several years before.

He was the Chief of Detectives for Guangzhou, fourth largest city in China with nearly 12 million people. He served as a technical advisor for the film. We had an instant rapport and I noted something about his demeanor that fascinated me. While outwardly optimistic and enthusiastic, in rare moments an overwhelming sadness showed, only in glimpses and only obliquely. As I came to learn his story it all made perfect sense. As an actor I tried to show such rare glimpses of an underlying difference in my character. Viewers had noted it and reported it was one of the things that kept them watching, trying to learn what were the events that led to that different hidden, but glimpsed persona.

"Xian. Are you free to talk?" I began.

"Desmond. Desperate, my friend, call middle day for you."

"Its late afternoon and we're finished shooting for the day. I have a scene coming up and I'm not sure how to play it."

"Always advise, ask heart how reasonable man do and find other extreme express anger and disappointment with life."

"Such is the path of the prudent man. But as you know I've never been prudent. I'm looking for a different means of expressing the futility of seeking success. You know this better than most men. How should I play such a scene?"

"What situation?"

"My character, Rory Gallagher, has discovered the Federal Reserve Bank has been intruded by a terrorist group seeking to paralyze the US economy. The hacker has captured the entire overnight Repurchase Agreement funds flow. That has put nearly every US bank out of balance with the Federal Reserve and created chaos in the markets."

"Rory? Mean red-haired?"

"Yeah. They're dying my hair color these days. I know. Let's just drop it."

"What dilemma?"

"Rory must find the man responsible and put him in jail. End the threat. Move on."

"Realize one man not threat. Society dependent upon systems, threat. You protect systems from attacks. Disagree with producers. Only want sensationalize. Find cheap solution."

"Why do you see so clearly what my writers and producers don't?"

Xian was quiet for a long moment, then responded, "You world... sensationalize gain attention. Real world, hide. Real world not want people see it bends reality, serve own interests. Convince writer only successful road less traveled. Character go lonely road fix problem not symptom."

"How?"

"In China, government tell writer what he do. America different. You find lever. You find sponsors, producers and writers value. Convince change direction, story. Real events have occurred? Bring someone talk invested in outcome?"

Xian always made so much sense, but he always proscribed a solution that was extremely hard to effect or achieve. I knew that when I called. He confirmed what I knew to be the problem and the difficulty of the solution. But he was right, as always, and I had to follow the hard road to the right solution.

"The easy path is to do what they want. It will neither be satisfying nor result in any real world actions. Finding the right person who can change their mind is a whole different problem. At the moment I have no idea who could do that."

"Follow money."

"You mean the sponsor?"

"Or customer of sponsor. Convince expend capital your cause. Only influence real events people with you, understand stakes, willing take personal action change events."

"Sounds like you're speaking from experience."

"China very different America. But more different, more same. Tactics different, but strategy same."

I thanked Xian for his perfect insight and his willingness to take my call so early in the morning. I knew his life had changed since he retired from the police force in Guangzhou. It had not been a voluntary retirement. A new mayor had been appointed by the central government. The mayor had a close associate who wanted Xian's job. It had become high profile because of his Hollywood connections. We both knew that his successor wouldn't gain the same notoriety as Xian because he didn't have the same experience or insights from a lifetime of compromises and decisions. Xian's successor had never been a detective, never even served a police force. He was a political appointee and would fail miserably. Xian had already picked up consulting contracts to several of the major businesses in Guangzhou who wanted to protect themselves in a coming wave of lawlessness foreseen by those who understood the nature of politics in China.

As I put away my phone, Robert re-entered the stage. His disheveled look confirmed my suspicions about his relationship with Mimi. I needed to keep that in mind as I negotiated the changes I would want him to make to his scripts. I had always longed to change world events, even if only indirectly. I'd never succeeded in doing anything more than causing politicians to ask questions they may not have otherwise. I'd listened intently to the public discussions that had resulted, but had no idea how the private discussions went. In thinking back, I was convinced no change of direction had ever resulted from the most pointed suggestions made on my shows. However, I wasn't about to give up. If the means of changing world events didn't appear on Robert's pages, then I needed to find a way to put the questions out there such that politicians and world leaders couldn't ignore them. Only doing so had just become infinitely more complex, since Mimi had the upper hand in influencing Robert.

Chapter Three

About eight o'clock the Googlecar arrived to pick me up. Mimi and the dapper Alistair Wright, our agent, as we both used Alistair, were in the car. We had reservations at the Ivy for 8:30 even though it was usually impossible to get in then. Alistair prided himself in his connections. This was just another display of why Mimi and I chose him. He could get things done most agents couldn't.

As always, Alistair was on his cell phone. "I don't care about his feelings. This has nothing to do with that. It's business. The sooner he understands the sooner we get to a deal. Now I know we've been hard on him. But he hasn't delivered the audiences the studio has been paying him to deliver. It's all about demographics. Sure the old ladies still watch, but he's not picking up the kids. Without them the whole spending profile changes. He's seen his wallet share decline from three percent to two. Now I understand he wasn't big in wallet share to begin with, but the fact it has declined by thirty-three percent is alarming to the people who are trying to push their products on his show. So he's got to get a new stylist. He needs someone who can breathe fresh air into his look. You know what I mean? Younger! Yes, much younger."

Mimi air kissed me. She looked relaxed as if she'd had a great orgasm and wasn't about to let Alistair spoil her perfect mood.

"So did you win?" I asked her.

"Of course." As if the question didn't need asking.

"So we going to rename it the St. Julian Mysteries next season?" St. Julian was the last name of her character, Samantha St. Julian, Senior Investigator with Interpol.

"But of course. And I'll have Robert write you out so you can go live on a Caribbean beach somewhere."

I was afraid after our split that she might be serious. "Please don't. I need the paycheck."

"I guess I can put up with you for one more season, but only one." I knew she wasn't serious in that case. If she was willing to continue working with me in the short run, the long run wouldn't be a problem for her as she never looked at the long run. She was relaxed, probably had more than one glass of wine. I thought she was probably annoyed that she had to spend a perfectly good evening with Alistair and me rather than having another orgasm with Robert.

Alistair turned his attention to us. "Have you looked at your latest Nielsens?" He was talking about the ratings on our show. It was our show in that both of our contracts were riding on its success.

"Steady at twenty-eight percent of the audience." I noted

"Studio thinks the show can do better."

Mimi turned to Alistair. She wasn't up for renewal for another year, but my contract was up at the end of this season. Sounded like she might get her wish about retiring me to a beach somewhere. "What are they saying?"

"They threw out a prequel. 'Mister hot commodity of the moment' is like twenty-two and should have been a beach lifeguard. And he's about as smart. You know the type. And there's only about two-hundred-thousand young wannabes who want to take your spot, Mimi."

"This any different than the tactic they took last time Mimi was negotiating? What was it then? Something about wanting her to show more skin?" I asked.

"Can't tell. They might be serious this time. They signed Johnny

Hollywood to a contract. They need to figure out what to do with him now that they're paying him to go party and have a good time. I think your series is one option they have, but not the only one." Alistair answered another cell call.

Mimi looked at me and her mellowness had disappeared. "So Johnny Hollywood could be a legitimate threat to another season?"

I nodded in realization. This was not going to be an easy contract negotiation. None had been, and each season had gotten harder and harder as the studio imposed more and more requirements on me. So far I'd been able to stay one step ahead, but I never knew when they'd come up with something that would just make my continued success untenable. Alistair ended his call and looked at me curiously.

"What's wrong with twenty-eight percent? Isn't that the highest percentage?" I asked Alistair.

"It is, but amongst the wrong demographic. You need to attract the kids. They're watching reality programming opposite you. They're the ones with the discretionary income and that's who the advertisers want to capture. So far you've held your own because you've still got the top half of the desirables. But they spend less than the younger half on useless shit, you know what I mean. The problem is to get advertisers for your demographic. They aren't spending the money right now."

"And here all I thought I had to worry about was my performance. Now I have to be a god-damn marketing machine." Mimi was getting angry.

I needed to get her off the subject and back to being mellow. "Honey, you sell sex better than anyone I know. Agree to a topless scene and we'll be at a fifty share with the entire younger half of the demographic."

She lifted her breasts and smiled at me. "Amazing what these can do for a girl."

"Amazing what they do to a guy." I winked at her.

The Googlecar stopped in front of the Ivy. It was time for us to make an entrance. The ever ready Alphonso greeted us as usual and led the parade to show us off to the other guests as he escorted us to our favorite table in the back. The trick at the Ivy was if you wanted to be noticed you sat in the back. If you sat in the courtyard where everyone could see you, it was an indication you were a wannabe and not someone of consequence. Sitting in the back brought more eyes as everyone deliberately went to the rest rooms to see who was back there. It was also much harder to get a table in the back as they were always reserved for people of stature.

At the table next to us was Walter Marsden, studio head of Twenty-first Century Fox with Jaime Alonzo Randolph, studio head of Disney - Columbia. Jaime was a gorgeous actress, who proved to actually be more shrewd than beautiful. She formed her own production company. She was so successful picking winners that Disney bought her company and made her their studio head. Her dinner with Walter would start the gossip mills turning. All the media feeds would be in a frenzy.

Alistair greeted them both individually and introduced us before taking his seat across from us. Our show was produced at Lone Star studios across town, which was one of the independents.

Walter went back to the conversation they apparently were having as we approached. "The question is how'd they ever plant a bomb at the repair facility? Did someone leave a package in one of the Googlecars? Did they get past the security? How'd it happen?"

"I'm sure you'll announce a mini-series on it before I get back to the office." Jaime responded.

"No, I'm serious. Everyone is dependent on the autonomous cars. Googlecar is now the largest transportation stock on the exchange. The impact on the economy is huge. A lot of jobs are at stake. You have the production jobs where they make the cars, the maintenance jobs where they repair them, the administrative jobs billing and collecting payments. And every one of those jobs enables someone to watch what we produce. We have to take this seriously. If the transport sector falters, so do revenues."

Jaime took a sip of her white wine. I glanced at the bottle and saw it was a Torrontes from Salta in Argentina. "What are you going to do? Lower your revenue forecast by what? One or two percent?"

Walter leaned across the table. I wasn't sure if it was to get a better look at Jaime's spectacular breasts or to reveal a deep, dark secret he didn't want anyone else to hear, even though our table was right next to theirs. "I'm not doing a mini-series, but I have the news division on a story about Googlecar. We're going to do a special on it next week."

Jaime leaned back to ensure his motivation wasn't the former and hit him with: "Ours appears tomorrow night. Didn't you have anything in the can you could use?" She made it sound like Walter wasn't prepared to deliver the news, which made him dive into his scotch and water.

Mimi leaned over towards Walter, ensuring he had a direct view of her assets before asking, "Do you think anyone cares about cars? They're like electricity or cell phones or water or garbage pickup. They're always there. Why should anyone care someone blew up a repair facility? Come on. Probably some guy found out a mechanic was banging his wife and he wanted revenge. It's probably not something anyone other than the police need to worry about."

Jaime seemed more interested in Mimi's opinion than Walter, who still hadn't looked above her assets. "You make a good point. We could be blowing this whole incident out of proportion. At this point there's no telling the real cause."

Not to be outdone by Mimi I joined in, "Why are we still afraid of the dark?"

Mimi turned to me as if I were a Martian. Jaime looked at me too, but she was considering the comment more seriously than Mimi.

"A singular event. Unusual, I'll admit, and our antenna are up trying to divine the potential importance of an otherwise unimportant event. For most of our history as a nation we weren't looking over our shoulders in fear. We simply went about our business, growing our economy, building giant cities, solving unsolvable problems and enabling prosperity for ever more people."

"But what about our world leadership?" Jaime asked to blow a hole through my rosy scenario.

"Our record there is uneven, I'll admit. But I don't see anyone else stepping up and providing the moral guidance we have over the past century. We did things for moral reasons, once. But somewhere along the way we lost our moral compass. If you find it would you please return it as things have been touch and go since."

Jaime turned to me with a smile, "I didn't know you were a student of our political history. You may cause me to want to watch your show. If nothing else just to see what direction you've been able to impose on your writers."

I glanced at Mimi thinking about Robert and knowing she had a lot more influence over him at the moment than I did. "You may want to look at picking us up in syndication. If nothing else in ten years we'll be a good period piece."

"You were still driving your own car that first season, weren't you?"

"I really didn't drive it. The studio wouldn't let me for insurance reasons. It's been a decade since any man or woman drove their own car." I pointed out.

Walter finally realized he'd been left behind and joined in, "I still think it's a plot. Someone's trying to send us a message. This isn't the end of the affair. I'm sure we'll be dealing with this for a long time to come."

Jaime turned away and I felt the loss of her attention immediately. If the studio really was intending a reboot with a prequel of my series would there be another opportunity with Disney –Columbia? From what I observed of Walter, without tits, I had no chance of getting in 21st Century Fox.

Alistair decided it was time to re-engage us. With two studio heads sitting next to us, he had a chance to plant seeds and he seemed determined to do so. "Do you really think your plan could take us from twenty-eight to fifty?"

I noticed that Jaime blinked twice and resisted turning back to us, preferring to listen and not engage us.

"Absolutely." I responded.

Chapter Four

The Googlecar pulled up in front of my apartment. Mimi seemed at loose ends and a little unstable at the moment. "You want to come in?"

She nodded and I put my arm around her to guide her in. She was enjoying the effects of most of a bottle of wine on top of the several joints she'd had before dinner. Once inside my Spartan apartment, I deposited her on my couch and put on soft background music. I returned to sit beside her. She pushed me down and lay on top of me with her head on my chest as she had when we were together. I inhaled her soft soapy smell, the Obsession perfume, which was her trademark, and rubbed her head as I had done so many times before. I felt the fine texture of her hair. I was transported back to the days before Alison Andress and the rift between us. I felt the happiness I had when we were together, filling the void that had been my life for more than a year now.

"Why?" she asked.

"Does it make any difference?"

"No."

"Then why do you want to know?"

"I want to know if you know why."

I couldn't tell where she was going with this discussion. She wasn't looking for answers. She seemed scattered and not focused. "Did I make a conscious decision that I didn't want to be with you anymore? The answer is no. And the year we've been together at work and not at home has just killed me."

She patted my chest twice without opening her eyes. "I've seen that. You're sad. Are you sad about us?"

I kissed the top of her head but couldn't answer her question. She seemed to understand. We just lay together for a long time. I felt her breathing and weight upon me, reinforcing the fact that she was there after so long of not having been.

"You want to sleep with me, don't you?" she asked.

"I have no expectations."

"But you wouldn't say no if I offered."

"I've never stopped loving you."

She turned to look directly into my eyes. "Not even when you were fucking Alison?"

I held her gaze, "I didn't fuck Alison."

She started to get up, but I wouldn't let her, holding her against me. "Give me a break. You spent the night."

"Did I?" We'd not spoken of the events of that night.

"I left at dawn and you still hadn't come home." She noted.

"I got home about nine-thirty." I remember looking at the clock.

"In the morning."

"Yes."

"You made your choice." She was done with the conversation.

"I made a choice."

"You chose her over me." None of the alternatives to answer this would solve the problem.

"For that night, she needed me more than you did." I finally answered.

Mimi pulled away and sat up, running her hands through her long blonde hair, pulling her dress back into place. "You betrayed me. I simply can't trust you and I can't be with you."

"Even though you love me, and I love you?"

"Love isn't enough. I can't wonder if every starlet you meet is going to take you away from me. I can't let myself be hurt like I was when you didn't come home. I can't do that." She teared up.

"You don't have to." I offered, knowing it wouldn't make any difference, but hoping nonetheless.

She looked down at me, clearly not sure of what I was saying, but unwilling to explore the mystery I lay before her.

I wanted to tell her the events of that night, but I knew she wouldn't believe me, nor would it make any difference. So I said nothing. Mimi would come to accept me or not. At the moment it was 'or not'. While I desperately hoped things would change in the future, I didn't expect they would. I knew Mimi too well. She would have to discover the truth for herself, and not through me. Would she be curious enough to seek that truth? Tonight gave me some limited hope. She had asked a question about it. I had created some doubt of what she thought happened. It was now up to her to want to find the truth. I had done all I could.

She rose and went to the bathroom. She would leave soon and I would be left with my loneliness. As she approached the door to leave, she glanced around. "You really ought to do something with this place or move. It's depressing." And she was gone.

Chapter Five

The morning after Mimi's first visit in over a year I watched the mid-morning news. Another Googlecar repair facility had been destroyed in the night. This time it was in Chicago. The news reporter was at the scene. The fire was out but not much was left of the building in the background. "We still have no word as to the cause of the earlier destruction of a Googlecar repair center in Los Angeles recently. Some have questioned whether two such incidents is more than a coincidence. For the time being, we simply do not have enough information to know the answer to that question." The reporter seemed uneasy to me, as if he didn't agree with what he was reporting. Was I reading too much into his body language? The one thing I did know was I was usually right about body language. That made me momentarily return to Mimi's the night before. Her body language was that she longed for me as much as I did her, but she simply wasn't going to put herself into a situation where she could be hurt again.

The reporter interviewed the Chicago Chief of Police. "What can you tell us about what happened here last night?"

"You can see our forensics team is walking the scene as we speak. We have very little we can report on at the moment, but we will release a full report once our experts have gathered the facts and concluded their analysis."

"Do you think there's a link between this incident and the one in LA?" The reporter was taking us right where I wanted him to go, good job!

"I did speak to the Chief in LA and got his take on things there, but it's really too soon to know if this has any relationship whatsoever to those events."

He didn't answer the question. I was listening even more carefully now.

"Could it be something to do with the batteries in the Googlecars? I remember there were fires in Lithium Ion batteries a long time ago."

"Nothing we've found so far would point in that direction, but we haven't ruled it out either."

The Chief was finished with the interview, stepping out of frame before the reporter could ask another question. That sent my antenna even higher. Why wouldn't the Chief want to give out any more information? A lot of tension there and the Chief was clearly, in my mind, very uncomfortable talking about the incident.

But then my phone rang.

"Mister Jensen, my name is Albert Gaydos of Gaydos, Keebaugh and Mutek in Dallas, Texas. I'm the attorney for your uncle, James Jensen."

I had to get my head out of the mystery in Chicago to focus on this new mystery. "Attorney? Is there some problem?" My uncle was an attorney, so what could this be all about?

"Might you be aware your Uncle passed over the weekend? Only sixty-four. A real shame."

I hadn't heard and felt guilty I was so disconnected from my family that no one had called to tell me. "Is there some problem?" I repeated, not wanting to confirm my distance from the family.

"You're named… in his will."

I breathed a sigh of relief. At least I wasn't being pulled into some litigation that was going to cost me a wheelbarrow full of money. "Uncle Jim never mentioned anything about a will."

"You must be very busy and all, but could you appear in Dallas next Tuesday at 11:00 am? I'll be reading his will in our offices at Bryan Tower in downtown Dallas."

I first thought of all the reasons why I shouldn't go. But then realized I needed to make amends with the family. The best way was to go to them. This would be an opening. I knew I'd be inundated with requests for loans and gifts of money. But I'd become an expert at dodging them. The whole family thought I was a tightwad. Here was a chance to reinforce that notion. Particularly if this might be my last year on the series. I had the perfect excuse not to lend or give money to anyone.

"I'll have to confirm with the studio, but I'll do everything I can to attend."

"I understand you were his favorite nephew."

I thought about all the fishing trips I'd taken with Uncle Jim. He was free with his advice, even though as an attorney he usually charged for such insights. Somehow he figured out early that of all my siblings and cousins I was the one most likely to make it in the world. He was right. My family could best be described as underachievers, although I knew many simply described them as trailer trash. It had nothing to do with the fact that most of them lived in mobile homes and drove fork lifts, loading and unloading cargo at trucking companies for a living; or married those who did. Somehow I'd escaped that culture. Was it a happenstance of genetics, or was I one of those people who simply wasn't going to go along with the group? Was I one of those people who wouldn't take no for an answer and kept pushing until I got one that was more acceptable?

I was lucky. I went to college and met people who were more like me than my family. At college I met people who had dreams. We envisioned a future that changed the world as we knew it. I had no idea that in other parts of the country there were people who had bigger dreams of transformation than I did, but that was alright with me. I rose as my talents permitted. I was much better off than my parents and siblings. I was much better off than I knew. It was just what I did and the rewards followed.

I kept in touch with Uncle Jim. We would text when something happened in the family. Someone died, or someone was sentenced to prison. Those were the ones I remembered. But he'd also texted when he bought his Tesla. He'd suggested I should buy one. Green energy and all that. But when he bought his Tesla, I still couldn't make a living as an actor, waiting tables and doing Community Theater. I couldn't afford any car at that point. It wasn't long afterwards that the autonomous cars finally caught on and people, other than the very rich, no longer thought of buying cars.

The Tesla was Uncle Jim's pride and joy. He was more proud of that car than he was of my cousins, Adam and Leslie. Said the car was his contribution to changing the world. The jury was still out on Adam and Leslie even though they were now in their forties.

I had promised Uncle Jim I would go for a ride in his Tesla the next time I was home. The problem was I never went home between the purchase of the car and his passing, a period of more than twenty years. I had meant to go home, but the proper occasion just never presented itself. The occasion had arrived, but I wouldn't be tooling around Dallas in his Tesla with him behind the wheel. Besides it would have been illegal.

In an age where computers manage everything, driving your own car was dangerous. The computers plot out the best route, the safest speed and ensure that the unpredictability of a human driver never enters into the equation. It was a minor inconvenience given that the autonomous cars ensure you arrive at your destination safely and on time every time. Why worry about traffic or tickets or any of the annoyances that come with transporting yourself from one location to another? Some people, mostly in Texas, for some curious reason I never understood, talk incessantly on the radio about freedom. Driving yourself is some kind of civil right of passage or something. I never understood their arguments. Calling a Googlecar to pick you up and deliver you where you were going just seemed to be the way it was now. Driving your own car involved finding a place to park, maintaining the car, insurance, licenses, a garage, buying gasoline. Why in the world would anyone want to add all that to their lives when a simple text message produces a car that takes you where you want to go and is gone once it delivers you there?

I felt badly that I never came and appeased Uncle Jim's desire to give me a ride in his electric car. At least I wouldn't be dealing with his disappointment. The funeral was scheduled to be the day before the reading of the will. Just like Uncle Jim. He wanted his eulogy to be positive and not tinged by the nasty overtones that would emerge once he divided his estate not as his heirs would want it.

I expected nothing from Uncle Jim. He was a great guy, who I greatly admired and respected. But I didn't expect him to give me anything. I had most of the things I wanted. Most of all, I didn't want to become embroiled in family disputes. I set aside the whole question of the inheritance and thought more about the trip being a time to heal the wounds I'd inflicted on the family by withdrawing to Hollywood and not getting engaged in the spats and disputes that inevitably arose. I was happy to be far away and wanted to keep it that way.

So why did I agree to go to the funeral? Being alone since Mimi left me, I was looking for connections. Even though I wasn't much interested in the connections my family provided, they were my family and I needed to start the process of reconnecting.

I thought about Adam and Leslie. They were set in their ways. Both were corporate attorneys like their father. Both had invested wisely and were actually quite well off from everything I'd been told. Given that Uncle Jim was reputed to be a tyrant when it came to his own family, there was little doubt that Adam and Leslie would toe their father's line. Was that the reason that Uncle Jim decided to pass along something to me? I hoped it would be something merely sentimental to him that his kids wouldn't care about so there wouldn't be a hassle with them. I never wanted to be in an adversarial position with an attorney, let alone the possibility of dealing with two of them. And one thing I was certain of, knowing my uncle, they were both well trained in the law and also disciplined. Uncle Jim wouldn't permit them to work in his firm if they weren't. They were a reflection on him. They were also his legacy.

"Mister Gaydos? I assume you prepared the will?"

"I did."

"So you know its contents."

"I do."

"Did my uncle do something in his will that will end up being controversial with Adam and Leslie?"

Mister Gaydos considered my question before responding, "I don't know. I do know Adam and Leslie well. Almost as well as I knew their father. But it's a funny thing about families. When someone passes on people react differently than you'd normally predict. Some people are passive. They simply want what the deceased wanted. Others are never satisfied. And the worst thing? There's almost no way of tellin' in advance which way certain people will go. I've even had relatives come out of the woodwork to challenge a will they weren't named in and probably for good reason. But it usually ends up in court. Nobody wins then, not after all the court costs and legal fees."

"I take it you're not expecting someone to come out of the woodwork in this case."

"Never can tell." He started. "You know your family much better than I do. What do you think?"

Back on the spot, asking for an opinion about my family and not really wanting to discuss them since whatever I said would probably be wrong. "Guess we'll have to wait and see."

"Won't have to wait long. Not like in some states where things get hung up for months or years even. Your uncle was fastidious about the law. He made sure nothin' could subvert his wishes. Everythin' is very clear. He made sure any of the usual grounds for a challenge were tied off early. So if anyone wants to challenge, all I have to say is good luck."

"I take it you liked my uncle?"

"He was a good man. Fair, reasonable and an advocate for his clients. Always made sure when a deal was done everyone walked away feeling like it wasn't all one-sided. Don't know anyone who didn't like your uncle, and mostly for that reason."

"What about Adam and Leslie? Did they adopt their father's approach to the law?"

Mr. Gaydos laughed. "No, and I know your uncle wished they had. Adam's a technician. He never meets with clients, or voices an opinion. Cautious is how I'd describe Adam. He's a wiz at research. He'll give you every side of an argument and all of the relevant case law in his written opinions. Air tight is how people have described his briefs."

"What about Leslie?"

"Leslie, now there's a piece of work. Leslie's the client manager for the firm. She doesn't do law, not really. She builds relationships for the firm and makes sure Adam and the others all have work to do. She's out nearly every night havin' dinner with one client or another. She gives great parties, but don't expect to find Adam at them. And it's Adam's work that she sells, mostly."

"Why did you call her a piece of work?"

"Leslie knows everyone and all about everyone. She's not someone you'd want sitting across the table from you. She's a tough negotiator and won't leave a nickel on the table that she thinks belongs to her. She'll rattle off relevant case law, and even when you're sure it doesn't apply, somehow she finds a connection or nexus and there you are tryin' to figure out how she ever came up with that one."

"I take it you've had the pleasure of sitting across from her?"

"I have." He sounded regretful. "And my record is perfect. I've never won a case or an argument with her. I don't know anyone who has for that matter."

"I thought she was married."

"To Judge Stephens. I think the only thing that keeps them together is she can't appear in his court. I personally think he married her just so he could learn all the secrets she knows."

"Sounds like Tuesday's going to be a real experience." I summarized.

Chapter Six

Mountain View Estates looks out from the peak of a rise on a back country road just outside Dallas. There are neither mountains nor a view, and the estates are tiny since they are generally single or family plots. But in North Texas, you find things that seem incongruous if you've ever been any place else. This was one, more an attempt to make family believe they were doing something wonderful for a departed family member, giving them a fake mountain top and a non-existent view, even though neither would be appreciated nor enjoyed by the newly departed.

I can only assume Uncle Jim chose this place for his final rest because it was close to where he had lived, yet far enough away that the urban growth wouldn't encompass this place any time soon. His grave was next to his wife's, who had predeceased him by three years. Zelda was the opposite of Uncle Jim, as I recall. She was as warm and loving as he was strict and disciplined. Aunt Z was a homebody. She had no wanderlust and just enjoyed all that Texas had to offer, including drought, heat and congested roads. Even with the drought and heat she managed to keep a flower garden growing around her backyard pool. In the summers she and Uncle Jim entertained friends and neighbors. They had an outdoor kitchen and enough shade around the pool that folks would come over nearly every summer weekend to float in the pool, eat munchies that Aunt Z floated on rafts on the water and drink Uncle Jim's well stocked reserves of wine, mostly European and South American.

Aunt Z read everything that wasn't moving faster than she was. And sometimes she'd read that too. She always had some topic to discuss with anyone who happened to show up. Whether it was about gardening when water was restricted, schools and how to get kids to read and do their math, or world events. She had something to say and discuss with everyone. And one of the best things was she listened first and asked questions as folks went along. Only when others had said their piece would she venture her own well-reasoned opinions. I was sorry I'd let time get away from me and I'd not been back to see my aunt before she passed on. I remember many a weekend at their house, floating, eating and talking with Adam and Leslie or their friends.

Adam and Leslie always wanted to talk about people. I often wondered what so fascinated them about people we knew and those we knew about. But when I learned that they had gone into law like their father it became more understandable. The law is relatively straight forward. What complicates the law is how people interpret it and what they do to reinterpret it so it permits them to do what they want. People are Adam and Leslie's stock in trade. How to exploit weakness, how to counter strength, how to devise arguments that obfuscate your real intentions and how to achieve your objectives when in a contested situation.

I probably could have learned a lot from Adam and Leslie, since I was in the people business myself. The major difference was I studied people so I could portray and interpret them to others. I sought to help people understand people, whereas Adam and Leslie sought to fight legal battles for them and find a way to win every time. As I thought about it, it seemed like being a lawyer would have been something I could have been good at as well. I just wasn't sure how I would deal with the need to be callous about prevailing when you probably should not have and losing when you should have won. I had a high moral sense of right and wrong from my parents, which seemed to get me into trouble sometimes when I found myself conflicted about decisions my characters would make that I knew I never could. Those were the instances when I showed the glimpses of another persona below the surface.

Adam and Leslie wore expensive black suits. I couldn't tell if the clothing matched, but it was instantly obvious they were related. He had graying dark hair and her full blonde mane seemed to fly everywhere at once. It was their eyes that reminded me of Uncle Jim, but both had Aunt Z's nose. He was taller and she was slightly heavier, although not displeasingly so. She had a ready reassuring smile for all who greeted them. Not once did I see any expression on Adam's face.

"Well, well, if it's not our prodigal cousin." Leslie greeted me before the kiss I knew would be coming. "You look well."

"All that California artificial sun, tofu and vitamin water." I responded knowing she wouldn't have time to pursue my comments. "Adam, I'm sorry for your loss." I shook his hand, although he looked away rather than at me.

"We'll need to catch up. Are you staying?" Leslie asked, although I was sure she knew the answer.

"Definitely. My schedule is kind of fluid as I'm trying to see as many folks as I can while I'm here. But we'll find a time to sit."

"You… you don't sound… like your character." Adam stammered, surprised.

"Hollywood goes to great lengths to get you to do something that's totally unlike you, whether in how you talk, or in the nature of the character you play. That's what makes a great actor, someone who can reach to comprehend and become totally different than he or she really is."

Adam nodded although I wasn't sure if he really understood what I'd said. "You… you sound the same… as when… you were growin' up… here."

"I'm pretty much the same person, only older, and wiser I hope."

"Why… why'd you never come… and go… for that ride… in Dad's car?"

Adam made me feel bad, which I was sure was his intent. "Why'd you never come visit with me in LA? I guess takin' care of today, and

35

life, gets in the way of your best intentions."

Leslie, now. "Why'd you never marry? Seems I read you were with what's her name for the longest time."

"Meredith. I understand you married Judge Stephens," who had to be at least fifteen years older than she was.

Knowing where I was going she responded, "There's lots of reasons to get married."

"And just as many to know when not to," was all I'd give her.

"Rumor is you've turned gay. Is that even possible?"

I'd seen the tabloid that made the accusation. "Not that I'm aware of, and if you have any questions look at all the women I've been associated with. Not the resume of someone who has different preferences." This was going to be a really fun two days.

"Hear the studio's gonna cancel your show." Leslie wanted to make sure I was on the defensive.

"Looks like the Rev's getting ready to start." I nodded to the gravesite, not wanting to continue the conversation just then.

I followed them to the graveside, but stood a short distance away since I wasn't immediate family. While waiting for the Reverend Smythe to begin, I felt a poke in my rib. I turned to find Petra Smerno standing behind me. She'd been my high school Prom Queen and head football cheerleader. That meant she had the choice of any guy she wanted in my whole graduating class. She was cute, but not beautiful as I'd come to appreciate in Hollywood. She was athletic and had retained her wiry stance that made her look like she was always waiting for a starting gun to go off. "Petra. How are you?"

"Great. How's the Hollywood big shot?"

"Don't know, I'll ask the next time I see one."

"Ha, ha. You know what I mean." She pushed me away. Making contact I'd noted.

I was surprised to see her and something didn't make sense. "Didn't know you knew my uncle."

"I'm the office manager for his law firm."

Without thinking I responded, "You always were good at organizing things. I can see how a job like that would be something you'd like to do."

"I actually hate my job and my life, but the money's reasonable."

I looked around for her spouse, "Where's Gordo? He coaching a practice today?" Gordo had been the captain of our high school football team. He and Petra were the class couple. They'd married when he washed out of college football. I understood they'd struggled while they finished their degrees. He became the football coach at our old high school, when coach Grayson had finally called it quits.

"We're not together any more. He got a wanderin' eye, which I never minded. It was when somethin' else started wanderin' that I threw him out and took him for every cent he had."

"Didn't you have kids?"

"Gordo, Jr. He's quarterback's coach on his daddy's team."

"Must be hard for you." I wasn't really sure what else to say. She didn't want to continue down that path.

"What about you? Heard you're not with what's her name any more."

"Meredith. I'm good. Busy."

Petra didn't hesitate an instant, but then again, I'd practically invited her response. "I read they're thinking of replacing you. With a kid, no less."

I went for what had become my stock answer. "Trial balloon. Studio does that every few years to see what reaction they get."

"The article I read said your writers had run out of fresh ideas and your character doesn't hold any surprise for the audience anymore. Said the studio expects your numbers to drop drastically this season if they renew you."

I didn't realize everyone read the same stories. "The Rev's gonna start."

We turned to watch and listen as they interred my uncle. The ceremony was short and I could tell the eulogy the Rev delivered had been written by my uncle. It sounded just like him. Factual, unemotional and just the right and precise words were chosen.

Adam threw the first shovel full of dirt, followed by Leslie. Neither appeared to have shed a tear. This was all business. And it was a good place for Leslie to make contacts with folks for legal work.

As we walked away from the grave, Petra surprised me. "Aren't you gonna ask me out while you're here?"

"I..." didn't know what to say, not expecting Petra to be available or to have any interest in me. She never had in high school.

"You know I always wanted you and not Gordo." She began what seemed the most surreal discussion I'd ever had. "But you were always with Natalie. What ever happened there?"

"Natalie outgrew me," was all I could come up with. How do you sum up a long time romance when things fall apart? Natalie wanted to get married and have kids right away. I knew if I followed my dream I'd not be able to support her in the style she wanted for a long time. She didn't want to wait. Said she didn't want to be old when her kids grew up. She wanted to relive her high school years through her kids while still young enough to really enjoy them. I often thought she wanted to enjoy the years more than she wanted to enjoy the kids, but that's another story.

"You know she has a kid?"

No, I didn't. "We didn't keep in touch."

"And her husband just left her for Mr. Taylor."

What? "The high school band director?"

"A kid and no husband. Sometimes life just sucks, you know?"

I was stuck on the band director being gay. There had been rumors, but nothing was ever substantiated. I felt bad for Natalie. She'd gotten what she wanted when Ronnie Walsh stepped up to the plate to take my place in our senior year. Ronnie had it made because his father owned the Chevy dealership in town. Ronnie was already working as a service advisor in high school. He bragged that he'd be running the whole department before he was twenty. Back then he'd been expecting his father would leave the dealership to him when his father retired. With the rise of the Googlecars the dealership went out of business.

Then something else clicked. Ronnie had been in the marching band in high school under Mr. Taylor's direction. Had something been going on all those years between them? And Ronnie had a kid besides? Wow. I couldn't imagine how Natalie had coped.

Petra got tired of waiting for me to respond. "So I thought we could do something tonight. I'm sure you don't really want to go to the reception and listen to all those boring people talk good about your uncle when they all seriously hated his guts. Everyone thought he should have retired when he bought that god-damn car."

I couldn't understand why my uncle's car kept coming up. "What's the deal with his car?"

"You know he drove that thing every day? Even when it became illegal to drive your own car he drove it on his farm every day. Sometimes he'd sneak it out on the roads and scare people half to death, passing them at high speed on back country roads. Then he started driving it down to the Police Department for meetings with the Police Chief. They didn't give him a ticket or anything. It was like he was above the law. People really resented that. It became like a symbol that he was better than the rest of us. You know what I mean?"

"Never heard that story." I knew the car meant a lot to him, but not that much.

"So come on. We can go to Billy Bob's. I haven't been dancin' in forever."

I was intrigued. "Still the Texas Two-step? I haven't danced that in I can't remember."

"So let's cruise through the reception and head on over there. No one will miss us."

But reality set back in. "I haven't seen my parents yet."

She looked around realizing they weren't there. "Where are they? I thought they'd be here for sure. Your father was close to his brother, wasn't he?"

"Yes and no. Their health isn't very good. Didn't think they could handle the heat. They're gonna be at the reception, so it will be kinda hard to cruise through." I could see she'd been planning this escape for quite some time. She was crestfallen and tried to regroup quickly. She evidently thought I'd be her ticket out of Dallas and sugar daddy since she'd always been the high school queen bee.

"Why don't you come by after the reception? If it's not too late we could still go, and if it's late you could just come in for a cup of coffee... or something."

I knew what she meant by 'or something'. "No promises. I haven't seen my parents in a while so I need to spend some quality time with them while I have the chance. Don't know when I'll be back."

She understood, turned and kissed me, engaging my tongue with hers as a preview. She grabbed my ass and pressed into me. Not to be rude, I went along, returned the compliment of grabbing her ass as well. She made sure she'd fully communicated her intent before allowing me to disengage from our full body assault upon each other. When we parted I winked at her, but gave her no further reassurance.

Chapter Seven

Bryan Tower sits just off the Woodall Rodgers Freeway that runs through the heart of Dallas. A forty-five story building, the top floors have broad views of the Trinity River and the city that grew around it. The law offices of Gaydos, Keebaugh and Mutek occupied the seventeenth floor. High enough to have good views, but low enough not to pay top floor rent. The wood paneling looked worn and in need of a refresh or something. The furniture was likewise not the latest fashion and although not dull like the wood walls, clearly not what you would have found higher up.

A pleasant receptionist showed me to a large conference room. Seats for at least thirty people around the large oak table. It had a highly lustrous finish. I saw it had been used only for occasions like this. Not much chance it would experience much in the way of abuse. Adam and Leslie sat opposite each other at one end of the table. Mr. Gaydos sat between them on the end, talking to Leslie. Adam looked bored, as usual, noted as I entered the room and he gave me a head nod of recognition.

I sat next to Leslie. I knew that would piss her off because she would want someone who might be a future client to sit next to her and not me. But I didn't care.

"Morning Leslie, Adam. Mister Gaydos, I'm Desmond Jensen. We spoke."

Mr. Gaydos came around behind Leslie to shake my hand. "Thanks for comin'. I'm sure Jim would have been pleased."

Mr. Gaydos consulted the clock on the back wall. "It's time we begin. This is a sad occasion and I'm sure we all feel the loss of James

Harrison Jensen. He was a great man who we shall all miss. I have been privileged to know James for nearly thirty years. It's an honor for me to read the last will and testament of my friend and colleague. 'I James Harrison Jensen, residing at 101 Liberty Stables, Dallas, Texas, being of sound mind, hereby bequeath all of my stock in Jensen, Wilson and Molina, LLP in equal shares to my children, Adam Jensen and Leslie Jensen Stephens, both of Dallas, Texas and both currently partners in the firm. I hereby also direct that all of my worldly possessions, with one exception, shall be liquidated and the proceeds equally divided between my two children, Adam and Leslie. The one item that shall not be liquidated is my 2012 Tesla Model S automobile. I bequeath this one item to my nephew, Desmond Jensen, of Los Angeles, California on the condition that he drive the vehicle back to California. These enumerated items constitute the sum and total of my worldly possessions and the clear intent and expressed desire of James Harrison Jensen.' There you have it. Everythin' with the exception of his automobile shall be equally divided between his surviving children and the automobile to his nephew."

Just like Uncle Jim. Short, precise and to the point. He left absolutely no ambiguity as to what he wanted to happen to his possessions or how they would be transferred to his kids. For some reason he gave his prized car to me. Probably because I'd never come out to take a ride with him as I'd promised. This way he could be sure I'd ride in it at least once. But curious that the one condition to obtain the car was that I would have to break the law to do so. It would take two to three days to get home with it and most likely I'd be arrested and the car confiscated. He certainly wasn't going to make it easy on me. That's what I get for not coming out and taking that ride with him.

Leslie leaned over to me. "Adam wants the car. Why don't you just refuse to drive it out? That would violate the condition of gift."

Even though the absolute last thing I wanted to do was drive the car back to California, just the way Leslie put it to me got my back up. And I could see if I tried to drive it home, she or Adam, or both would notify every sheriff along the way. I'd have to puzzle on this one. But the more I thought about it, the more I wanted to ensure Leslie and Adam didn't get everything.

"Since Adam is the one who wants the car, he's gonna have to ask me. A proxy request is insufficient counselor." I knew Adam would struggle with my condition. He couldn't confront anyone.

Chapter Eight

Uncle Jim's barn… well, it smelled like… yeah, like a barn. I guess a place where horses and cows take a crap and it sits on the wood floor until you clean it out the next day… well, you get the picture. I held my breath as I strode into the semi-darkness. I had forgotten barns didn't have windows. But then again, maybe I never knew that. In my own defense, I didn't tend to hang out in barns when I was a kid, and I still didn't as an adult. Going into the barn reminded me I had really put a lot of distance between myself and Uncle Jim. Too much distance. I'd forgotten what it was like to be a kid in Dallas. I'd forgotten what it was like to be connected to people who weren't trying to get today's takes done. I regretted I'd let that happen. Uncle Jim, I'm sure, would have had some fascinating things to tell me if I'd ever taken the time to come by and just chat. But then again, I was all about me. Had been ever since I left Dallas. I'd pulled in all my receptors and just plowed on ahead, full steam towards the sunset. I'd convinced myself that in a business as competitive as acting if I wasn't one hundred and ten percent engaged, I'd be run over by those who were willing to do just one percent more. So I never let up. I never gave anyone an opportunity to wedge that one percent between me and the job. I'd made up my mind early no one would ever take away a job from me once I'd secured it. But Alistair had indicated maybe someone else had found a way to get one percent over me. Younger stud. All the rage. I'd heard those words spoken about me, but not in a long time. Too long. I needed a new strategy. But what? How was I going to keep what was mine? I'd created the character. I was the only one who'd ever played him. How could I walk away now and watch someone else re-interpret what I'd done?

Once my eyes adjusted to the darkness I was able to see the Tesla was under a tarp, or actually a fitted canvas cover. Uncle Jim was taking no chances an owl or bird or something would take a crap on his prized possession. Yeah, someone had said something about crap was acidic and would eat into the paint. Got all that, but I still thought Uncle Jim was a bit anal about a car.

Going around it, I grabbed the cover and lifted it off. And there it stood, a shimmering black jewel of a car. The wax was thick enough bees probably could have made a honeycomb. As I opened the door, Adam and Leslie entered the barn. They'd obviously been here often as their eyes adjusted almost at once. "So you found it with no trouble." Leslie observed. I was glad she was observant. Would have hated for her to have to tell me the obvious.

"This it?" I thought I'd play with her.

"Dad's pride and joy. Only one anyone can point to that's still road worthy."

"Thought it was illegal to drive yourself."

"It is, technically. But no one ever said a word to Dad when he'd drive it into town."

That reminded me of a question that had come to me in listening to Petra, "When was the last time? That he drove into town?"

"Last week. He'd go in on Sunday to attend church. No one wanted to discourage church attendance. Dad was always figuring the angles." I wondered, based on Petra's comments whether the meetings at the Police department were on Sundays too.

Adam slid in on the passenger side as if that was his side of the car. I realized he probably had ridden with his father all those years and probably did think of the passenger side as his. But he slid across into the driver's side as if he'd been waiting his whole life to sit there, the lord and master… finally.

I left the driver's door open and walked around behind as if inspecting the vehicle. The stylized T caught my attention. I wondered

46

why cars needed a symbol. Was it so people could tell what kind of car it was? Or was it something more symbolic, like invoking the lord god of war or something? I couldn't tell and no one was giving me lessons about hood ornaments, so I needed to move on.

"Your dad ever let you drive it?" I casually asked Leslie as I inspected the passenger side. Not a scratch, dent or ding on it anywhere. I marveled how well Uncle Jim had kept it since he was reputed to have driven it so often.

"Are you kidding me?" Guess not.

"So you don't have your pilot's license?"

"Dad drove fast, but I never saw it leave the ground." She confirmed my inquiry.

"It's a beautiful machine, no doubt about it. Particularly when you compare it to a Googlecar or one of the other autonomous cars." I mused, wondering what kind of reaction that was going to bring from Leslie. I had to assume they'd come out here so Adam could ask me his big question. So I thought I'd speed things up. I walked back over to the driver's side and motioned for Adam to move back over to the passenger seat. He looked up at me as if I'd just struck him with a knife. "I want to take it out. I'm assuming it's fully charged."

Adam grabbed the wheel and wasn't about to surrender his position of control.

"Adam!" I was much more emphatic now. But he leaned down as if to protect the steering wheel. I looked to Leslie who simply shrugged.

I grabbed Adam roughly and yanked him out of the car. He fell prostrate on the ground, so I stepped over him and slid in behind the steering wheel. Having no idea what I was doing I fumbled with the buttons, pedals and indicators until I heard a high pitched hum and all the dash lights came on showing me that indeed the ancient vehicle had once more risen to the occasion and was ready to carry me into the past where people ruled machines rather than the other way around.

I took my foot off the brake and gently touched the pedal. The Tesla leapt forward effortlessly and I needed all my concentration to steer it through the wide barn door and into the yard outside. I realized I had no idea what I was doing and if I wasn't careful I was certain to wreck my uncle's pride and joy. So I took my foot off the accelerator and the car quickly came to a stop, even without touching the brake. I thought the safest thing was to back it into the barn, but looking around I was far from certain I could maneuver it successfully. I'd need to keep going forward, but I realized at some point I was going to have to back it into the barn or I'd never be able to get it out the next time I wanted to. Or I could go back in, get the tarp and simply leave it out for the night. But I quickly realized Uncle Jim would never accept that. So I put it into reverse gear, touched the pedal ever so gently and slowly backed straight back to where I started.

When I took my foot off the accelerator I had completed a journey that was much shorter than the Wright Brother's first flight. Oh well, I guess you have to start somewhere. I had a fifteen hundred mile trip ahead of me, so I figured I'd have a lot of time to learn how to actually drive it.

Adam opened the door, "Mine!" he nearly screamed in my face.

"Not according to your father or Mister Gaydos." I observed.

"Mine!" This time it was more threatening.

"I'll make you a deal. I swap this here car for all the shares in your law firm your father left you."

Adam was getting ready to yell 'Mine' one more time when my words sunk in. He shook his head and backed away from the door.

"If this car is the most important thing to you, then you should be willing to swap that which is not as important to get that which is the most important. How about it?"

Leslie cut in as I expected she would, "That's not realistic."

"What's not realistic? This car has invaluable sentimental value. So you can't say my swap isn't equivalent. You can't put a value on this car, so anything I ask has to be reasonable by definition."

She came back with the expected counterattack. Gaydos warned me she was good. I was about to find out how good. "This car has no sentimental value to you. So anything you ask by definition is too much."

"But all that has changed by the mere fact that your father wanted me to have it and as Mister Gaydos pointed out, Uncle Jim was my favorite uncle."

Adam suddenly joined the conversation, "Why do you... want my car?"

I decided to be honest with him, which was less than either of them were being with me, "Twenty years ago your father called me and suggested that I needed to buy one of these. I couldn't afford to buy enough food to eat at that particular time in my career. He asked me every time we talked thereafter when I was going to come home and go for a ride with him. I disappointed your father by not doing as he asked. The least that I can do is honor his wishes by driving his Tesla now."

"He's dead." Adam was most emphatic.

"He is, but the least I can do is honor his memory by fulfilling his long time wish for me."

"It's not fair. He knew...knew I wanted it. He was just... punishing... punishing me."

"That's between you and him and really has nothing to do with me."

Leslie had become quiet, too quiet. She had to be working out the next means of attacking my unwillingness to give them what they wanted.

"So you're determined to break the law."

"In driving it back to California?"

She nodded.

"I could always drive it to church and then home, just like your father."

"It's a longer drive home from church, for you." She said it in a curious way. Not threatening in an outright manner, but there was no mistaking what she was implying.

I got out of the car and replaced the cover, keeping it exactly as Uncle Jim had for twenty years. We walked out together.

"So when are you going back?" Leslie asked, again making her point.

"Don't know. I've still got a few connections I'd like to make while I'm here. Just never know when I'll be coming this way again.

"Soon....Tabloids say soon." Adam was making his point that I was finished in Hollywood.

I put an arm around Adam's shoulder, which nearly drove him crazy. He didn't know what to do, but his eyes betrayed his extreme discomfort. "You obviously haven't been following my career, Adam. The tabloids have been saying that about me since before I got the show. I was washed up and with no prospects a week before the first episode aired. It was amazing how quickly that negativity disappeared when the people got a chance to vote with their viewing habits, proving the gossipers wrong."

"Not wrong. You're... all washed up."

"You may be right. And if that's my fate, then I'll have more time to drive Uncle Jim's car, won't I? And since I'll be broke, I'll actually need to drive it to the unemployment line since I won't be able to afford a Googlecar."

Leslie rolled her eyes. I knew I hadn't heard the last from her on the subject, but she was clearly saving it for a time when I'd be least prepared. Uncle Jim had taught her well.

Chapter Nine

Mom and Dad wanted me to stay with them at their house, but I just couldn't do it. I'd been on my own for so many years, to spend a night in my old room would have been just too spooky. It would have forced me to experience remembrances and emotions I'd been trying to forget since the day I left that house. Just being back in town was bad enough. Visiting the house was almost overwhelming. Staying in my old room. Nope. I just couldn't endure those emotions, feelings and recollections.

The Fairmont Hotel was downtown, within walking distance of Mr. Gaydos' offices, the Arts Center and the Klyde Warren Park, which had been a favorite place I liked to hang out when growing up. As with most things in Dallas, it wasn't just a park. It was built over the expressway that cut through the heart of downtown and was built with mostly private money. It linked the uptown and downtown areas, and that was why people congregated there. The park was only two blocks from the Fairmont, so of course, after I returned to my hotel from visiting with my parents that was the first place I went.

The grass, as I remembered it, was manicured so it almost looked like a carpet, but it was real. Flowering shrubs lined the area next to the enclosed children's play area. The water spouts were still working and I watched a mother remove the blouses from her two daughters and send them into the spray. Good grief, topless women in downtown Dallas. What would the Junior League and Women's Christian Temperance Union members say about that? But then again, the girls were probably less than two, so you actually had to look twice to be sure they weren't boys.

I walked over by the covered stage where Jazz groups and local garage bands used to perform in the summers when I came by. The Booker T Washington Magnet High School for the Performing Arts was just a couple blocks away. Student groups used to come here to perform. It was always a great time and the price was right. Like I said, I had to earn the money to pay for anything I did when I was a kid. Still do for that matter, but it's a whole lot easier at the moment. Then again, that might change too.

Next to the stage was Savor, a restaurant with walls that were entirely glass windows. No matter where you sat in the restaurant, you had a great view of the outdoors and the park was on three sides, with the street on the other.

I took a seat at the chess table. There were racks with magazines and newspapers, tables where visitors ate a lunch from the many food trucks that lined up on the other side of the park, and a small selection of books that people would donate to the park. People either read there or took the book home and returned it when finished. It always amazed me people respected the park and didn't take things without returning them.

A woman in what I surmised was her late twenties sat down opposite me. "You looking for a game or are you just sitting here?"

"Game." I responded.

She opened with a classic move, so she clearly knew what she was doing. I was going to have to pay attention here or quickly lose. Before I made my move I looked up to see who my opponent was. She was attractive in a plain sort of way. Long brown hair pulled behind her. I tried to place the clothes. Didn't look expensive, but were clearly quality. No jewelry of any kind. She kept it simple.

I made my usual counter move.

"Going defensive on me right off the bat?" she observed.

"You work down town?"

She nodded, "Live down here too, over at Cirque by the American

Airlines Center."

"What do you do, besides play chess with people you don't know?"

"I know you alright. Desmond Jensen, also known as Rory Gallagher, Chief of Detectives for the Los Angeles Police Department. What brings you to Dallas?"

"Family."

"I didn't know you were from here."

"I keep it a secret. Wouldn't want anyone making a snap judgment about me on that basis."

"But I already have. You're not at all what you portray each week. That makes you a good actor. Probably underappreciated."

"Clearly when I'm negotiating a contract renewal."

"I read that." She made her next move. She was following the pattern I expected, so I countered in such a way that I could have options depending on how she continued.

"What was that I saw on the news about an explosion at a Googlecar repair facility here? We had one in LA, and I read something about other explosions. I think they were in New York and Chicago and now Dallas. Looks like a pattern."

She looked at me as if surprised I was interested in real world events. "I talked with the Chief of Police about that. He has an investigative team working it, but the FBI is in there too since, as you pointed out, there seems to be an emerging pattern."

"He say anything about who might be behind it?"

"No, and he wouldn't until they complete their investigation." I knew that would be the response, but was wondering about her relationship to the chief.

"You didn't say what you do."

"I'm the Mayor. Judith Hanson." I clearly showed my surprise because she laughed. "That happens to me a lot. People think I'm young for a mayor. But I'm passionate about this city. I want to make it the equal of all the other great cities in this country. I want it to be a city that rivals London, or Rome or Buenos Aires, but in its own unique way."

I was surprised, and interested in her enthusiasm. She left no doubt why she'd been elected. "I thought it was."

"We have a ways to go. But I'm happy to say we're making progress."

"So where'd you learn to play chess?"

"My daddy. Taught me when I was three years old. I was regularly beating him by the time I was six. I compete at the Master level in tournaments. Even in one I sponsor through the city. We're working hard to make Chess something kids here in Dallas want to participate in. It's great to help them understand strategy, patience and self-control."

"I'm afraid I won't be able to give you much of a match." I conceded I wasn't going to win.

"I'll let you out of your commitment to play me if you'll stop by City Hall tomorrow at 9:00 am and participate in my morning press conference."

"What would I say to the press?"

"You'll say that as a proud Texan, who grew up in Dallas, graduated from Booker T. Washington High School and went on to international fame and fortune, that you're a huge supporter of the arts here in Dallas, and you'll give me a donation for our Arts Center in whatever amount you consider reasonable."

I hadn't expected her to blackmail me quite so effectively. "I'll have to remember that Chess can be a costly game to play."

She laughed, shook my hand and left me wondering what her next move would have been.

Chapter Ten

Since my free time at the park, hadn't ended up being free, I decided to move to a table away from the chess set and pull out my tablet to see what I could find in the way of instructions on how to drive a Tesla. I was going to need to figure out how to drive it back to LA without getting arrested. I searched for a while and was able to finally find a video game that was a driver's adventure that had a Tesla as one of the cars that could be chosen. When a car was chosen the program went through a quick tutorial on what controls were where, so I figured out quickly what I needed to know to drive a Tesla. I tried a couple of times to navigate the game. It wasn't the same since the controls were proxies for the real thing. Consequently the car didn't respond the way it would if I were actually driving it. That may have been a good thing since I ended up crashing both times. I kept telling myself it was the proxy controls that didn't respond properly, but I knew I probably wouldn't be much better if I were actually driving.

I needed to get some time behind the wheel to figure it out, and even though I was tired from the trip and the long day, I texted for a Googlecar and went back out to the ranch. As I suspected neither Leslie nor Adam was there. The lights were out at the big house as they had their own homes in the city. I walked over to the barn after the Googlecar had left. I searched just inside the door and eventually found the light switch. The Tesla was right where I'd left it. I drove it out of the barn. The headlights came on automatically but it took a few minutes to get used to only being able to see a short distance ahead. I slowly drove down the long driveway. At the end I backed up a ways, and turned the car around. This wasn't so bad. Of course I was doing all this maneuvering at very slow speed, but I was getting the hang of it. I drove back up to the big house and circled around the yard in front of the barn.

I wondered what to do next? I needed to get it out on the highway and up to speed, but how to do that without causing a disturbance and possibly ending up in jail? Oh what the hell, I decided that no one would be looking for me and if I stayed on back roads I had a better chance of not being detected. But where to go? Then Natalie came to mind. Was that an encounter I could handle? She had chosen Ronnie Walsh over me. It was much to my relief at the time, because her action had saved me from having to be the bad guy. I knew I couldn't do what she wanted. As much as I loved her then, I had a deep conviction I could be more than I would have been if I'd stayed in Dallas. I could have been the King of Theatre Three, or the Kitchen Dog Theater. Maybe I would have made it big and done Casa Manana in Fort Worth. People had actually ended up on Broadway from there, but I probably wouldn't have. I would have had to pay the bills reading the news or sports. Since I didn't get a meteorology degree I never could have done the weather. Yes, I loved Natalie, but I couldn't give up my dreams for her, when hers were so parochial in comparison. Do you really need to have a mate who shares your dreams? I'd decided the answer was yes. Your mate doesn't have to share a specific dream, but has to share an understanding and willingness to do what it will take to realize the dream you have. And that's where Natalie and I'd parted ways.

I don't think I really decided to go see Natalie, at least not consciously, but I was soon turning onto her street. I'd never been to this part of Dallas, even when I was growing up. Siri had given me the address and guided me here on the big screen in the middle of the Tesla dash. I didn't know Tesla had used the Apple convention of a synthesized voice to respond to inquiries. The driver didn't have to take his or her hands off the car's controls when driving.

"Twenty-seven- nineteen?" I asked Siri as I let the Tesla roll to a stop in front of the small brick two-story house with two live oak trees in the front yard.

"Yes, Desmond. That is the address of Ronald and Natalie Walsh and their son, Desmond…"

"Thanks, Siri. Don't really need to know the kid's name." So she'd named their son after me. I wondered how Ronnie felt about that. Maybe this wasn't such a good idea. But the porch light came on and in only a moment there she was in the doorway. She had to be ten pounds heavier, which probably wasn't much, given she'd had a kid. The streaks of gray in her hair weren't flattering. She was wearing a one piece zip up jogging suit. She was looking at the car and me as if she couldn't figure out who had come to her home. She was evidently expecting someone, but I had no idea who.

I opened the door and as I stepped out, the biggest smile I'd ever seen on her appeared. She ran to me, throwing her arms around my neck and hugging me tightly. "I hoped it was you. I can't believe you're actually here. Do you have any idea how much I've missed you?"

She kissed me and it was almost as if the intervening years hadn't occurred. Her lips were still soft and her tongue eager to find mine. Holding her was so familiar. Her soapy smells, the same perfume, same lustrous soft long hair I used to love touching. I'd often helped her find split ends.

"Can you go for a ride with me, or do you need to stay here?"

She looked around at the house, then back to me. "Give me a minute. Just need to tell Des I've gone out."

"Des?" I asked as I let her go.

She didn't look back as she answered, "My son."

I went around the car and opened the passenger door while I waited. She was right back, seated in the passenger seat and a moment later I was driving her away from her home. She leaned towards me and rubbed my right arm with both hands. "It really is you. Here. In Dallas. With me. Why'd you wait so long to come home?"

Time for my pat answer, "Life gets in the way of your best intentions. Petra told me you'd had a son."

"You talked with Petra?" Oops, that wasn't smart.

"Today at the burial." I tried to clarify and minimize the damage I'd done at the same time.

"You know she threw Gordo out? The irony was that he was sleeping with the cheerleading coach, who's about half Petra's age. Just out of college. Hard body. You know the type."

"I don't think Petra weighs an ounce more than she did in high school." I disagreed.

Natalie sounded disgusted with herself, "You know she still runs her ten miles every day before she goes in to work. She's just amazing. Won a triathlon for her age group last year. Gordo didn't even place on his side. Too much weed. He's lost that edge."

"Didn't know that about Gordo." I admitted.

"Buys it from the kids on his team. Not much wonder why they haven't won the championship in forever."

"What about you and Ronnie?"

Natalie sat back in her seat and pulled inward. She evidently knew we'd have this discussion, but now that it was here, she wasn't quite sure how to respond to me. I understood she had to be feeling she'd made a mistake with Ronnie, but we never would have been together and she had to know that.

"You remember Mister Taylor, the Band Director?"

I nodded without saying anything, knowing this was hard for her.

"Well... he and Ronnie are living together."

"That many problems with his Chevy?" I couldn't help myself, it just came out.

"No, that many problems with Ronnie's self-esteem. You remember Ronnie was the marching band major all four years in high school? No one else ever had that honor for more than one year. I should have known it meant something, but no. I just ignored all the warning signs. They were there, but I just ignored them all." She dropped her head into her hand and started sobbing.

I touched her shoulder as I kept on driving. "When did you first know?"

"Not until I got the note after he'd moved out. That was about a week ago."

"So this just happened."

"What am I going to do now that everyone knows he loves a man more than he loves me or his son?"

"You can't let your son think that. Ronnie loves his son more than he loves Mr. Taylor. You son's a part of him that Mr. Taylor never will be. You've got to make sure your son believes that."

"Bullshit. How would you know? He's sleeping with Mr. Taylor. It's pure lust. This has been going on since high school, probably during high school, if the facts were known, which they never will be. How could I ever have let him blind me like he did?"

"You saw what you wanted to see." I began. "He was a good husband and father, wasn't he... at least until now?"

"He ran off with his gay lover, what am I supposed to think?"

I pulled into a Walgreens parking lot and shut down the Tesla. I tried to face her as best I could with a console between us. "You're supposed to think of your kid first and not your feelings about Ronnie. Wasn't he a good husband and father all those years?"

"We had good times." Her voice was small and she seemed to be thinking of something she wasn't about to share.

"You had more good times than bad times."

She looked at me clearly not expecting I'd have taken this tactic. "You're supposed to come riding in on your white horse, or Tesla, or whatever, and save me from this nightmare."

"I can't save you from anything, and it's not a nightmare. It's life. When you said for better or worse, this is what you signed up for. You had some great times, judging by the fact you have a son. But you have a challenge to get through. How you respond now is really the measure of your character, not how you took the good times for granted."

"But you're not with what's her name anymore."

"Meredith. No, I'm not with her anymore. The reason you and I went our separate ways isn't any different today than it was then."

"What do you mean?" she clearly doesn't want to revisit ancient history.

"Did you ever go on to college?"

She looked away. "No, I got pregnant right out of high school. Once Des came along there wasn't time."

"You didn't work?"

"No. I had a baby to look after."

"Why didn't you have a bigger family? I thought you wanted a half dozen."

She smiled apparently remembering the conversation where she'd laid out her expectations of our life together before I disagreed with that prospect. "Ronnie said we couldn't afford a bigger family until his dad retired from the business. And then the Googlecars started replacing everything and it just never happened."

"Our dreams weren't the same then and they still aren't. I would expect you to be a full partner in my career. To dive into the business side of what I do, manage things for us. Your dream is to be a woman who raises kids and then has a life of charity events to keep her busy. Ronnie was the perfect husband because someday he was going to own the Chevy dealership. You'd have the money to be comfortable and do your charity events. That's not me. That's not Hollywood. And I'm not coming back to Dallas."

I blew that. Should have stopped sooner. "Not what I've been reading. Looks like this is your last season. They've got Johnny Hollywood all lined up to replace you."

I couldn't believe everyone seemed to have the same thoughts about my career. "Where are people reading all that?"

"Hollywood Reporter."

I was surprised. "I didn't think anyone outside Hollywood read that."

"Everyone in town reads it now. Particularly when the rumors about you started circulating."

"They're just rumors."

"Where there's smoke, there's fire. I learned that the hard way." She drew inward.

I had to get the conversation back to her. "So there were rumors?"

"Even before I married Ronnie, people said I needed to be careful. Something just wasn't right with him. But I never saw it. Not until last week."

She'd only looked at the money from the dealership. Good to know that it wasn't how good Ronnie was in bed. That would have been a real blow to my ego. "I'm sorry you have to go through all that's coming."

She reached across and put her hand on mine. "You were always able to see things I couldn't."

"I remember it a little differently. You saw things but chose to ignore them because you always thought you'd find some way to make it right. I remember that confidence about you I so loved."

"Did you? Love me?"

I had to admit that I did, then. "You'll never know how hard it was for me to see you with Ronnie that last year."

"Why didn't you say something? I thought you hated me."

I had to be honest. "Never hated you, but simply came to the realization you weren't willing to do what it was going to take for me to realize my dreams."

She looked at me strangely, "What do you mean?"

I let it all come out. "We talked about it endlessly, or so it seemed to me. I'd talk about how I couldn't marry you right away because I had to go to Hollywood and do menial jobs until I could get acting work and build a resume. I told you it would be ten years or more before I could commit to having kids. You said you wanted them right away and couldn't wait that long."

"I was testing you. Did you really love me enough to compromise and do what was important to me?"

I wondered why we never had an open discussion like this back them, unless it was because back then neither of us understood what we do now. "If I had, I wouldn't have a series now. I'd be doing the local news and Kitchen Dog Theater."

That same strange look returned, as if she'd never considered the impact of choosing her over my career. "I don't buy that. You never would have let anything stop you. You would have made it and my son would have been ours. And I'd be happy rather than a total wreck."

She was going to believe what she wanted to believe, even though I saw it much differently. I'd confirmed what I wanted to know. She was exactly the same, even with her whole world imploding around her. She'd been blind to the obvious, as she had been when we were together. I'd made the right choice then and I had to stay strong now that we were inches apart. It was hard as I knew I still loved her as much as I did then. But we weren't a match. We'd never be a match. And I had to accept that and go back to Hollywood and a life she could only fantasize about. It isn't like her fantasy. No fantasy ever is. And I had to be the adult here and make the hard decision she never would.

"I need to get you home and get some sleep. Tomorrow's another full day and I return to LA tomorrow night. We're shooting next week and I haven't even looked at the script yet."

"What happened to you?"

Her question totally caught me off guard. "Pardon?"

"You're not the Des I remember. You're hard somehow. Like you don't really care anymore. Not like you did when we were together."

I could see where she was going. I had to head it off before she backed me into a corner. I could never explain to her what had happened to me, although I had a pretty good idea of what had happened to her since I left. I hated to think things were that obvious, but in her case they were. "I told you when I left that the road I was taking was going to be hard. Much harder than the one you chose. If I seem harder, it's because that's what it takes to survive in Hollywood. You've read they're talking about bringing in Johnny Hollywood to replace me. It may happen. But I have to find a way to prevent that. If I just accept things as you seem to, I'll be the one out of a job and soon forgotten. I don't intend to let that be my fate."

"That's what I mean. You would have found a way if we'd

married and had kids like I wanted. I know you better than you do. Someone backs you in a corner, you'll find a way to reverse positions and come out on top. That's you. Desmond Jensen. No one defeats you. Look at Rory Gallagher. He's the perfect character for you because he always wins in the end. That's you. You win."

I had to stop and think about what she was saying. If I'd chosen differently would it have been any different? Could we have had kids and could I have been successful at the same time? I didn't think so then and I still didn't. But she made me think about the choices I'd made. She'd made hers and regretted it, now. I'd made my choice and maybe I didn't have to make that choice. Maybe if I'd been more confident in myself I could have been right where I was in my career and had her and six kids to fill the hole that existed in my life. I would have been complete, but would I have kept the edge I needed to succeed? Would I have been content so I would have lost the series years ago? I didn't know the answer to that question. I never would. But Natalie presented me with a past that as a future could have been very different, and may have been more rewarding personally for me, but in different ways.

I didn't want to contemplate the past and future connections, so I started up the Tesla and re-entered traffic. I took back roads to her house. The whole trip back had been in silence as we individually contemplated a different set of options that we both were faced with. Hers were all negative and mine were equally negative, but for very different reasons. I wasn't the savior coming to save her in a white Tesla, particularly since this one was black. I was her fantasy. The one who once loved her. If she'd only held on, she could have shared in my success. But she'd taken what was then the more obvious successful route, only to be disappointed that the end results were not as anyone, except maybe Ronnie, could foresee. A son named Desmond Walsh. I'd have to keep in touch with her and him just to find out what choices he made and how that determined his future. Would I take him under my wing and help him in Hollywood as the son I never had? No. He would have to make it on his own if Hollywood was the destination he chose. After this season, for all I knew, I might not have any influence.

Chapter Eleven

I'd taken Interstate 35 north to Oklahoma City and then across Interstate 40 to LA, leaving right after I left Natalie at her house. I'd gambled that Leslie and Adam had expected me to wait until Sunday and then to take I-20 to I-10 and across along the southern border as it was the shortest route. But in many respects the route I took was nearly as direct although much more boring as the only cities along the way were Oklahoma City and Albuquerque. I traveled through both cities at off hours so I didn't encounter police waiting for me. I only stopped to recharge at the Tesla stations along the way, which also afforded a bladder break. Apparently Adam and Leslie didn't think they could intimidate VISA to give them information on my charges. I half expected they would request the information, but by Wednesday I was at the studio, ready to film my scenes, although very tired. The Tesla was in the garage I'd rented to keep it safe. No scratches, dents or other imperfections that would have invoked a concern from Uncle Jim. And since the vehicle was now in my garage, Adam and Leslie weren't in a position to claim I hadn't driven it all the way to LA as required by Uncle Jim's will. I'd won this round, but retained an uneasy feeling I wasn't finished with Adam and Leslie. I was convinced they would be knocking on my door at some point claiming I'd done something that violated the will of Uncle Jim. Then they would drive off into the sunset with my Tesla.

Mimi came onto the set. God, she's a gorgeous woman. I regretted all the more that we'd gone our separate ways. And I had no one to blame except myself for the state of affairs. I'd had her love. I'd had her commitment to me. I'd screwed it up. And now I'd lost the one person who meant more to me than Petra and Natalie together. I had to go visit my past and come back face-to-face with her to realize just how much she meant to me.

Robert came onto the set carrying the script for today. I wondered how Mimi had influenced him to change the story line to favor her character as she had last week. The producers had chosen to show the episode as she reworked it, hoping the unexpected changes to the story line would bring back viewers who thought we'd become predictable. I didn't think predictability was our problem. I thought Robert being too close to Mimi was the problem. No one else would have agreed with me. I went to Mimi and put my arm around her, leading her away from Robert, whispered into her ear: "Judging from the size of Robert's cock, he can't possibly be as pleasing as I was."

Mimi laughed despite her best efforts not to. She looked at me and kissed my cheek. "If it was only size you'd win. But there are collateral benefits to sleeping with the writer."

"I think Alistair has made it clear our interests are more aligned than yours with Robert. He'll write the series whether it's you and me or Johnny Hollywood. He has nothing to lose. We do."

"This a business proposition or are you hoping to reestablish the relationship you fucked up last year?"

"Let's just say I've come to appreciate you in ways that I'd previously taken for granted."

She surprised me with, "This new found appreciation have anything to do with encountering those you left behind?"

"I appreciated your uniqueness before, but this past weekend certainly brought home a number of things I'd been overlooking." I was being absolutely honest, but didn't expect her to appreciate my honesty.

"Still doesn't make up for Alison Andress." Came like a cold slap in the face. I dropped my grasp of her waist and looked down at my shoes. We were still in the same place. Nothing I could say would make any difference. She kissed me with her usual good morning passionless kiss, a constant reminder I'd fucked up. She was going to make me pay for what she saw as my indiscretion for the rest of my life.

She could see what she was doing to me, and she used that to her advantage. "I need to straighten Robert out, and not in the sense you'd like me to straighten you out, but in the sense of a script that works, since you never really fight with them."

She was on her way to confront Robert and John and beyond my grasp. I'd tried to communicate with her and found nothing had changed for her even as everything had become clear for me. I should have known, but hoped I could get back in her good graces. No such luck. Welcome back to paradise.

We started filming the episode.

On the set, Mimi as Samantha and I came into the lab where the actor who played Randy, our tech wizard, was waiting to answer my often inane questions. "Someone's trying to kill Samantha."

"What do you know about this person?" Randy took the stance of an absent minded professor.

"Tried to ambush her when she arrived at the office this morning. If Samantha hadn't been early probably would have succeeded."

"Someone who knows your routine." Randy observed. "What else?"

"Left this note." Samantha handed the note to Randy who read it out loud.

"'Die bitch'. Not much to go on."

"She's been trying to identify the leader of the sick bastards who blew up Le Gare Nord, the Paris North Train Station, but we never caught him." I noted.

"Possible. Would the bomber have crossed the pond to find you?"

"Probably depends on whether he thinks I can pick him out in a lineup." Samantha offered.

"Could you?" Randy asked, but then added, "I mean, do you have a suspect from the evidence you gathered at the scene?"

Mimi looked at me as she was supposed to according to the script. "A profile, not a name if that's what you're getting at. And from the profile we've identified literally hundreds of suspects. We're working our way through the list, but it's taking a long time and the trail is getting cold."

"We're helping from our national persons of interest databases, but she's right. The profile fits a lot of people." Rory Gallagher responded through me.

"You'll have to keep working that, but in the meantime, is there anyone else who'd want you dead? Anyone who seems out of place when you look around?" Randy asked.

Samantha did her best to remember, "I don't know. I haven't really paid any attention. This case we've been working has just been all consuming."

"Tell me about it."

"White collar criminal. You know the type. Selling technology to the highest bidder, only the bidder isn't on the approved government lists."

"And the technology blows stuff up?" Randy followed along.

"More like helps those things that blow up, do so close to the right target."

"If it was him, his technology must not be worth much, since it didn't get you." Randy's character wasn't being particularly insightful. I hated when the script was so predictable.

"What If he was on his way to bomb something, and diverted to find you? Maybe he thought he might get two for the price of one."

Rory asked through me.

"Possible." Samantha responded, now looking at it differently.

"Who else could have been involved?" Rory asked still in command of the scene.

"What about Daniel Dixson?" she offered.

Mimi and I looked at each other as if the name had some special significance.

"I thought he was dead." Rory tried to confirm with Samantha.

"Suppose he isn't," Randy responded.

"Do you know something we don't? As former LAPD, he would be a clear security threat." Rory answered. "Why did you rebuff his advances?" Rory turned to Samantha

"I didn't love him."

"He threatened you once, could this be him again?" Rory asked without asking the more obvious question.

"No one ever found the body." Samantha responded.

"Randy, what do you think?"

"I just sent my 'bots' out. Let's see what they come back with."

In only a moment he came up with an address. "Nineteen–twelve Somerset Avenue in Long Beach."

"What's there?" Rory asked.

"His cell phone."

"Whose?" Samantha questioned Randy.

"Daniel Dixson's. According to this, it's been used daily since his reputed death."

John called out, "Cut. Set up the next scene. Quickly, time is money, people."

In the next scene Samantha and I are at a beach house in Long Beach. We confront the tall and laconic actor who plays Daniel Dixson, dressed in swim trunks and flower shirt.

"Why did you threaten to kill Samantha, Daniel?" Rory confronted him.

"That was a long time ago." Daniel dismissed the question.

Rory showed him the note, "She received this last week."

Daniel reacted as if he'd seen a ghost. "That didn't come from me."

"Who did it come from, then?" Samantha asked, unsatisfied.

"The Russian Mafia. See this symbol in the upper right hand corner?"

"Why would they want to kill Samantha?" Rory asked.

"I arrested their head of Paris operations before I came to LA. That was a long time ago." Samantha answered for Daniel.

"Guess it took that long for them to find you." Daniel observed. "You need to take out Sergei Andropov. He's the guy here in LA."

"You willing to help us?" Rory asked.

"I could be convinced."

"Why?" Samantha was still not buying his story.

"Sergei Andropov killed my wife and son."

His response surprised me in the script. Rory would have thought he would have done something before now, so Rory wasn't completely buying his explanation. "So this is personal for you." Rory observed skeptically.

Daniel Dixson nodded grimly.

"Cut." John directed the reset to: The Final scene.

We descended upon Andropov's lair in a West LA warehouse. Local police, CIA, DEA, FBI. We were all there. The gunfire coming from the building pinned us down. Daniel and I circled to the left as the police circled to the right. The fire from the building traced the police's progress, but those inside evidently didn't see Daniel and myself.

As we broke into the room where Andropov was holed up, Daniel took a shot to the chest, but I was right behind and able to take down the shooters, except Andropov who raised his hands in surrender.

"Why should I take you in Sergei?" Rory asked.

"You must. You are police. My lawyers will have me out in the hour. I have done nothing that you can prove."

"But what about those things we can't prove, but we know you did?"

"They never happened in your country."

Sergei reached into his suit coat pocket. Rory saw metal coming out. No time to think, only to react. In a moment one of us would be dead. If Rory hesitated it would be me. Rory fired only one shot, but my arm was fully extended and the gun was aimed at his forehead. The force of the bullet whipped his head back with blood flowing away. He fell straight backwards.

Rory approached the dead Russian. The metal in his pocket was a small bore handgun. Rory had been justified, but now he would never know if Sergei was the one who had threatened Samantha.

Rory went over to Daniel, who was barely alive, but asked, "He dead?"

"Yes."

"My wife and son are vindicated, and now I go to join them."

"Rest easy, Daniel."

"You mean final rest." And Daniel was gone.

Samantha entered the room to find Sergei and Daniel both dead.

"Guess it doesn't make any difference which one wanted me dead." Samantha observed to Rory.

"I just hope it wasn't someone else we haven't thought of." Rory concluded.

John called out, "Cut. You got it. Let's call it a wrap for tonight. Next episode starts production on Monday. Great work everyone."

Mimi walked right past me without acknowledging or looking at me. She simply left her scent behind, which she knew would torture me more than anything else she could do. She approached Robert Anderson who was in a conversation with John about the shoot.

"That sucked. You've got to come up with something more gripping than a shoot-out that's over before it even begins. Give me a break. You take Daniel out and Rory gets everyone else except Sergei? What's the drama to that? I could write a better script than what you had us just do. Besides I had basically nothing to do in that whole scene."

"Now, Mimi. Don't get that way." Robert responded.

"What way? I'm speaking the truth here. I'm going back to my trailer and write the next episode. Why don't you go on vacation or something? You need to get inspired again. I can't think of an inspired script from you in the last two seasons. You're just going through the motions and making us all look bad."

John intervened, "Be fair, Mimi. You want to take a shot at writing a script? Go for it. I'll take it to the producers and if they buy it, we'll make it. That way you can get a screenwriting credit."

Robert didn't like John's offer, "Now wait a moment. She's not in the screenwriter's guild. Can't write for the show unless she's in the guild."

"And she can't get in the guild until she sells a script. So back off Robert. If she writes something we all like, she'll join. Won't you Mimi?"

"If that's the only way you turkeys will make what I write."

"You want a collaborator?" I asked pretty much expecting a strong 'no'.

"Sure. Bring your tablet and keyboard."

That was a surprise. But then I realized it sounded like she was putting Robert in his place. Evidently he was getting too possessive for Mimi, so she was putting some distance between them. Hard to do when you're dependent upon him for your lines. She had to put him on the defensive so he wouldn't minimize her role on the series and give her nothing to do. I wasn't complaining because she'd invited me in, although I expected a frosty reception once I got there.

John stopped her, "What's your premise?"

"I'd rather it be a surprise or Robert will do his take on it and make it harder for anyone to take me seriously."

"We take you dead seriously, Mimi." I offered.

She looked at me as if I had challenged her in some mysterious way I couldn't fathom. But then she softened, "Bring your ideas, I want to make sure this is a collaborative script, since we never seem to get them from Robert." She looked Robert right in the eye and passed on, heading to her trailer.

Chapter Twelve

Jake Goodbody had the perfect name for a torturer. A personal trainer by profession, he thoroughly enjoyed pushing actors to their limits as he made sure we were in the proper shape for the roles we contracted to play. As an action mystery hero, I had to be able to do whatever physical stuff Robert threw into his script. It seemed to me in the last year or so Robert reduced the action sequences. At first I thought the studio had instructed him to do so as they wanted to save money. Any time the studio blew something up, it was bound to be expensive. Especially if it was a car or a house. But Mimi told me that Robert was in one of his cerebral periods. The stories he was imagining were more head crimes than shoot outs and car chases. Maybe that was why the younger demographic was getting bored, Robert wanted them to think, and that wasn't always something popular when someone was trying to relax. Alistair may be right about what the studio was saying to him. If indeed it was Robert behind the shift in my demographic, how could the studio hold me responsible? The fact that we were holding our numbers should indicate I was doing a tremendous job, given the material I had to work with. I'd need to remember that in negotiations.

Jake had me on my back on the sit-ups bench. My feet were hooked so my legs wouldn't move as I sat up. Twisting as I came up, I touched my right elbow to my left knee and back and then left elbow to right knee in an alternating fashion.

"Work your core." Jake encouraged me, although I never saw him doing any of the exercises he had me doing. But looking at Jake, it was clear he spent more time working on his own body than he did mine.

I finished the fifth set of one hundred and lay back. "Tell, me Jake. Why am I doing all this?"

"Your contract. Says you have to be able to do whatever your script calls for you to do, physically. And there's a standard in the industry. I've got to make sure you meet that standard of strength, endurance and lean body mass."

"Since my writer's in a cerebral period, what are you doing to help me exercise my head muscle to be able to follow Robert's logic?"

Jake helped me up with one hand. He was a lot stronger than I was. "Not in my contract or yours, so I wouldn't worry about it."

"So, what am I supposed to do if Robert suddenly gets the brain storm I need to lift a car off a victim? You going to be able to build me up to do that?"

"There's a 'real world' clause in the contract. Says you only have to be able to do the physical things that a person of your age and stature would be expected to be able to do in the real world. So, no. Don't have to worry about lifting cars, or leaping tall buildings in a single bound for that matter. I want you to get down for push-ups. I'm gonna put fifty pounds on your back and I want two sets of two hundred and fifty."

"Taking me up ten pounds. You think I'm ready?"

"If you're not, we'll know before you finish the first set."

I got down on the mat. Jake brought over a fifty-pound weight, stood across me and put the weight down on my back. He kept his hands on both sides as I did the exercise to make sure the weight wouldn't slide off as I did the push-ups.

The first set went fine. I struggled a little more than usual on the last fifty, but got through and Jake lifted the weight off while I rested on my chest on the floor.

"Only a minute." Jake reminded me.

When the time was up, I pushed back up into position and Jake rested the weight on my back once more. I started straining at one-hundred and fifty. Another hundred to go, but I wasn't going to fail to complete the exercise. Jake evidently thought I was ready, so I had to make sure I was. With fifty to go, I knew it was going to be a struggle to get the last ones out. But I gritted my teeth, breathed through my mouth with strong exhales on each up phase, and pushed it out. When I hit two-fifty, I held the top position long enough for Jake to remove the weight and collapsed onto the mat.

"Not so bad, now was it?" Jake could see how much I struggled, but as I said he enjoyed his role as a torturer of actors.

"This amuse you?" I inquired.

"Why do you ask?"

"I mean, you watch our shows. You see us do the stunts. You know which ones require a stunt double and which ones require a little technology to get us through. And then you put us through our paces here in your studio and know we could never do some of the things you see on television."

"I've never seen you do anything on television you couldn't have really done if you'd had to."

"I don't agree." And I didn't. My character had done some things I'd have never attempted in reality.

"Give me an example then." Jake wasn't going to let me skate on this comment.

"Episode one-nineteen, 'The Case of the Runaway Heiress'. I have to run down the kidnapper who's in an autonomous cars, with a block long head start in Manhattan. Those are long blocks, by the way. I've walked them in reality. No way could I have run fast enough to catch an autonomous car with that head start."

But Jake was ready, "Disagree. With a stop light at every block, each with an average dwell time of ninety seconds, the average speed up or down a Manhattan street is only about seven miles an hour. You ran a fifteen kilometer race last year at an average pace of ten miles an hour. So you would have caught that autonomous car in six blocks if you'd only maintained that same pace you ran last year."

"The script called for me to catch it in five, but as you know I didn't run that whole distance. We broke it up into camera shots, which made it look like I caught up in five. Okay, you made your point."

"I have to be right about your fitness level. I'm under contract to deliver you in condition that would permit you to do anything needed by the script and that's what I do."

"I just don't think I need to be in quite that good shape."

"You can think anything you'd like. The contract calls for it, that's what I deliver. A better you. One who the audience looks at and says, yeah, he could do that. Can't create cognitive dissonance now, can we?"

"Cognitive who?" was all I could think of to say.

Chapter Thirteen

Alistair came to my trailer at the studio. Not a good sign. He only came to me when it was bad news. Otherwise he expected Mohammed to come to the mountain. And over the past decade, I'd been a regular visitor at his offices just off Wilshire Boulevard.

When he arrived I was watching the news… again. Another Googlecar repair facility had exploded in the middle of the night. This time in Atlanta. What was going on? The reporter stood off to the side as the firemen rained water on the still smoldering building. He had the fire chief pinned and wasn't going to let him get away without a statement. "What can you tell us Chief Wilcox?"

"We have an eye witness."

"And??" the reporter isn't wasting any words.

"A video, showing that someone put a missile through a window."

"Missile? Like a rocket?"

"It only flew about a quarter of a mile, so it wasn't a very big device, but it carried a lot of explosives. As you can see, it leveled the garage."

"Are you calling this a terrorist event?" The reporter asked the question everyone wanted to know.

"No. We don't have enough information yet on who would possess such devices."

"But a rocket. Isn't that like a military grade weapon?" good follow-up question by the reporter.

The Chief looked away, apparently trying to decide how to answer this question. I knew that whatever he said was going to be pure bullshit from his physical response, so I listened carefully to understand what he didn't want me or anyone to know. "We don't know what we're dealing with yet. Hobbyists have been building model rockets for decades, just as hobbyists built model airplanes before drones and model computers before laptops. We don't want people to draw the wrong conclusions. There are indications of a coordinated set of events. But we simply don't know who or why these are taking place."

I was wrong, it wasn't completely bullshit. He knows something he can't discuss. Probably a coordinated attack using sophisticated weapons. I didn't buy that whole hobbyist thing, even though what he said was true enough. But hobbyists wouldn't be putting that much explosives on their homebuilt rockets. I believed him when he said they didn't know who or why. So what was I to think?

Alistair brought me back into the moment. "Curious, don't you think? But not relevant to what the studio has in mind for you and Mimi."

Alistair was in a talent agency with fifteen partners. That meant he was only one of many, and he wasn't the top dog in the agency. His partners had people who had much more studio clout than I did. Alistair seemed to have gotten stuck with people like me, from whom he could expect to make a decent living, but he'd never have the yacht or private plane his senior partners had. Alistair had chosen to represent people he liked. Several of his partners had people in their portfolio who had infamous reputations as general pains in the ass, but who were enormously popular. The pains in the ass made those partners a lot more money, but they had to work for it. Alistair wasn't hurting by any stretch of the imagination. But neither was he going home to a trophy wife in his privately owned autonomous Lamborghini like some of Alistair's partners.

Alistair settled into his favorite chair in my trailer, which just happened to be my favorite chair in my trailer. "I just met with Jack and

Stan." Jack and Stan were the producers of my show, along with Regina, who was the Executive Producer.

"Regina not there?"

"She was in China or Thailand or some damn place over there." Alistair waved in a westerly direction and sounded annoyed. I'd apparently hit a sensitive point with him. Regina had sent her lower level guys to deliver whatever the bad news was, but didn't participate herself. She probably expected to be hearing from me shortly and wanted to say she wasn't in the meeting.

"So who did most of the talking, Jack or Stan?" Jack was more senior, but Stan was much brighter and had a better feel for what made a good show.

"Jack." It was an official meeting, not a conversation, then.

"And?"

"You're the highest paid actor on the set." Something I already knew, although Mimi constantly complained about just that fact, thinking she should get what I got paid as a co-star, even if only in her mind. I had top billing and top salary as a result.

"How much do they want me to give back?" I could see where the discussion had gone.

"They don't think of it as a give back. They think of it as an adjustment to market rates." Alistair was parroting the discussion to give me insight into how it had gone.

"And they think the market has gone south, even though we're delivering the same market share and they're charging the advertisers more for our show than last year."

Alistair was in full parrot mode, "You can't look at it that way. Your client has held market share, we'll acknowledge, but the components of that share have changed. He's lost the age bottom end who are the ones who spend. He just doesn't have the same draw there anymore. I think he needs to shave his head by the way. It would change the whole dynamic of his face. You see what I mean? It would give him a whole new look that just might appeal to the folks under thirty."

"And you asked Jack if he'd done any focus group studies to support his suggestion?" I asked Alistair, knowing him as well as I did.

"No, I didn't have to. He volunteered that they hadn't done any kind of studies to find out what you need to do. They'd rather you spend the money to do that and give them the results. Said they'd be happy to consider any third party evaluations of how to get your demographic back where it needs to be. But even if you do that, they still intend to adjust you to market, and they've already decided what market is without the benefit of any studies or analysis."

This was going to be a longer conversation than I'd first thought. Alistair rose from my favorite chair, went over to the bar and poured a glass of Italian red wine. He turned to look at me, raised his glass without making a toast and proceeded to drink the entire glass in one long continuous drink. Not a good sign. He refilled the glass and then came over to stand where I normally did at my stand-up desk.

"This isn't a negotiation. They think Johnny Wonderful…."

"Hollywood." I corrected.

"Johnny Hollywood can step in and take your place, not miss a beat, and bring in the lower end of the demographic."

"So why aren't they doing it?"

"Desmond's been a great draw for us. He's still got the essentials." Alistair parroted.

"Which means?"

"They have another show they think they can plug Johnny Wonderful, er… Hollywood, or whatever, into and make even more money, than if they have him replace you."

I nodded. The logic followed. Of course they want to make as much money as they could, but "Why is it a take it or leave it if they have someplace else for Johnny Wonderful?"

"Jack said the modeling shows they should be indifferent as to whether they put Johnny in your spot or the other one. The other actor might be willing to take even less than you to keep his job."

"They didn't tell you who it was?"

"Of course not. I'm not convinced there is another position for Johnny Hollywood. This might be all a big bluff to see how low they can drive you. If you're cheaper than whatever they signed Johnny to, they'll keep you as a better deal."

It was all economics. Nothing about I'd delivered millions of dollars of profits to the network and studio over the past decade. It was all about would I be cheaper than Johnny Hollywood? If so they'd keep me, if not, then I was history. "How much?"

"Of a reduction? Fifty percent. Said that if Mimi was up this year it could have been less if they could have convinced her to participate in the reductions. But she's locked in for another year."

"So I make about two-thirds of what Mimi makes. They going to rename the show the St. Julian Mysteries since she'll be the higher paid star?"

"No, but only because they expect to whack her completely next year."

"Does she know?" I had to ask. Poor Mimi.

"No, and I'm not telling her. She'll be insufferable is she knows." I knew she would.

I walked over to the bar and filled a glass with the same Italian red that Alistair had started. A fifty percent reduction still ended up a whole lot of money. But it sent the message I was willing to go along with their conception of the world. Another studio might be willing to pay me more to do a different role. But was I willing to walk away from a paycheck and hope I could make more doing something I'd never done, and have to go find a whole new audience? "What's your recommendation?"

"Do I think this is the best deal you can get? No. I think you can do better, but it's a crap shoot. Do I have something in my pocket for you? No, because I haven't been shopping you. I always thought they'd come back and want to keep you. Never thought they'd low ball you to this degree. Always thought it would be ten or twenty percent, or something we could negotiate back up. But fifty percent? Not going to happen. I didn't see Johnny Hollywood doing so well with that sequel. It was awful, by the way, but I'm sure you didn't see it."

I hadn't. "Should we walk?" I asked, thinking I already knew the answer.

"My recommendation?" Alistair drained a second glass of wine. This is worse than I thought. "I think we have to play for time. They'll know what we're doing. Can't go very long. But at worst it will give me a chance to have a few conversations and see where the other studios are. Not many have been able to hold a market share as high as you have for as long as you have. The problem is the track record of folks after that long a streak aren't nearly as strong."

I was well aware of those who had left a long running series and tried to go to another series. It never went well. "So you don't expect anyone will stand up with a better deal?"

"I don't know. Several of the studios are in droughts right now. Nothing new has come out in a while. They've got to be scrambling.

There might be an opportunity. Until I make the calls, I just don't know."

I was getting depressed. "When do we have to get back to them?"

"A week, maybe more." Alistair wasn't giving me much maneuvering room.

So the studio thought they had me where they wanted me. I had to find a way to change the dynamic of the negotiations, but would need some time to come up with a plan. "Make your calls. See what's out there."

Alistair looked at me curiously. "Have I lowered your expectations sufficiently?"

"Much lower and I'll be paying them to work here." I answered truthfully.

"They mentioned that, not in the sense of how low they're going with you, but that you ought to be grateful they're willing to consider keeping you when they have other options."

Could this get much worse? I didn't know. I wondered where the real number was where everything went south. Alistair evidently didn't know either. Worst case scenario was I'd be out of work with no paycheck. Best case was something more than half of what I was making this season. What could I do to drive that number higher? I didn't know.

Chapter Fourteen

I needed to talk with Mimi. She was my touchstone. She always had a view of the world I never saw, and for that reason alone, I needed to understand what she saw as my options. All of the information I had said I'd have to just take it and be happy with what I expected would be a one year contract. While Alistair hadn't said anything, I expected the studio would want to reboot when both Mimi and I were off the payroll. That was one more year. I was also curious as to what Johnny Hollywood's contract had been. I wasn't sure they were paying him all that much, given he was essentially a one hit wonder, and they certainly weren't giving me the benefit of the doubt after a decade of delivering profits. Alistair was more than willing to go find out the answer for me.

I picked up Mimi in the Tesla. When I arrived at her apartment, she came out and took one look at the car with me driving. I wasn't sure she would get in. "What's this? A relic from our past?"

"Just get in and don't give me all your shit about breaking a law."

Before she got in she had to ask, "But if they arrest you will they arrest me as an accomplice?"

"Innocent bystander." I assured her.

She got in, but was still not comfortable with the situation. "How do I know you're not kidnapping me and taking me away to some mountain lair where you'll ravish me until I have nothing more to give you?"

"There was a time, but I have no such grand expectations anymore. I just need your insights on what the studio is doing to me and will do to you next year." I had to put it into the self-interest terms that she couldn't refuse to discuss with me. If it had been just me, she probably would have told me good luck and let her know how it all turned out. But now she would see what I was able to negotiate would affect her directly. She couldn't refuse to talk with me about it in such circumstances.

I watched her expectations deflate, "What's Alistair saying?"

"They're piece-mealing it as usual. They want a fifty percent cut. That's as far as they've gone so far. I expect it will only be a one year deal and they say goodbye to both of us."

I watched her deflate another level. She clearly hadn't thought this next season would be the last year, but now she was adjusting to the reality of the situation. "A final season."

"That's my read." I admitted. "They could go to a prequel reboot this season and not do the final season. But it's all a matter of how much money they can make with either option."

She looked at me in horror, "You mean I might have to do this season with Johnny Hollywood?"

I shook my head. "I think if I go, they'll buy you out and go directly to the reboot without either of us."

My observation was even harder for her to take. Alistair had warned us, but it was just a negotiations tactic in Mimi's mind. We'd been here before and it was always the same. Find some way to drive down the price of our contracts so they could make even more money. But now she saw there was a very real prospect that we wouldn't even be back for one more season.

She sat quietly thinking through the situation. I drove us out of the city. She was no longer thinking about the fact I was breaking the law, or that she was riding in a car that legally no longer existed. She was confronting the future and it was suddenly painted in terms she'd not considered.

I drove us out towards the airport and into the wilds of El Segundo. This was a misnomer in that most of the beach area was built out, but there were lots of back streets where I could drive and probably avoid detection. I went to the Manhattan Beach waterfront. It was a high end community with small but very expensive homes and big incomes. It was the kind of place no one could imagine a law breaker tooling down their well landscaped streets and through manicured lawns and gardens. Even though California was in the midst of a decade long draught, money made it possible to buy the water individuals needed to keep their tiny lawns and gardens growing.

I drove us to the pier and parked out front of the Williams Sonoma store. Every car around us was an autonomous car owned by an individual. That was highly unusual. Most people took the Googlecars everywhere. Not here. Money was a strange thing. Those who had it spent it on things the rest of us wouldn't consider. But then I was driving an old Tesla which few, if any, of those with the expensive autonomous car would ever consider acquiring given they were illegal.

Mimi opened her door even before I had the car shut down. I'd ruined her whole day, just as Alistair had ruined mine. She headed off to the pier as if I weren't even there. So I gave her space and followed along behind until she turned to look for me. I saw in her eyes that she was afraid I hadn't followed, but then the smile I was hoping to see finally appeared. She slowed to wait for me to catch up, which took only a moment.

"You afraid I was going to just walk off the end of the pier?" she asked.

"Never considered it." I responded truthfully.

"If this were the end of my career, I would, you know."

I put my arm around her shoulders and slowed her walk to match mine. "It's only a blip in the road. If I do what they want we'll have another year and that will give us time to find that next thing."

She looked out over the Pacific Ocean. "Is this the high point of our careers or the end?"

She was still trying to absorb the reality of the situation. "This isn't the end for either of us." She looked up at me to gage what I was saying. I was the one looking out over the Pacific now, perfectly calm and not about to let the studio define who I was or what I'd do next.

We walked in silence out to the end of the pier. There she disengaged my arm around her and leaned over the railing looking directly down into the water. "Fifty percent give back, hunh?"

"Yes." Was my full and complete answer. I was happy she'd returned to my problem.

"What can we do to drive up ratings for the rest of this season?"

"You ready to do the topless scene?"

"I'm serious." So was I.

"You're the one with direct influence over Robert. We've got to have better scripts to make any difference."

She looked back at me, "We're supposed to write the next one, you and me. You got any ideas?"

"I thought you did, the way you negotiated that whole deal." I was surprised she was saying she didn't.

"I was just angry with Robert. He expects me to make all the decisions for him."

"Seems to me you'd scripted that whole change to the last episode. Did Robert do that for you and just not tell the studio?"

She nodded. Same old Mimi. She knew how to manipulate men better than anyone I'd ever known. She'd certainly manipulated me when we were together.

"So is Robert going to do the next script and let you present it as your own so you can get a screenwriting credit?"

"No. He didn't see that coming. I was just angry with him and it all just came out. Maybe I was finally seeing what the studio is saying, that the scripts aren't serious anymore. I don't know."

"Do you remember Grant Boerner?"

She raised one eyebrow and looked back at me.

"He's the Production Assistant who helped us with the ten year retrospective last year."

She shook her head. Guess Grant didn't make a big impression. "He talked to me about some ideas he had. Things he'd like to see us do on the show. I thought he had some good ideas. We ought to talk with him."

"We don't need any help. We can do this. Just you and me, like it used to be."

"It won't be like it used to be until you forgive me." I observed.

She looked back out to the ocean and the sun setting in the distance. "No, it won't be like it was. But we can do this. You just have to get your head around it."

"And what about you?"

"I'll edit your drafts." She coyly looked around to see my expression.

"So it will be like it used to be." I smiled.

She laughed and pushed me away. I stepped back towards her, put my arms around her and kissed her on the top of her head, as I knew that was about all she'd permit. We slowly walked back up the pier towards the waiting Tesla. We didn't talk as I was furiously trying to figure out what plot I'd want to use for an episode script. Even though Mimi didn't want to bring anyone else in, I knew I'd call Grant and discuss my ideas with him, just to get an outside perspective. I was far from confident that I could come up with a great script all by myself.

Once in the Tesla, Mimi was fidgety. She turned on the radio and the announcer was in the middle of a headline, "...shut down the plastics refinery in the Houston ships channel. No immediate indication of any injuries or casualties as yet. But the officials have just reached the site of the explosion. We will provide more information as it becomes available. To repeat, there has been an explosion at an oil refinery in Houston, Texas. This refinery produces the raw materials used in plastics manufacture. No indication at this time as to who might be responsible."

"What's that all about?" Mimi asked and I knew she didn't expect me to answer.

"Someone unhappy with our plastic society?" I answered only half seriously.

"But who? That's a pretty drastic step to take. Getting through security and all. Must have been pretty well organized. Could we use that as the premise of our script? You know? Someone blows up something and we have to go investigate and bring the guilty party to justice."

I listened to her plea. She had no idea what to write about. She was grasping at straws, but therein may lie an answer to our dilemma. "What if we do stories that are based on real events? Like this one."

"That's what I'm saying. This could be the plot. You and me, finding the people responsible and bringing them to justice."

"Where does Interpol fit in?" I asked, since her role had to make sense. Couldn't be just a plot that Interpol wouldn't participate in.

"Could be international terrorists. Maybe the Saudi's are mad that we've become independent of them for our oil. Trying to get back at us by shutting down our production of end products."

"I'd go with the French. They never liked us." I suggested.

"But people like the French. I'd go with the Germans. They always seemed like they were still angry about losing that last war against us."

"If we're going in that direction, let's say the Russians. They've always been against us."

"Except when they weren't." Mimi observed.

"Even when they weren't against us, they really weren't for us."

"I can live with the Russians as the bad guys." Mimi was getting into it.

I had to slow us down. "So why would the Russians want to blow up a plastics refinery?"

Mimi looked at me quizzically. "I think you need to answer that. You're the one who reads everything. What do you think?"

I had no answer to her question. So we sat in silence. She was expecting me to come up with something brilliant and I didn't know what it would be. Suddenly a dog wandered into the street. The autonomous cars all came to an immediate halt, but I had to swerve to miss the animal. By doing so I was forced to drive across a ditch and into a front yard before coming to a halt. My back tires were still in the ditch. I put the car into reverse and the tires spun. I wasn't going to be going anywhere. I really didn't want to go to the authorities to get help. That was a high probability of getting the car impounded and I might end up in jail, even if only for a short time.

"Now what?" Mimi looked around. People were getting out of the Googlecars and the homeowner came out his front door. The owner looked to be around forty and probably forty pounds overweight. He was wearing a t-shirt and jeans with bare feet. I got out of the Tesla and started walking towards him.

"You what's his name?"

"Rory Gallagher?" I answered. With that name out there the others who were gathering around seemed to take a second look at me and Mimi, who was still in the car.

The homeowner started looking around for the cameras, and the others seemed to take his cue to do the same. "You on a case here?"

It occurred to me that I might be able to bluff my way through this situation. "Think you could help me get my car back on the road?"

"What happened?" he was still looking around.

I answered truthfully, "Dog wandered into the street."

"Your autonomous car have a glitch or something?"

He seemed to be going along with me. "Yeah. Had to override to keep it from hitting the dog."

My explanation seemed to satisfy him, although the others who had come over from their autonomous cars seemed less satisfied with my answer. I went to the window and spoke to Mimi. "Can you steer it out for us? We're going to push it."

The homeowner came over, "I thought the autonomous car would steer itself out."

"Already glitched once. Don't think I want to take the chance if we're pushing it."

"That Samantha St. Julian?"

"Yeah."

"You working a case?" I had to respond in such a way that he wouldn't expect to see himself on television that night.

"Afraid I can't say much. You'll have to watch and everything will become clear."

"Didn't realize your show was a reality series."

"I get that a lot." I had to keep him focused on getting the car out. "Think if we push it forward we can steer it around to your driveway?"

"Probably easier to push it down and back up onto the street." The owner was taking charge.

I called over to the others who were watching, "Can you help us push it back down from the lawn?"

Half a dozen men came over and joined in. We pushed slowly knowing we had to push the back tires up and out of the ditch. Eventually the front tires would go down into the ditch and that would be the real test if we could get it back up on the street. The eight of us were enough. The back tires came up and out of the ditch.

"This is a heavy mother." The homeowner observed.

"The battery pack underneath." I answered.

In only a moment the front tires were in the ditch. Now came the hard part. Gravity wasn't going to help us push it down, because now we were in the ditch pushing up. We strained a lot more. Mimi turned on the car and put it into reverse. She pushed down on the accelerator. The tires spun, but the added force was just enough for us to push it up onto the street. Mimi slammed on the breaks to keep it from going into the ditch on the other side of the street.

The homeowner tapped me on the shoulder, "Did she do that?"

"Must have been the autonomous car kicking in."

"Why would it do that?" He was trying to figure out what was going on. I needed to get away before he asked many more questions.

I shrugged as Mimi returned to the passenger seat. I turned to the crowd and those who had helped. "Thanks very much. I really appreciate your help."

A teenaged girl came over to the window. Mimi opened it and the girl passed a piece of paper and pen through the window. Mimi autographed it for her and passed it back through. Several others came over and Mimi and I gave them each an autograph.

Chapter Fifteen

Mimi arrived at my trailer early to work on the script the next day. We had a premise and some ideas that we were fleshing out in an outline. I'd called Grant Boerner after I'd dropped Mimi off and returned to my apartment. He was willing to help for a credit, but I told him I couldn't give it to him as Mimi was the co-author and she didn't want anyone else involved. So we agreed on a fee for his suggestions, but he wouldn't do any of the actual writing.

"I don't like that idea. It marginalizes my character." Mimi was in her whole defensive role. She wanted to be the central character and she'd gotten away with it once. Since the episode hadn't aired yet, I had no idea how it would be received. So I was trying to convince her we needed to keep this episode more in line with the series format. That meant I was the lead character.

"The best I'm willing to give you is equal lines and equal air time. You want me to write it, so that means you have to accept what I come up with."

"No, I don't. This was my idea. I got John to guarantee he'd take it to the producers if I did it, not you."

"But then you told everyone you wanted me to help write it. So do you want to do this yourself or are you going to help me figure out how we do this?"

She was unhappy with me, but I knew she'd accept the situation and let me do what I needed to in order to come up with a good story. She knew I'd give her more than her due, which was more than Robert had been doing until she got him to help her rewrite the one episode. Even then she had to spring it on everyone to get it made and then refuse to redo the scene to get it on air. That option was closed now as they'd never let her do it again.

"I think the Russian angle works if we cast it as part of a larger conspiracy." I started out.

A knock at the door distracted us.

"Yes?" Mimi called out.

Mimi's young production assistant, Ellen opened the door. "Did you hear the news?"

"What news?" I asked.

"It's all over."

"What is?" Mimi inquired.

"The autonomous cars. They've shut down. Nobody can get anywhere."

Ellen's statement didn't make any sense to me. "What do you mean they've shut down?"

"They all just stopped," she responded.

I turned on the news station. "…stranded motorists are walking to their destinations. Officials at the Department of Transportation have confirmed that whatever has shut down the auto-drive systems is a global phenomenon."

I looked at Mimi, still not believing what I was hearing.

"Are you thinking what I am?" she asked.

"The conspiracy we were looking for?"

Mimi turned to Ellen. "I need you to research what's going on. Find out anything you can on the auto-drive systems. What could have caused this? Who would have been able to bring them down? Is there anywhere that wasn't affected? What about transport systems? Are they affected too, or are they still working? We need to know everything about what's happening."

"Why? I just stopped by to tell you that you can't go home until they get them back up."

Part Two: Changed Circumstances

Chapter Sixteen

Without the Googlecars to take us to dinner, Mimi called over to the canteen to see if they could deliver dinner to us in my trailer. That proved to be no problem, however, one dish Mimi wanted in particular wasn't available. They'd run out of the ingredients and weren't sure when the supplier would be able to restock them. "Jacques said they might get some in the next day or two, but call again early tomorrow if the car problem isn't solved. Said they've been getting a lot of calls, and they really aren't stocked up for this many people." Mimi informed me.

I was only half listening, trying to put the car problem into the context of a Russian conspiracy for our episode. I was becoming more and more excited about the possibilities. The more I thought about it, the more plausible a longer running story line seemed to me. The problem was going to be how to get Robert on board. "Tell me what you see happening after our one episode?"

"Were you listening to me?" Mimi demanded to know.

"Dinner's on its way. Were you listening to me?"

"I haven't eaten, we need an episode as quickly as we can produce it and you're asking philosophical questions."

Since she'd dismissed my question, I needed to make her understand why it was relevant. "The food's coming, isn't it?"

"Yes, but..."

I cut her off before she could finish her thought, "And we have a concept for an episode..."

"Yes, but…"

"In order for us to decide how to construct this episode, we have to know what happens afterwards."

I don't know if I wore her down, or she heard something in my voice, but she focused in, "Russian conspiracy… you thinking this might be more than a single episode?"

"If we construct this right, it might make it harder for the studio to end our contracts now."

"I see where you're going." Mimi sat back on the sofa, now fully on the same page with me. "We finish the season with this plot line and leave a cliff hanger on the season finale, they have to bring us back."

"Or we do our single episode, show the studio we can develop a script that jumps our market share and next year we may be back as writers."

"I'm out on that count. Robert lives and dies each week based solely on the numbers and not the merit of the script. You wouldn't believe how many times I've heard his complaint."

"So he talks right up to the climax?" I suggested, expecting her to refuse to answer.

Her eyes widened, "Through it. I mean he never shuts up and just enjoys the moment."

That was more than I wanted to know. At least if things ever changed and Mimi was willing to share a bed with me again, I knew how she felt about when to shut up.

Mimi looked at me strangely, she must have guessed what I was thinking. "Talk to me about how you see this plot line playing out." She wasn't going to comment on my reaction. Guess I could forget about sharing her bed any time soon.

"Series of explosions around the country. First the Googlecar repair complexes, then the Houston refinery."

"You thinking of using the actual events?" Her question was neutral. She hadn't thought of using actual events, but hadn't reacted negatively to the thought. That was good. She was open to trying something totally out of character with what the series had done so far. "That would make us more like the reality shows we're up against in our time slot."

"Reality seems to go well with the younger half of our demographic and that's where Alistair says the studio thinks we're weak."

"You were actually listening to Alistair. Sometimes I wonder about that." Her mocking words weren't supported by the tone of her voice. She was actually surprised. And that made me believe she hadn't thought Alistair was being given the facts by the studio. Often in negotiations they fed us a bunch of statistics they knew we couldn't confirm independently. The surveys were always random samples, and any other independent survey wouldn't ask the same questions of the same people. They might get different, although in theory they should be similar, results.

I flashed back to last weekend for a moment before answering. "You never met Natalie." Mimi looked at me like she was waiting for me to say more. I guess from the tone of my voice I hadn't asked a question. "My high school girl friend." Mimi frowned like she was wondering where I was going. "I saw her last weekend when I went to my Uncle's funeral." Mimi nodded. "She told me I never let anything stop me from doing what I wanted, or getting what was important to me. She was talking about the fact I wouldn't marry her. Have a half dozen kids right out of high school. But she was more right than I guess I'd realized. The series has me on autopilot. I haven't had to fight for what I wanted in the last ten years. Everything's been too easy. Was I different that first year to two of the series?"

Mimi thought back, "I didn't like you then."

"So nothing's changed." I inserted to see how she reacted.

"For different reasons. You were arrogant. Intense. I thought you had a chip on your shoulder and a need to make everyone else look like idiots."

She was looking through me to a different me, one she had to deal with a long time ago. "Did I make you look like an idiot?"

"I wouldn't let you. You certainly tried. Every good suggestion I had to improve the story, you poo, poo'd."

She showed me scars I didn't know she carried. Scars from me that I didn't even know I'd caused. "I'm sorry."

She leaned forward with her elbow on her knee and chin in her hand. It was a pose I'd seen often in the last ten years. It usually meant she was trying to work through something and had no idea what she might decide. "Are you really? Do you even know what I'm talking about?"

"How long did that go on?" I asked confirming her worst impression.

"Are you kidding me? It still goes on. To this very day. In fact, you're doing it right now. You don't know what you do to people. You walk into the room and everything stops because you have arrived. You're the king of the jungle. The top dog. Everyone should just listen to you and everything will be great. Bullshit. There are other ideas, better than yours. There are people who have needs to be important, just like you. And you don't care. You don't have any idea we're here, what we're feeling or what we need to get through the day. You just don't care because you're getting what you need."

I accepted Mimi's observations like a boxer who was being worked over by someone bigger and stronger as I looked for an opening to get in my shot. But when she finished, I couldn't do it. I couldn't take the shot. "I'm not."

"Not what?" She seemed confused by my response.

"Getting what I need." I hesitated before going on to see what she said. She said nothing so I continued. "Going home I got to see the alternative future I'd not chosen. I came to see that people who are meant to be together and stay together have to share each other's dreams. That's more important than anything else. I've not been with anyone since you left who shares my dreams, can really understand why I do what I do. Can help me to do what I do better. Can share the enjoyment of little things most people ignore. Everyone I meet just thinks I've got it made and I'd be a great meal ticket. I can't be with anyone like that, and neither can you."

Mimi reached out and straightened my hair, putting it back into place. "You probably need to go home more often," she said softly. "Reconnect with your roots and appreciate where you are in life."

I wanted to kiss her, but the television beeped to signal an important news broadcast was about to be made. We both looked at the set, to my right at the other end of the room.

The set came on automatically. The image was of a large night time city. Western hemisphere since it was night in LA. The missing information scrolled across the bottom of the screen, 'Sao Paolo, Brazil – Dr. Silmara Cardoso, Global Terrorism Threat Analysis Chief.' An attractive dark complexioned woman with long raven black hair blinked back at us. "I know everyone is wondering when things will get back to normal. Let me assure you that thousands of individual across the globe are working different aspects of the problem and we will do so as quickly as humanly possible."

"Humanly?" I asked Mimi.

"Wonder what she's trying to say." Mimi responded.

"They don't trust the machines to self-diagnose and solve this themselves." I responded, but Mimi didn't comment.

Chapter Seventeen

I didn't think to ask Alistair how he got to Da Fortunato's. He had called the next morning and said we needed to meet in person. He said he'd find a way to get to the nearby restaurant if we would walk over from the studio. I'd called Mimi, who had gone back to her own trailer right after dinner, to let her know of Alistair's request. "It's a long walk. Couldn't he come here and we could have the canteen bring dinner like last night?"

"You told me Jacques said he was running low on things. Not sure we'd have much choice tonight."

"I thought you weren't listening." She reminded me.

"I always listen to you." Was my stock reply.

She laughed, "You rarely listen to me."

"I always listen, I just don't always do what you ask." I clarified.

"That was your big mistake." She went right for the jugular. I took a moment to recover. Where did she want to go with this discussion? I decided she wanted to be alone.

"I'll come by your trailer at 6:30. We should be able to walk it in about thirty minutes."

"Why don't you walk to your garage and bring your Tesla by to pick me up?"

My garage was an hour away on foot. She was testing me for some reason, and I didn't quite know why. "Okay. Your chauffer will stop by to pick you up at 6:45." Mimi was gone. No good-bye, no thanks, no 'would you really do that for me?' Nothing.

Alistair was already at Da Fortunato's when we arrived at 7:00. The restaurant was busy, but Alistair had a way of getting us in when it seemed no one else could. A quick shake of the hands and a thank you for coming preceded sitting down and a glance at the new menu. They only had soup, salad, three entrées and two sides listed. No appetizers, no desserts.

"Not much choice," Alistair apologized. "We could try someplace else."

"It'll be the same problem everywhere." I offered to help him relax. He was clearly uptight about something and I expected we would learn the answer quicker if we just stayed put.

We ordered and waited for the waiter to retreat into the kitchen. "What's so important?" I asked.

"Stan told me off the record the reboot is the favored scenario right now. He said he disagrees. Thinks there's more life to the series and with a few tweaks we can get to where we need to be. Jack is death on his scenario and Regina hasn't weighed in yet."

Mimi inserted herself, "Regina always sides with Jack because he's the money guy."

"Not always." Alistair cautioned us. "Stan has picked the last five winners in a row. Jack turned them all down, but Stan convinced Regina to commission a pilot on each. They've all been successes. So Stan has her ear."

"But this is different. It's not a new series a pilot can prove. We're an established series whose demographics are changing." I noted.

"Regina likes you." Mimi said to me.

"Not as much as she likes making money." Alistair pointed out.

"What do you mean Regina likes me?" I had to ask Mimi since I had no such vibes from the woman.

"She told me. Regardless of how bad the script, you've always seemed to find a way to convey something interesting to the audience. That's why we haven't lost the demographic."

"The gross demographic, you have lost the specific sweet spot the studio is most interested in." Alistair wanted to make sure we didn't drink our own bathwater.

"So, if it was us or… Mystery Science Theater…"

"She'd go with Mystery Science Theater. You know what a big Science Fiction buff she is." Mimi brought me back to reality.

"But she cancelled Mystery Science Fiction Theater three years ago because it wasn't delivering the demographic and she couldn't find a sponsor who loved the story more than money." Alistair closed the discussion and deflated the rest of the air from my trial balloon.

The waiter brought the soup Mimi ordered. We sat silently as she tasted her cheddar cheese and cold avocado soup and waited for it to cool.

I couldn't believe the series would really end in the next few weeks, then I remembered, "What about Johnny Hollywood? You find out what the studio is paying him?" I asked Alistair.

"It's a per episode contract. So they have nothing out there until he goes to work and the contract is weighted to ratings. He can make a whole lot if it delivers a great demographic and not much if he doesn't."

"Specifics Alistair. How far down do I need to go to be equal to him?"

"You need to agree to something with the same formula. You get a flat rate to continue delivering the audience you bring now. You change the demographics favorably and you get a big check, but if you don't you make practically nothing."

"So I agree to my current salary for the current audience…" I started out, but Alistair cut me off.

"You agree to half your current salary to deliver the current audience on a one year deal. You change the demographic the way they want and you can get back to where you are. You don't and you're not renewed."

Alistair had the deal, but hadn't shared it until we pushed him. It was obvious why. The deal sucked and he knew I'd never accept such a humiliating proposal. I think Alistair thought we were done. That explained why we had to meet face-to-face. This was to be the last supper together.

"If I accept their terms, where does Johnny Hollywood go?" I asked, trying to understand the whole set of dynamics under the proposal.

"They don't have another spot for him. Stan told me Jack doesn't believe you'd ever accept such a deal, so they think your ego will hand them the opportunity to do the reboot for next season."

"Robert is already doing outlines for the first season." Mimi confirmed to my surprise.

"How long have you known that?" Alistair asked. I was too angry with her to respond.

"A month." She affirmed. "Robert said it was all just concept stuff and he didn't expect they'd ever really follow through." She could see how angry I'd become, even though I hadn't said a word. "I couldn't tell you because I knew you'd get upset and it was all just concept stuff. Nothing made it real or anything."

I couldn't look at her. She'd withheld something important from me. Why would she do that? Oh yeah, because I wasn't supposed to know she was sleeping with Robert. No one was supposed to know, even though everyone on the lot knew. Why didn't she want me to know she was sleeping with our writer? Oh yeah, because she was setting it up so she would be the one to solve the mystery. Maybe her endgame really was to have it be the St. Julian Mysteries next season, only the studio had different options it was exploring. She hadn't accounted for her neutering of the writer would have the effect of jeopardizing everything we'd worked a decade to secure.

Alistair finally responded, "When were you going to tell me?"

Mimi was fully in the defensive mode now. "I didn't think it was important, Alistair. Besides, what would you have done differently if you had known?"

Alistair was up on his feet looking down at Mimi, "I'd have started the dialog with them a month ago, specifically addressing the issue of Johnny Hollywood. I'd have been building a strategy to ensure he wasn't a credible alternative for the studio. I'd have been out there, working Regina and sponsors and finding you a new writer. Who in their right mind would have accepted an assignment that undercut his whole cast and crew?"

"Robert." I answered Alistair's question.

"Oh, yeah, we are talking about Robert here, aren't we." Alistair understood why I answered the way I did. We all shared the same opinion of Robert. He was easily influenced by everyone and he usually went with whatever the last person who spoke with him suggested. That was why I let Mimi argue with him for hours about how he portrayed her character in the script. When they were finished I'd go talk with Robert about how I wanted to change a few things, minor things that would move the story along a little better. I didn't challenge him, I didn't beat him up the way Mimi would in front of everyone. I wanted tweaks. I wanted to improve the story, not change it. I affirmed I valued what Robert did as the head writer. Mimi belittled him on the set. But in the end, Robert had gotten into Mimi's bed. Maybe his strategy was better than mine. Maybe the public humiliation was worth it when the reward was sleeping with this gorgeous woman. But that too had apparently come to an end. Did that mean Robert would start working on the reboot scripts while Mimi and I tried to produce something to keep us alive for another season? Maybe Mimi had played directly into Robert's hands. Maybe he'd made her angry on purpose so he could ensure his employment on the reboot. Robert didn't seem either that smart or that conniving. Maybe I'd been underestimating the guy all these years. No, I hadn't. But Robert still seemed to be coming out in better shape than we were.

"So what are we going to do?" Alistair asked.

"Do you remember the law and order series?" I asked him.

"Yeah. It was more popular than you are and lasted a whole lot longer. Why?"

"That's what I was going to ask you, why?"

"Blend of cops and courtroom. People liked that." Alistair reflected.

"It also based the stories on real events and people." Mimi answered for me.

"Did it? I don't remember that. So what are you suggesting?" Alistair looked confused.

"We're going to base the episodes on real people and events, things people have heard about." I responded this time.

Alistair sat back down, considering. "Your time slot is all reality shows on the other channels."

I nodded.

"What about your Tesla? Could you do something for real with the LA detectives? Go take them for a ride until the Googlecars come back up? We could film the whole thing. Do it live. You need to strike while the iron's hot. No telling how long the autonomous cars will be down." Alistair was getting excited.

Mimi and I looked at each other. "I should have thought of that." She said to me with a smile.

I turned to Alistair, "You want to make the call, or should I?"

Alistair had his phone out before I even finished the question.

Chapter Eighteen

The Walt Simmons, my cameraman, sat in the back with Detective Peter Jefferies, and Detective Kareem Hussain. Mimi rode in front with me. We'd been able to get a portable transmitter into the trunk so the studio could pick up our pictures live. They'd had to work with the news division to get use of their equipment. We thought a news feel would make the impact more immediate. The news division editors would also make the story flow differently than the hour segments we normally made. We hoped that would add to the appeal. What we didn't know was so many people were at home and unable to go anywhere that many all over the world were curious to see what we were up to.

Kareem asked me to drive over to Culver City first thing. He hadn't given me any specifics and I thought I needed to just reconfirm my understanding of how this drive would go down. "Full access to any crime scenes. We've signed all the releases your lawyers asked for, so if I can add something of value, we simply want you to listen to what we have to say. If it doesn't help, we understand and will back away."

Kareem was more uncomfortable with the situation than Peter. "Look. This ain't no circus. Somethings going down, I expect you to stay with the car and keep your head down. We're not goin' to do anything to help you get pretty pictures. We got jobs to do and you need to stay out of the way."

I stopped the car. No need to worry about anyone crashing into us, since the roads were empty.

"What's the deal?" Kareem wanted to know.

"The agreement here says I can drive this car anywhere without fear of arrest or prosecution under the automated highways act. If you'd like to ride along, we will be happy to take you wherever it makes sense. If you're going to change the deal we have with the commissioner, I'm afraid you're back walking my friends."

Kareem looked at me like I was the devil himself. He clearly wanted to say something to me, and I had a pretty good idea what, but he refrained. "Drive on."

"What's the address?"

"11222 Washington Place. Just off the 405"

Mimi asked, "Isn't that near Tito's Tacos?"

"That is Titos." Kareem confirmed.

"Why are we going there?" Mimi sounded suspicious.

"'Cause I'm hungry." Kareem wasn't going to make this easy.

When I pulled up, the line was long, as usual, people were walking away. I usually got the tacos with cheese, chips and salsa. But the line was discouraging because I'd end up wasting most of the evening just getting dinner. That didn't work for me when the studio team was over at the news bureau waiting for video to start coming in.

I went around the block, crossed under the 405.

"A crowd. Something happening there." Mimi pointed to a crowd standing over a man in the street. I came to a stop a very short distance away and we all converged on the fallen man. The crowd watched us suspiciously, especially Walt, with the camera.

"What's going down here?" Kareem asked the crowd.

A short Hispanic man in a leather jacket and jeans called out from the back of the crowd, "Someone shot Pepe. He was just crossing the street minding his own business."

Detective Jefferies went to the victim, but it was clear that Pepe, if indeed his name, wouldn't be going anywhere except the morgue. He'd taken a shot to the head.

"Now why would someone do that?" Kareem wanted to know of the leather clad man.

"Half these shootings don't make sense," came as the reply. "My guess, someone just wanting to show they're a man."

I looked around at the crowd. Then I looked back at the leather man in the back row who was doing all the talking. I caught him making eye contact with another man, similar leather jacket and jeans who was standing across the street and down a few buildings, in front of a Laundromat. I started walking in that direction and was soon able to see a young woman through the Laundromat window. She was over dressed to be washing her clothes, seemed upset and kept looking up at the man in the doorway.

I glanced around and Walt was following us, catching everything we were doing. I walked up to the second man, flashed my series badge, after all I was an LA Detective in the show, turned him around and, "Spread 'em."

"Hey, man. I'm just standing here."

"And I'm just Santa Claus. Where's the gun. Is it in one of the washing machines?" I was wrong, he had it tucked into the small of his back inside his pants belt, but under the jacket. "My. Now what do we have here?" I took a handkerchief from my pocket and then, the weapon from him with the handkerchief. I lifted the .38 six shooter to my nose. "Recently fired. You have anything to say?"

"I want a lawyer."

Detective Jefferies had seen what was happening and joined us. He handcuffed the man and then I handed the weapon to him. I called over to Kareem, "Hold him. He's part of this." Kareem turned to look at what we were doing and the first Leatherman took off. Kareem went after him. I nodded to the laundromat window. Mimi understood and went inside.

She approached the over-dressed young woman. Her eyes grew wide. "What did I do?"

"Is Pepe your boyfriend?" Mimi asked, guessing.

"His name is Enrique Esparza." The young woman responded, quietly.

"Why'd they kill him?"

She was afraid, just kept looking at the man in the window that I had cuffed.

"Who's the shooter?"

The young woman didn't want to answer, but changed her mind. "My brother."

"He have a name?" Mimi asked.

"Luis Rodriguez Matta."

"And you are?"

"Maria."

"I should have known." Mimi began. "So Enrique was trying to make peace between the Crips and the Bloods so he could marry you and live happily ever after? That the story?"

Maria shook her head. "Enrique wanted to give me drugs. Said it was just coke, so no big deal. Luis found out he'd been giving heroin to some girls over in Palms. Got them into prostitution to keep up their habit. Luis said he'd do the same to me."

"So Luis and his friend used you as bait to get Enrique out here?"

Mimi summarized.

"No one said anything about killing him. Luis just said he'd make sure he didn't bother me anymore."

"Alright, Maria Rodriguez Mata. You live at home with your brother?"

"Yeah, about two blocks over. You going to have to tell my parents?"

Mimi nodded as if she knew this question was coming.

"He deserved to die. The cops don't do nothin'. Don't we have a right to defend ourselves from predators like him?" Mimi could tell by the tremor in her voice she was trying to convince herself as well as Mimi.

"That's for the courts to decide. Come with me, Maria." Mimi and Maria went outside to where Detective Jefferies and I held Luis Rodriguez Mata.

"We have a weapon, a motive and a witness. All we need is Detective Hussain and Luis' accomplice and I think we'll be done here." I noted.

"What about the body?" Jefferies this time.

"I suspect Samantha and Detective Hussain will be happy to do the crime scene investigation."

Jefferies seemed to be wondering who Samantha was, but evidently put it together. "I'll take you, and our friends back in and then come back for Samantha, Detective Hussain and the body."

We started walking back to the Tesla when Kareem came around the corner with the accomplice. Luis turned to me and asked, "How'd you find us? Cars ain't supposed to be working."

"Don't believe everything you hear." I responded as we met up with Kareem. We put the three kids, for that was what they were, in the back of the Tesla.

"How do we keep them there?" Kareem asked.

"Child proof locks."

Jefferies had to ask, "How'd you know?"

I turned to Walt, my cameraman who was filming the whole thing and said, "Episode twelve, first season. Explains everything." Jefferies and I got into the Tesla and Walt filmed us driving away.

Chapter Nineteen

Dr. Silmara Cardoso, the Global Terrorism Threat Analysis Chief, sat in her office in a non-descript office building in the heart of Sao Paolo, Brazil. She was about to commence a teleconference with two members of her team, but she knew the time differences were a killer. Kalindi Jain, her Counter Terrorism Expert was eight and a half hours ahead of her in New Delhi and Bomani, her Forensic Software Analyst, was five and a half hours ahead in a suburb of Cairo. That explained why she always made these calls first thing in the morning for her.

"Good afternoon, everyone." She always tried to be upbeat on these calls, no matter how she actually felt about things.

"Good morning to you." Kalindi responded. Bomani held up his index finger and waved it at her, side-to-side, as he was his habit.

"Do you have any insights you wish to share today?" Silmara began.

Bomani raised the same index finger to indicate he wished to speak. Kalindi noticed in time to withhold her comments. "I can confirm it is a virus. It's not code I recognize. Whoever developed this went to great lengths to disguise the origin. The usual telltale signs of various coders are missing. That would mean this originates with someone new to this game, which I think unlikely, or the source wanted to make sure it would take us a long time to track them."

"Time is not on our side." Silmara noted aloud. "What else can you tell us so far?"

"Appears to be a Trojan. That means someone planted this inert, probably some time ago. I can't tell yet if it was activated internally or externally. I suspect it was external given all the autonomous cars stopped functioning at exactly the same moment. Would have been very difficult to have coordinated that so precisely across so many vehicles with an internal software clock, unless the software Trojan was uploaded to all machines simultaneously. That's a possibility, but again, I suspect it not as likely."

Kalindi observed, "Sounds like someone has planned this event for a long time."

"Their preparation was meticulous. Really well thought out and planned long in advance from what I can see." Bomani added.

Kalindi added, "My investigation has not detected any breaches of the firewalls at Googlecar or any of the other autonomous car manufacturers. I can find no evidence of hackers gaining entry through a trap door of any kind. This software has been screened using all of the most advanced tools for non-conformance to the master. I must come to only one conclusion. As Bomani has observed, this software virus is a Trojan. I believe it was uploaded at an update of the software. That would have distributed it across all systems at the same time. The conformity checks mean the virus was part of the code submitted for the update."

Silmara listened to her team mates stoically. "Then the code was tampered with at the factory?"

"At the software developer, yes. They submitted the software with the virus in place, probably inert. Someone was able to embed in the master early on, so it was seen as just part of the code in all conformity checks. I suspect the Trojan has been there a very long time." Bomani responded.

Silmara was curious with his choice of words, "Very long meaning weeks or months?"

"Very long meaning years or maybe even a decade or more." Bomani clarified.

"How is that even possible?" Silmara asked.

Kalindi offered a possibility, "Whoever is responsible must have known our software security tools would only improve over time. By embedding the code, inert in an early master, it would be seen as just part of the original code by all the subsequent sniffer tools. It would be seen as an integral part of the code by the conformity checker tools. It would raise less suspicion the longer it remained in place, inert. There would also be no investment in counter tools as long as it wasn't triggered. Someone was waiting for a confluence of events to do this. Probably one of the primary events was the retirement of the last remaining person driven vehicles, used by the police and first responders until two years ago. The perpetrator was waiting until we would experience the most pain from the lack of transport."

Silmara nodded. "Your theory makes sense. I will note it as one possible theory we must consider further. Now are there others we should focus on? We must bring this event to a close as quickly as possible. People will start running out of food in just a few days. Law enforcement will become more and more of a challenge without transport. Emergency response has shut down."

Bomani raised his finger again, seeking permission to speak. Silmara nodded. "My initial tests lead me to believe the virus must be removed from each machine individually in order for the system as a whole to be restored. From a virus to destroy the world perspective, that makes perfect sense. But someone so patient, to have waited this long, must have an agenda we cannot yet understand. I believe there is another possibility, a key of some sort that shuts down the virus. A key that once activated, the virus goes back to sleep and life resumes. This is the rosy scenario, as if it is the one contemplated by our perpetrators, we may be able to find the key and restore order to the world."

"And if you're wrong?" Kalindi asked.

"Then we will be cleaning the software on every vehicle globally and the system will not return until that entire task is completed."

Silmara had trouble contemplating how long that would take, so she asked, "And your estimate of time to restore under this scenario?"

"A decade, maybe more. I estimate it could take as long as five years to find the method necessary to remove the virus without destroying the software as well. You see, it is such an integral part of the code we have no idea of its extent, how it interacts with the rest of the code, what happens if we remove part of the code, but not all of it. It will be a very complex and delicate process."

"Can't we simply go back to an earlier version of the code and reload it?" Silmara asked.

"We don't know how far back we would need to go to find a defect free version. And the software company has not retained versions over five years old. I believe all the versions in existence have the virus. If we attempt to re-host the code on all of the vehicles, we will find we have simply re-infected the transport fleet with the same Trojan and end up with the same result."

Kalindi asked a question no one was ready for, "Is it possible whoever implanted this code was with the original software development team and could be dead by now?"

"If they acted alone, we could be chasing a ghost. And if it were a ghost, then that person would have been less likely to have a restore key built in, because she or he wouldn't have cared at all about what happened after they were gone." Silmara thought through aloud. "Okay, what other theories do we have?"

"It's entirely possible," Bomani began, "we could be looking at this all wrong."

Kalindi was used to Bomani coming up with far-fetched theories, so she always waited until he finished before making a comment.

"Go on." Silmara was still trying to look past the ghost theory.

"It could be this is a gift. As I said, the code is unrecognizable to me. It could be code that does something miraculous. It could be it was embedded in our autonomous cars and timed to bring notice to itself at this time and in this way to announce its arrival."

"The alien civilization theory?" Kalindi asked, having heard this theory before from code wonks other than Bomani. However, she wasn't prepared for Silmara's next comment.

"I wouldn't rule it out, but let's put it lower on the priority list. Do you understand Bomani? No working this theory until we've exhausted all, and I repeat, all of the others."

Bomani sounded like a whipped puppy, "Yes, I understand."

Silmara needed to refocus. "Okay, here are the assignments. Bomani, I want you attacking that code with all of the tools and teams you can apply. We have to find a way to get transport back up and running today, if at all possible."

"I understand." Bomani was back as his thoughtful self."

"And Kalindi, I need you to check into the software developer. You apparently have to go all the way back to the beginning. Check backgrounds on anyone who worked on this project, as a coder or even as an accountant. Anyone who would have had access to the code, we have to check them. Could have been someone who cleaned the toilets for all we know, and just happened to be a very twisted programmer with an agenda to end the world as we know it. Any questions?"

There was a moment of awkward silence, as neither team member responded.

"Then we need to solve this mystery today. Let's get to work."

Chapter Twenty

Mimi and I worked through the night and the next day with the editing team assembling the episode from the raw footage Walt had captured. We wanted to have something we could air if John and the producers signed off on it. I thought the story was going to be compelling, although a radical departure from where we'd been on the series. I was still trying to work in the whole Russian conspiracy plot. Walt, Mimi and I went outside and shot a few filler scenes we could insert where we discovered clues that would suggest such a possibility. We edited them in. We wanted to foreshadow where we thought we wanted to take the series, although we had no idea how people were going to respond to our vision. The whole night was just so energizing I'd not even gotten tired, although we'd been up almost thirty-six hours now.

"Yes, this is great stuff, but you've marginalized me again." Mimi was pointing out as I rubbed my eyes with the heels of my hands.

"If only my uncle had left me a Tesla X there would have been room."

"I know."

The whole discussion before the first drive with the LAPD had been brutal. Mimi even suggested I should stay behind and she'd drive the car. If it wasn't for the fact that it was my car, she might have won that argument. We'd compromised by putting Walt in the far back, which was less than comfortable for him. But Mimi was not going to be denied.

"I know." I reiterated.

"You're giving me lip service. I know that tone in your voice. You're placating me and not really agreeing. I'm not going to let you get away with doing that. We're in this together and we're going to pull equal weight here."

I looked up from the Avid machine where I was doing the editing and looked at her, shaking my head. "Mimi. Listen to yourself."

"Why should I when you aren't"

"What? Listening to myself?" She'd confused me.

"No, listening to me."

I shook my head again and went back to editing.

"See. You're ignoring me. You can't do that. I simply won't let you." She came around behind the machine so she could stand over me and be face-to-face when I looked up. I did so when I finished the edit. She moved in close. Probably only an inch or two from me.

I kissed her, which caught her completely by surprise. I kissed her longer the second time. She looked at me with the strangest look when I pulled back. "What?" I asked.

"Who gave you permission to kiss me?"

"You just did." I observed.

"No I didn't. You assumed I'd let you."

"I assumed the first time, I didn't the second." I didn't intend to let her dismiss me as she had every day since she moved out of my apartment.

"You assumed, because you don't have my permission to kiss me. Not since Alison took my place at the top of your all-time hit parade."

"Alison never took your place. She's not in the same class as you. Not even close."

Mimi regarded me with a sideways glance as if she were

126

considering what I was saying, but I knew it wouldn't make any difference. Words were just words to her, with no more validity than the wind. Words pass by. They leave nothing more than a remembrance. They might leave an evoked emotion or fact to store away. But words were nothing that should cause a change in behavior as far as Mimi was concerned and I understood. Actors express words that suggest a meaning, but in fact have none. Mimi had pointed this out to me when we were together one night over a shared bottle of expensive red wine from Italy. Gaja, I think. Might have been Biondi Santi. Tuscan, I know that for a fact. We'd talked that same night about going to Tuscany. We planned to stay at one of the wineries if possible. It was less than a week later that I'd not returned until the next morning and my life had changed one more time, and not for the better.

I went for a third kiss, but Mimi pushed me away, or started to. I'd expected her reaction and took her into my arms and didn't give her the choice to resist. She resisted the kiss, at first, but the longer it lasted, the less push back I felt. She finally put her arms around me and accepted the kiss for what it was. A genuine expression of how I felt about her.

When I let her go, her expression had changed again. She was trying to figure out why I wasn't simply accepting her sentence and walking around like the condemned man I was. I acted like someone who had the right to be familiar with her. I knew she didn't think I had that right any longer. But I simply wasn't going to accept her sentence.

"I need to get ready. LAPD is expecting us to pick them up in an hour or so." I deliberately left it at that to see what she did next. I didn't have to wait long to find out. Her reaction was immediate.

"Can we get Shawn from makeup in the car or do I need to stop there on the way?"

Chapter Twenty-One

Walt Simmons was stuffed between Peter Jefferies and Kareem Hussain in the back seat. It wouldn't have been so bad if it hadn't been for the camera system Walt carried. He needed to get each of them into frame from a distance of less than 24 inches, which was tough. Now Mimi was in perfect frame given she was three feet or so from Walt, sitting in the front seat next to me. She wasn't happy with the close ups as Shawn wasn't in the third row with her makeup kit and Mimi had to do her own makeup. On the other hand, I had none on, and didn't care about the lines on my face that the lack of makeup revealed.

Mimi signaled to Walt she wanted the camera on her. "What do we know about the crime scene?"

Kareem answered, "Small house in Torrance. Quiet neighborhood. Victim has rented there for about five months. She lived alone even though the neighbors mentioned there had been a steady stream of guests, some overnight."

"Paying customers?" I asked.

"Speculation." Detective Jefferies offered.

"Motive?" Mimi asked, after all she was being filmed.

"Leading candidate?" Kareem asked, "Probably wasn't kinky enough for somebody."

"So you think a John did her in?" I asked.

"That's what we usually find in deals like this. But I'll be able to tell you better once we've seen the murder scene." Kareem answered. He was being filmed as well and acted for the camera.

I pulled up in front of the house in Torrance. Small, beige in color. Mediterranean tiles on the roof, so no solar panels. Obviously not a tree hugger. Yard was neat, the sparse lawn had been mowed. A few low water plants, but not much color. "Who discovered her?" Mimi asked.

"Neighbor. Said whoever had been here left in a hurry about three am. So he called to see if everything was alright and she didn't answer. So he came over and found her."

"Was he a customer?" I asked.

"No way of telling until we meet him." Kareem responded.

The front door was unlocked and we entered the house. Sparsely decorated. Looked like she didn't bring much with her. We went through the kitchen. Table and four chairs in a corner. A few appliances and dishes in the sink. She'd not cleaned up from dinner. Service was for one. Pizza. Deep dish, so Chicago style. Was she from Chicago or just addicted to Pizzeria Uno? Wine glass. I opened the refrigerator. The cheap red wine bottle was still in the door. Looked like only one glass from the bottle. Didn't appear to be an alcoholic. No extra slices of the pizza. A bottle of orange juice. A package of English Muffins. Nothing else. She apparently didn't cook at home.

Kareem hadn't waited and entered the bedroom with Mimi just ahead of me. I heard her gasp. She had her hand over her mouth when I came up beside her. The body was in the bed. Nude of course. Blood everywhere. Brown hair, her pubics anyway. On her head it was reddish. Attractive hair color, I thought. Her face was covered with light freckles. Her chest was covered with her blood that had bled out from the deep slash cross her throat. Someone had nearly decapitated her. The woman was slender. Full breasts. Firm even in death. Probably augmented. Her legs were spread as if assuming the position to receive someone. Above her on the wall was the word, 'SLUT', written in her blood.

I looked around the room. She had a white silk wrap and

underwear neatly piled on a bedside chair. The dresser had a single picture. Apparently her mother, younger brother and her with brown hair and smaller breasts. Looked to be about ten years ago. Would guess the father had taken the picture. Something about the brother caught my attention. He was standing partially behind his sister and had his right hand on her breast. She looked like she wasn't concerned or was going along with it. Why had she kept that picture?

Kareem began taking pictures with his cell phone, which he sent back to the station. Mimi needed to say something to lessen the shock and refocus the camera on her. "Why 'slut' if she was a prostitute?"

I couldn't wait any longer if that was all Mimi was bringing. "Detective Hussain."

Kareem stopped taking pictures to look up at me.

"Check on a boyfriend. I'd estimate she broke up with him three to four months ago."

"Why a boyfriend?" Kareem asked like I had to be a complete idiot.

"You said she's lived here about five months."

"That's right."

"She probably was augmented about that time. Moved her upscale. She could entertain here and get a lot more for her services. My guess is she had a taste of a better life and wanted the fairy tale. Broke up with the guy from back home hoping she could get one of her new clients to either become a sugar daddy or marry her. From looking at her I'd guess she had a good technique. Johns were willing to pay for the new improved version."

Mimi couldn't be outdone. "How do you get to the good technique?"

"Muscle tone. This lady was in good shape. She was spending a lot of time in a gym for some reason and I'd guess it was professionally motivated."

Mimi reexamined the young woman, as did Kareem and Detective Jefferies. Walt brought the camera closer as well to focus in on my observation.

"How do you get all that from a two minute look around?" Kareem asked.

"Episode twenty-one, 'The case of the jagged edge'." I responded, looking directly into Walt's camera.

Mimi didn't like where this episode was going. She'd marginalized herself. She was in episode twenty-one. She knew the plot as well as I did, but didn't see what I'd seen. She was either still in shock about the body, or she just didn't make the same calculations.

"Why slut? The boyfriend had to know what she was doing here. I disagree. This was a John. Someone who felt he was cheated by her somehow. Someone who felt maybe she should be his alone. Maybe that Sugar Daddy you spoke of. Maybe he came here and found she'd been doing tricks again and flew into a rage. He did her in because he wanted to keep her for himself."

I shook my head. "Not enough time. For a Sugar Daddy to get possessive to the point he'd risk jail to vent rage would take more than the three or four months at most he'd been doing her. Has to be the boyfriend from back home, who'd been with her for three, four years maybe. Besides. Look at her. She didn't struggle. It was someone she loved. Someone she trusted."

Mimi looked at me when I said 'trusted.'

Kareem found her wallet, handed it to Jefferies, who called it in. "Christine Kyhl. Age 27. Of 1317 Hickory Lane in Torrance. Deceased. Can we find a boyfriend?" Walt got it all on tape.

Chapter Twenty-Two

The episode Mimi and I cobbled together of the murder of the drug pusher garnered only a twenty-one market share. Less than our usual. There had been no advance publicity about the episode so what could we expect? But it had over a million hits on You-tube for replays. Word of mouth spread and the second episode we developed, that showed the murdered prostitute, went all the way to forty-nine market share. Unbelievable. Almost half of the audience watching television at that time slot watched us. Mimi still wasn't happy when LAPD discovered the boyfriend had broken up with the victim four months before and had no reasonable alibi that evening. The boyfriend also rambled on about the fact she'd ditched him for some rich guy that had come around, even though she lived in Torrance and not Beverly Hills or Malibu. His interview had been worked into the show. We'd found a new format the producers and the audience liked. But could we keep it up? I had absolutely no idea. But it was time to take another drive with my new best friends from the LAPD and Mimi.

The next filming started at LAPD headquarters. Kareem asked Mimi and me to join him in a Spartan briefing room.

"This is a cold case. We've had no leads on it for almost four years until last week." Kareem began. "Andrea Timmerman was a nanny to producer Julius Roberts. She disappeared without a trace four years ago. Born in Heidelburg, Germany, she graduated from a top German University in Philosophy. Seemed to have a brilliant future in teaching, but after a single semester at Berlin University graduate school, withdrew and took a position as a nanny to the children of a University professor. That lasted all of one year, at which time she moved to the US to become a nanny to the children of Mr. Roberts. According to our records, Mr. Roberts has three children ages nine, seven and three. Ms. Timmerman was fluent in five European languages and Mr. Roberts wanted his children to be fluent in at least three. She seemed to be the perfect fit."

I nodded in understanding, but Mimi wasn't ready to move on. "Okay. The producer obviously did her in, but why?"

Kareem listened to Mimi and responded with cool detachment. "Mr. Roberts had absolutely no motive to harm Ms. Timmerman in any way. They had no relationship anyone has been able to document, other than her initial hiring interview. After that they had no contact as Mr. Roberts was traveling on set for film shoots nearly the entire time. So he is currently not a suspect."

"Then who else in the household had contact with Ms. Timmerman?" Mimi wasn't going to let me upstage her this time around.

"We questioned the other domestics. No one saw Ms. Timmerman with anyone other than the children." Kareem responded.

"What about the professor in Germany? Was there something there?" Mimi was reaching.

"Nothing we could determine. Seems she had the professor for a class. She got a B that semester, but took the position as his nanny, according to the University, as a result of a posting the professor had made on a career center bulletin board. No indications of a quid pro quo. No indications the professor had ever strayed from his relationship with his family and wife."

Mimi seemed at a loss as to where to go. "Anything else in her background that could have motivated harm to her?"

"Nothing we've been able to substantiate."

"What about anything you couldn't substantiate? You know, where there's smoke?"

"Nothing there either." Detective Jefferies offered to close the discussion.

"But someone did her in. So what's the new evidence?"

Jefferies continued, "A neighbor to Mr. Roberts, by the name of Scottsdale was snorkeling in his pond. Seems his land has a pond for watering the horses and cattle. Not a small estate if you know what I mean. Anyway, Mr. Scottsdale was getting ready for a vacation in Italy and decided to practice his snorkeling in his pond and came across the badly decomposed body of Ms. Timmerman."

"Missing four years." Mimi wanted to confirm.

"Yes."

"Were the indications that the body had been in that pond the whole time?"

Jefferies again, "It would seem so, yes."

"So someone removed her from the Roberts Estate and dumped her into the pond of the estate next door. Why didn't she come to the surface with all that time?"

"Body was wrapped like a mummy with weights to keep it down on the bottom. Whoever did this knew that no one used the pond for anything other than water for the horses and cattle." Kareem concluded.

"The killer must have worked in the neighborhood, studied the area to know what to expect and planned the killing in such a way as to reduce dramatically the probability of discovery." I noted.

Mimi wasn't happy with my observation. "So the key question remains why would someone do her in?"

Kareem liked this line of inquiry better than me just pronouncing the solution to the case after they had invested multiples of calories into solving it with no results. I didn't intend to make it easy on him, but I also didn't have enough information yet. I didn't want him to know that as it might be pretext for not sharing with us. Anything to keep them from seeming even more incompetent.

"So far, we've not identified a specific motive in this case. Is there anything that jumps out at you we've overlooked?" Detective Jefferies was showing more resolve than he had to this point.

"Not enough information yet," Mimi responded. "We need to interview the domestic help of Mr. Roberts and also Mr. Scottsdale."

Mimi, Walt and Detective Jefferies left us to go interview the domestic help of both tycoons. I did not expect such interviews would provide much in the way of specifics in this case. But Mimi wanted the air time, so I was willing to play along.

I turned to Detective Hussain, "Tell me about the chauffer to Mr. Roberts."

Kareem had to consult his notes, after all, it had been four years since the original interviews had been conducted. "Here it is. Henri Simpson."

"That his real name?" I asked.

Kareem genuinely seemed surprised by my question. "As far as we know."

"Suggest you look into that. I think you will find he is German, has a different name and a record in Germany."

"What makes you think that?"
I shook my head, "Just check it out."

Kareem didn't want to do so, but because Walt wasn't taping this discussion he relaxed and realized he might be able to spin the outcome of this line of questioning. Kareem gave the assignment to a uniformed Sergeant.

"Why the chauffer?" Kareem asked.

"The chauffer has a lot of time where he's not driving someone. He can wash and wax his car, or he can wash and wax his firm member on a staff member. Which do you think is more fun for the chauffer?"

"I'm a little out of my depth when it comes to rich people and domesticated servants. Why are you able to divine what's going on behind closed gates here?" Kareem admitted and questioned.

I waved Kareem off, not answering his question.

Jefferies returned at that moment without Mimi, who was apparently still questioning the staff. "Chauffer has a record. Name's really Horst Mueller. Born in Russelsheim, Germany. Age is thirty-nine. Was convicted of petty theft, then robbery, and finally kidnapping in Munich ten years ago. Came to the US upon his release from prison and has been working for Mr. Roberts for the last five years. No record of criminal activity since his employment here."

Kareem glanced at me and shook his head. "We need to have a conversation with the Chauffer."

Jefferies went to make that happen. At the same time, Kareem approached me. "Which episode was this?"

"Forty-four, 'The case of the domesticated domestic.'" I responded without trying to spin it in any way.

"How many episodes have you done?"

"This will be one – hundred and eighteen." I replied.

"Guess I need to set aside some serious television watching time to catch up."

"I had mentors who taught me all kinds of things about law enforcement that you only get from years on the street." I responded.

Kareem nodded apparently thinking having mentors wasn't the same as being out on the streets and looked up to see Walt was filming this conversation.

Chapter Twenty-Three

Silmara sat in a room full of men at the Brazilian counterterrorism operations center. The wall behind the speaker displayed a map of the world with flags noting different countries and suspects. Silmara felt a vibration on her cell phone, looked down and saw it was Kalindi. She responded with a text that she was in a meeting and would call when it concluded. At that point the speaker summarized, "And unfortunately we have not been able to determine at what point a re-host would be effective. None of the independent teams we have working to isolate the code has been successful in fully doing so. From all appearances, this malware has been in place since the original release."

A man sitting four seats down from Silmara responded, "How is that possible? This code has been inspected and validated literally thousands of times. The best of the best have had a shot at trying to corrupt, compromise or bring it down. Every time it's passed with flying colors. A sunset virus just doesn't make sense."

The main speaker responded, "While I may agree with your observations, they don't get us any closer to our objective of getting transport moving again. Does anyone have anything constructive to say?"

Silmara nodded to the speaker to gain the floor, "Gentlemen. My experts suggest the only way to get transport moving again will be to leave the code in place, but return it to its hibernation state. I have my best people working the hibernation angle at the moment. That isn't to say hibernation will ultimately be the approach to return transport, but we are working it harder than any other at the moment. My people say they have never seen code like what we found in this instance. The implications are staggering. From a law enforcement perspective, if someone or some group has devised a new computer language we may be working to solve this mystery for quite some time. We have to bring in resources from different fields, like commercial software development, transport control systems, wireless communications, maybe even anthropologists. We have to open up our minds to understand the challenge before us. We're not faced with a crime we've seen thousands of times before. This is a very different type of opponent. We have to be prepared to use unusual methods to succeed. And we have very little time before people start running out of food, medicine and toilet paper."

The speaker responded, "Chief Cardoso has made some very important points. Who else is working on the hibernation angle?" He looked for a show of hands, but no one else raised one. "Curious, I thought there were at least three hibernation projects going on." Silmara scanned the room, but no one would make eye contact. "Is anyone doing anything except trying to isolate the embedded code?" The speaker asked.

A man across the room from Silmara nodded to the speaker, "We are examining ways to permanently render the embedded code inoperable. Logic faults, perpetual loops, things of that nature. If we can isolate the code so it does not interoperate with the larger program but perpetually tries to solve for pi or something similar, we may be able to bring transport back up, even if some of the compute power is siphoned off in these perpetual loops."

Silmara acknowledged the approach, "Not ideal, but you may get there first and if so we will definitely employ your solution."

The speaker scanned the room. No one else wished to discuss what they may or may not be doing. Silmara felt a growing uneasiness. If only two teams were looking at alternative approaches, it would take much longer to find a solution. She nodded to the speaker once more, "Is anyone else here as uncomfortable as I am? We have a dozen teams working this, but apparently only two have sought out alternative approaches. If the rest are all doing the same work, it is not additive, but duplicative. And we all know people doing the same thing all seem to come to the same conclusion. I think we should use the remaining time to identify and assign teams to work other alternative approaches."

Silmara's phone vibrated again. She looked down and saw Kalindi was calling again, even after the text. She thought it must be something important. "Excuse me, Gentlemen. I need to respond to this." She held up her phone and left the conference room.

Once outside, Silmara called Kalindi, "Yes?"

"Silmara. Thank you for stepping out. Yes we've found something important you need to know about. Have you ever heard of Gabriel Von Horn?"

Of course Silmara knew the name, "The Bronx Bomber. Blew up the new Yankee Stadium." She remembered the stadium had been full for an opening day game. April 5th and it snowed in the second inning. The media had replayed the scene of the Yankee's pitcher, snow accumulating on his neck and melting as he pitched. He'd tried to wipe it away multiple times, but he shivered none-the-less. The Yankees were behind three to two. The bomb had been concealed in a shipment of beer kegs, which had been packed with high explosives and wired together. Silmara had seen photos of Von Horn's loft apartment which was only two blocks from the stadium. He had a radio transmitter attached to the bomb and detonated at the beginning of the seventh inning stretch. It was the worst sporting disaster ever, at the time. Von Horn had never been found. He simply disappeared into the subway system, or at least that was the theory as several witnesses said they remembered seeing him enter a subway station within a few minutes after the explosion.

"We think he may have worked on developing the code for transport. One of the core team members was a man who loosely fit his description. No one knows where he was for the five years after the Bronx bombing. It could have been him."

Silmara remembered that Von Horn was a brilliant software guru.

He had worked for several of the major software companies developing tools that revolutionized social media in the early days. But he became bitter when the owners became fabulously wealthy and they gave him only a salary to live on along with stock options that were worthless by the time they vested. Von Horn had gone off on his own to start a company, but it failed within a year. Von Horn was brilliant, but not a good business person. He insisted on pushing his developers to create leading edge solutions. The problem arose when the tools were delayed and seriously over budget. He lost his backers and found himself in a serious cash flow squeeze. One of his customers seized the company in payment for loans they'd advanced to gain tools he promised but couldn't deliver. Von Horn became even more embittered when that company subsequently finished his tool suite and made a fortune when it became the industry standard.

"Von Horn would seem to be the kind of person who could have developed the code. He certainly had motivation. How do we confirm?" Silmara asked.

"We're working on it now. Interviewing people who worked with Von Horn before he disappeared along with people who worked with our person of interest on the transport code project."

"Distinguishing marks?" Silmara tried to remember but nothing came to her.

"We don't know yet, but will get the answer to that as part of the first group interviews."

"Not being able to do interviews in person is just such a limitation. If we could sit across a table from someone, study how they're reacting, we'd get so much more information."

Kalindi understood, "We're trying to do videoconferences as much as possible. Not always possible, however."

"Do we have any idea where Von Horn might be?"

"As you apparently remember, he surfaced about five years after the bombing. Gave the world his integration code that allowed anyone to access any social media from one device without having to switch back and forth between programs. Everything fed into a single interface. I still use it since no one's come out with anything better since."

"I do remember and also that he never came out of where he had gone. He delivered a virtual message with a download site. One and a half billion people downloaded that code within a month."

Kalindi's voice changed, fear crept in. "Do you think there might be some connection between the transport and integration codes?"

"Might be. Do you mind calling Bomani and have him look into it? I really need to get back to my meeting."

"Of course." Kalindi was now all apologetic. I'll ring him up just now."

"And tell him Von Horn's a much more likely suspect than space aliens."

Kalindi knew what Silmara was saying. They both knew Bomani would never adhere to the priorities Silmara had given him. Bomani would be looking for signs of intelligent life in the universe in the code. After all, there were fewer and fewer signs of intelligent life on Earth from what Silmara could see. But then again, she kept reminding herself her job kept her from looking at the good things that were happening.

As Silmara re-entered the meeting room, she heard the speaker concluding his remarks. "...disappointed that we can't identify any other approaches to solving this problem." Silmara was already unhappy she hadn't stayed in the room to make sure they got results. "If we are unsuccessful millions or billions will suffer and most likely die. We are the last defense against those who would take away the standard of living we have been able to achieve. Take away the liberties and freedoms we have come to enjoy. Take away a future for our

142

children every person in this room has worked hard and long to ensure. Do you have any concluding remarks, Chief Cardoso?"

Silmara walked over to her chair before addressing the group. "We have identified a potential source of the code. If that proves correct, your job is much harder than you imagine."

Chapter Twenty-Four

Mimi and I drove up the long circular drive to the home of billionaire Steve Boys. Kareem and Detective Jefferies sandwiched Walt Simmons, who shot footage of our arrival though the window next to Kareem, who was not at all happy to have a camera in his face, but pointing away from him.

"How many homes does this guy have?" Detective Jefferies asked no one in particular.

Mimi responded, "I've been to three. This is the smallest."

"Social visit?" I asked.

"Arts council. Mr. Boys was donating to a capital campaign to build a new center for film making arts."

"I thought the American Society for Motion Picture Arts and Sciences took care of that." I responded.

"They're more of a museum with a preservation focus. This new center is for experimental film making techniques. Looking for ways to revolutionize film making."

"And Mr. Boys gets the Intellectual Property on any new devices created at his center?" I was being snide as I always wondered why rich people gave money away to causes that didn't seem to have anything to do with what they did to make all their money.

"Only if he funds the actual development work."

"Didn't know he was interested in films." I wasn't going to let go yet.

"He's interested in projects that affect large audiences. Films affect millions or billions of people. They convey messages, and emotions and stories of human exploits to stir the imagination."

"I can see you really got into that little project." Kareem offered from the back seat.

Mimi looked over her shoulder, noted his lack of smile and turned around again. To me she said, "You know what I mean."

"I do." I responded, not wanting to carry the discussion any further. After parking the Tesla, we approached the front door of the Boys residence. We expected a butler, but were surprised to find Mr. Boys, blue jeans, dockers, black t-shirt and pony tail for his greying hair answered the door himself.

"Mimi. So nice to see you again." He reached for my co-star and gave her a warm kiss on the cheek. He then offered his hand to me. "Desmond Jensen. I'm a big fan. Think I've seen every episode."

"Detective Hussain." Kareem introduced himself.

"Detective Jefferies." Jefferies introduced himself.

I waited to see if Walt would introduce himself, but Mr. Boys was playing to the camera and led us into his den.

"This is where it hung." We found a wall with no art work in comparison to all the other walls which were covered with paintings, photos and lithographs.

"Could you describe the article?" Kareem began.

"The Andy Warhol Self-Portrait? You're kidding me. You really don't know the piece?" Boys was incredulous.

Mimi interjected, "Red on black, the older Andy with his hair all spiked out in comparison to the earlier self-portrait where he was younger and had short hair." She looked at me, accepted my look of surprise and responded quietly just to me, "I saw it when I was here to pick up the check. His prized piece."

I turned to Mr. Boys, "How did they get it out of the house? You have alarm systems."

Mr. Boys turned to me, "That's the curious part. The alarm was engaged, but never sent an alert. No signs of forced entry, nothing else missing. Almost seems like it was an inside job. Someone who knew all the codes, how to get in and out, when to do it and all that."

"I take it you've carefully vetted your staff?" Kareem this time. Didn't want me to get credit for this one too. He was already feeling the heat that an actor had solved three crimes while he'd struck out each time.

"I have a service that does the screenings and makes recommendations. No gaps in employment histories, no criminal records. For most of them, not so much as a speeding ticket in the last five years."

"So you're comfortable with the staff." I stated. He nodded. "Then how do you think the painting came to disappear?"

"Mission Impossible, suspended wires from the ceiling. Anything's possible, but that's really your department and not mine."

Suspended wires caused me to look up and around the room, looking for anything that might give away how the painting was removed. But the more I looked the more I realized there hadn't been any Hollywood effects used to get the painting out. Someone had bypassed the alarms and simply walked out carrying the priceless painting. I walked over to the wall, looked at the security camera, and read the name of the security company and phone number. I wrote that information on a piece of paper and handed it to Detective Jefferies. "Need you to have someone check the background of every employee at that company who was involved in the installation of this security system. They must have some records about that. Also need a comparison of public profiles. Anything that shows a discrepancy."

Kareem glanced over to us with a disapproving look. "What are you plotting?"

"I'll let you know if we find anything. Just running down possibilities."

"It's a reasonable request." Detective Jefferies responded before leaving to make the call.

Mimi needed some face time with the camera. "Mr. Boys, do you have any other art work that would be in the same value class as the Warhol?"

"I have several, yes."

"But they were not disturbed?"

"No. They are where they have always been."

I felt a suspicion nagging. "Could you show us?"

Mr. Boys led us to a small gallery in a hallway between the living room and the dining room. Dark paneled walls, plush dark brown carpet. Spot lights on the art works. The first was a jeweled prayer rug. I couldn't even count the number of stones on that rug.

"Have you had someone confirm this is the rug you purchased?" I asked.

"Of course not. I recognize it instantly."

"Mr. Boys. Do you have any idea how many identical rugs to this exist? I would assume that not many had stones as valuable as yours. But stones are much easier to sell than an original Andy Warhol." I responded.

Mr. Boys looked closer at the rug, but shrugged. "I'm sure you're right that there may be many that look like my rug. It looks like my rug and that is all I can tell you."

"What else do you have of similar value?" I asked. Kareem was still looking at the prayer rug.

"My whaler's lamp. The base is solid gold." He took us to a lamp off to the side. The base was a figurine, holding a vase on her shoulder. Above the vase a glass oil globe and lamp shade rested. The sculpture of the base was intricate and detailed. The globe and shade didn't seem to be extraordinary.

"You're sure the base is solid gold?" Kareem asked picking up on my line of questioning.

"I have a certificate of authenticity. This lamp is Roman period. Was produced on the Island of Rhodes and was recovered from the home of a Roman merchant after a fire around the time of Christ."

"What do you do, Mr. Boys, that you keep such valuable pieces of artwork in your home?" I asked.

Mimi answered for him, "You really don't know who he is? Why he founded five high tech start-ups, selling each one for many times more than the previous one. He's now a philanthropist, giving away millions of dollars every year from the Boys Foundation for the Arts."

"Including your capital campaign." I answered.

"His foundation gave twenty-five million dollars." Mimi was very protective of Mr. Boys. I wondered why.

Detective Jefferies returned to the room with a piece of paper. I quickly scanned the document and looked up. "Detective Jefferies has learned that one of the installation team for the security system on this house had a degree in software development and worked for a defense contractor for seven years. He masked his background as his application showed he'd owned his own security company for ten years before going to work for the contractor. With a software background, I think we need to bring in Mr...." I had to look at the paper, "Awani, and see if he ever took the time to look at the code on these security systems. He could have easily installed a trap door that would have let him walk in here and carry out anything he chose." I looked at Mr. Boys again, "And I'd get an expert in to take a look at everything. I suspect that if Mr. Awani took your Warhol, it was to cover up the fact that he's robbed you blind and you don't even know how much of value you're really missing."

"Which episode was this?" Kareem asked.

Chapter Twenty-Five

The night the episode solving the Boys art theft showed Alistair had arranged to join Mimi and myself in my trailer to watch. I wasn't crazy about some of the editing. I know the editor had to get it down to fit the time slot, but the cuts were too abrupt for my taste. I wanted it to be a smooth transition from one event to the next. But that wasn't the style they were teaching in film school, so it was all quick cuts and instantly changed perspectives that accelerated the pace of the piece, but sometimes made it hard to follow everything. Particularly how much was really stolen.

"You look unhappy." Mimi noted.

"Collaboration sometimes leaves me unfulfilled."

"You're not talking about me, are you?" Mimi wanted to know instantly.

"The editor. It's not my style."

Alistair looked at me funny. "The studio lets you completely revamp the format of the show, write your own scripts, go unscripted for much of it and still you're complaining?"

"What are you hearing about next year?" I asked.

"All's been quiet since your first new show. I think they're tracking how high this will go and whether it's gonna last or crash and burn. I think the jury's still out on that front and they won't move until they know what they've got."

"So the reboot's still on the table?" Mimi asked.

"I haven't heard of them committing Johnny Hollywood any place else."

"We broke a fifty share last week. No one's done that in forever." Mimi noted for Alistair.

"But what happens when transport comes back on? Will people stay home to watch you solve another mystery or crime? No one knows."

"I understand they've been able to transport some food and medicine by old trains that still had the manual controls in place. They'd been mothballed but not destroyed." Alistair offered.

"We always adapt, but the lack of food is getting scary. So much of what we grow has been automated. While we're getting some crops out, it's not at anywhere near what we're used to."

"More reports of old people and young children dying for lack of nutrition." Mimi mentioned to add to the commentary.

"People can't get out so how do people know the old folks and kids are dying?" I asked.

"Family calls and gets no answer. They ride bicycles or walk if it's close enough. They call neighbors and ask them to check in. When they do they find the old folks." Alistair reported.

"Has there been anything more from that woman they put in charge of solving the transport problem. What was her name?" I asked.

"Cardoso, I think. No. I've not seen anything." Alistair offered.

"That's not good news. I don't know how much longer this can go on before lots of people start dying." Mimi was getting depressed. When she got depressed, she wanted a glass of wine. She went over to the cabinet where I kept my supply, "What's this? No wine?"

"Sorry. We finished the last bottle last night." I confirmed.

She returned to the chair where she'd been watching the show. "Is this how it's going to be? First the wine is gone, then the canteen will be out of everything except granola bars and pretty soon we'll be surviving by eating the production assistants."

"I think there'll be some intermediate steps before we get to the Production Assistants." I responded to cheer her up, knowing it was going to be a miserable evening for her without wine.

"At least you have lots of production assistants here. All we have over at my shop is paralegals. They're usually tough old birds because all the young and tasty ones have gotten married and left to raise kids." Alistair was also trying to cheer up Mimi.

"Doesn't Jack have a full bar in his office?" Mimi was getting desperate.

"He only drinks Bourbon. Something about being raised in Tennessee as I remember." Alistair wanted to squash any thoughts Mimi was having about breaking and entering, even if it was only Jack's office.

"Do I like Bourbon?" Mimi asked herself out loud, not expecting any of us to know the answer.

"I've been getting reacquainted with water. Did you know you can actually drink the water that comes out of a tap? I always thought bottled water was the only kind safe to drink. Must have been some advertising campaign someone ran got me to thinking that." I reflected for Mimi's benefit.

"Really?" Alistair sounded genuinely surprised. "I'll have to try that."

Mimi got up and came over to sit on my lap. "Do you have a joint or do I have to go beg from Richard?"

"I thought you weren't talking to him." I'd noticed Mimi hadn't gone off to see Richard since we turned in our first episode. Until then she'd kept her options open to go back to him, but now she was spending her time with me, but only because we'd put Richard on the shelf with our episodes and she had no place else to go, or at least that was how I was interpreting her behavior. I think she also wanted to be sure I didn't go shoot an episode without her.

"I'm mostly not talking to him. But if he asks me a question I need to be civil, don't I? After all, Alistair just told us we don't know what's going to happen next season. I may have to go do it with Johnny Hollywood. I wonder how that young stud is in bed? The tabloids say he's wonderful, but somehow I haven't seen even one story where the girl has had anything to say afterwards. That always bothers me, when someone kisses and tells, but doesn't give details. You know what I mean?"

"I didn't see you singing my praises when we were together. What should I make of that?"

"If you give me a joint, you can interpret anything you want and I won't have anything negative to say about you in bed." She's getting desperate.

"And if I don't give you the joint?" I'm playing with her now.

"You can read all about it on the morning blogs."

"It's been so long I can't remember what you used to say about it." Continuing the thread.

"You're not giving me a joint, are you?" now she's getting pissed.

I opened the drawer to my desk, which was right next to the chair I was sitting in. She saw what she wanted and helped herself to more than one.

"Now that I know where you keep them, you better stock up." Mimi was off to find a lighter.

"What are you hearing from your supplier?" I asked Alistair. We didn't share the same source as his was more uptown and mine was on the lot.

"Says not to worry. He'll get me a supply if he has to walk to the border and bring it back himself."

"Good to know some things aren't affected by the world going to shit."

Alistair changed the channel to watch the news. I expected he was going to stay the night unless things were relatively calm out on the streets. The riots were happening more and more frequently. Usually later at night and usually as far from the police stations as possible. The studio had brought in rent-a-cops to provide protection on the lot. They were afraid people would simply assume that the studio had back up supplies to keep them going during prolonged shoots. That wasn't the case since Kraft Services were known for bringing in fresh fruit and vegetables and baked goods nearly every day. So I hadn't seen a fresh anything now in about a week. Mimi's comment about granola bars had struck closer to home than I wanted to admit. Now on the other hand, there were a few tasty production assistants, but I had to expect they would be long gone before I crossed that line.

I wasn't paying attention to the news since I wasn't planning on going out that night. I could have gone out every night with the LAPD, but we had to stay in to get the episode in shape every other night.

"Hey, isn't that the mayor?" Alistair asked. Mimi came back in with her joint and I could see she'd already taken the edge off.

"What about him?" I asked. Alistair turned up the volume.

"I am publicly asking Desmond Jensen to join the LAPD as Chief of Detectives. Over the last two weeks he's demonstrated over and over, as you've all seen, the ability to quickly solve crimes, both current and even our cold cases. We need that kind of leadership in this city until our Federal and International authorities are able to solve the transport crisis."

I couldn't believe what I'd heard, so I asked the question, "Did he just offer me a job?"

"You know any other Desmond Jensen?" Mimi responded.

"If you think the studio was going to cut your pay…" was Alistair's response.

Chapter Twenty-Six

When the call came from Dr. Silmara Cardoso I knew the world indeed was going to hell in a handbasket. "Mr. Jensen, I've been looking for someone who can bring a fresh set of eyes to our investigation. You've shown an ability to see things before the LAPD does. We're working as fast as we can to solve the transport problem, but the investigation is lagging because most of the resources are working the code issue."

"As well they should. Things are getting pretty desperate out on the street. Ms. Cardoso."

"If you were to work with my team where would you start?" All of a sudden I realized this discussion was a discussion, and not necessarily a done deal. But I instantly knew if I could help solve the transport issue in some small way, it would certainly help my case to keep my show.

"I'm sure you're aware of the infamous Xian Zhe."

"In fact, we've met." She confirmed.

"Xian is my mentor."

"You could have done a lot worse." Was less than a ringing endorsement. I thought that curious and noted I needed to probe that further at some point in time.

"Xian taught me everything I know about detecting."

"Don't you mean investigating?" Dr. Cardoso asked.

"Xian taught me you have to detect things first. Detecting is all about going places where investigators never look, into the heart of men. When you go detecting, you must never blink, you must never look away and you must never be afraid. When you truly know what someone is capable of, then the investigation begins, looking for the evidence of what you detect."

"I'm not sure I completely agree with the esteemed Xian Zhe. Especially in this case where we have few leads as to who is really behind the transport virus."

"Do you have any suspects?" I wasn't comfortable with her read on Xian. Was there some professional rivalry or something? I felt the tension in her voice, but maybe that was just the tension of being in charge and having made little progress even after two weeks of the transport stoppage.

"We have a theory more than a suspect since the person we think involved hasn't been seen for more than a decade."

"Doesn't mean he's not out there."

She hesitated before continuing, probably wondering if this call might be monitored. It was encrypted, but she, better than most, probably understood the limits of commercial encryption. "We have no time to solve this mystery. I have no time to sit on this call and answer your questions. So I must ask you directly, are you available to work with my team, as a member of my team and not as some rogue cowboy going off and doing things on your own?"

"So a job offer with conditions."

"Not a job offer. A request for you to consult with us as a private citizen. You will not become a law enforcement officer. You will be given special access to information, but you will not be able to release it or use it in your television show."

"Now that's a condition I don't think I can accept. If I'm going to have the greatest value to you and your team as a private citizen consultant and not a law enforcement officer, it will be as a conduit to those responsible. If they see me as part of your team, doing things to narrow the search for them, time delayed of course, I can act as a sheep dog, herding them to you and your team."

My suggestion was greeted by silence. She'd not considered the larger value I could provide, only the possible value of a fresh set of eyes. Maybe it was intended to be something that would reduce the public pressure on her and her team. Get the people to think they were not leaving any stone unturned. But I'd turned the proposition around.

"I'll have to get back to you on your suggestion. In the meantime, we have interest in your assistance. But I can't commit to defining your role at this moment, since you have a different perception of what your true value might be."

"Do you watch the show?" I asked curious as to whether she had any idea of what she was asking.

"It's shallow and unrealistic in many ways." Ah, she has at least watched one or more episodes.

"Our writer. Never was a cop. We have to keep adding depth to the scripts beyond what he wants to show. But what about the recent episodes, where they're reality based?"

"Those are the episodes I've watched. Previously they weren't worth watching."

"So we're still shallow? They're realistic given they are really happening when we tape them."

"Your episode where the prostitute was found dead. That is where you showed people what it is like to be in law enforcement. That was a good show."

"Thank you."

"I will call again, once I have clear direction about your suggestion. I can't promise anything and I am requesting that you not mention this conversation to anyone. We may still chose to go in a different direction and if people think we are grasping at straws that would not be good."

"Are you? Grasping at straws?"

"I hope not. I will call tomorrow about this same time, if that is all right with you?"

I ended the call and dropped my cell phone onto the desk in my trailer. A fresh set of eyes? From an actor? Who was she kidding? She really was grasping at straws. At least she admitted it at the end. The question was, what value could I bring to the investigation? She said they don't have suspects. This was clearly outside my area of prior episode expertise, so I really had nothing to draw upon. But if I could find some way to pull off being involved with the investigation, it would seal the deal on next year's contract. I had to look at it from that perspective. While I wasn't eating as much as usual since the food at the canteen was mostly frozen or canned, my first priority had to be renewing my contract.

I needed to call Xian, what time was it? Oh, the middle of the night in China. I'd have to wait and call him later. Who could I talk to about my off the cuff brainstorm? Would it work? Could it work? Would it be of any value at all, or would I become just a side show that no one cared about? I hoped the mystery would be solved soon as we needed to get the transport moving again or the deaths would begin to mount up. Even someone as removed from things as I was could see things couldn't go on much longer. But for my own selfish reasons, I had a chance to not only extend my contract, but if I played my cards right, might get a big increase. I would need that if I wanted to stay a step or two ahead of Johnny Hollywood.

I called Mimi, "You want to come over and discuss another change to our story line?"

"Right now? For all you know I might be in the middle of

something with Robert."

"That'll only take a minute. I can wait." She cut me off.

She opened my door and walked in without knocking or anything, as she always did, about ten minutes later. She wasn't mussed up so she hadn't been in bed.

I took her hands and led her over to her favorite chair to sit.

"What's going on?" She was suspicious.

"We have a chance to work on the transport virus, for real."

She took in my statement, but didn't process it right away. "What do you mean, for real?"

"You remember that woman on television – Dr. Cardoso who's the head of the investigation?"

"Vaguely."

"She called and wants us as fresh eyes on her investigation team. I pitched us making it into a series, delayed by a week or so to ensure they can stay ahead of those involved, but to build up pressure and public awareness of what they're doing."

"Did she buy that?" Mimi was incredulous.

"She has to go talk with others since that wasn't what she was authorized to offer. But she's watched our show. Even said the prostitute episode was a good show."

"That was the best one so far, I agree. But what are you saying? We're supposed to get to someplace somehow to go work on the case?"

"Didn't get that far. But nobody's traveling at the moment so I don't think so, but you need to start thinking about what can we do? How do we structure this so we get our contracts renewed and get a bigger say in the production?"

"And get residuals for all the things we're doing. Did you know they're still paying Robert for scripts they're not using?"

I wasn't concerned about Robert. I was trying to figure out how I was going to pull this off.

Chapter Twenty-Seven

Xian answered the call on the second ring. That was unusual for him. It normally took many more. In my mind's eye I thought he seldom would be near his phone working on one case or another, if that was indeed what a retired chief of detectives would do. I couldn't imagine my friend doing anything other than seeking to solve crimes.

"Calling about virus." He started. I didn't need to answer and in fact he continued as if I'd done so in the affirmative. "Looking someone unleash calamity upon mankind."

"So it's everywhere?" I asked, not having picked up that detail.

"Yes, everywhere. Even nations responsible."

"Why would anyone bring down their own transport?" I asked more for my own clarification than really expecting an answer from Xian.

"Staring into heart of darkness." Xian began. "Not looking government responsible to others."

"Why do you think that?" I asked not sure of his logic.

"Very old, very young starve to death. Food and medicine not reaching. Government cannot accept blame. Not survive as government."

His logic made perfect sense. But if he was correct, then it would be much harder to find whoever was behind the transport shut down. Probably the earlier attacks on the repair depots as well.

That reminded me of a question, "Why were the initial attacks on the repair depots only in the US? I never heard anything about them occurring elsewhere."

Xian had to think for a moment. "Not recall. Need check." I heard him entering a note into his iPad. "Suggest plot centered in US if linked attacks."

"Do you have any evidence that it might be coming from elsewhere?"

"People very smart. Announce with physical attacks. Then cripple with cyber-attack. Not looking where they intending go."

"What could possibly be their motivation?"

"Heart of darkness. Not peer inside. But loner, my estimation. Someone without vested interests. Want things change. Not lose in change situation."

Something about his description didn't seem to fit what little I knew. "Who benefits from bringing down transport? Everyone needs food and medicine. Everyone needs to be able to get from one place to another."

"Do they?" Xian asked and his question made me think all the harder.

"The obvious person would be a farmer, but even farmers need seeds and fertilizer and parts for their tractors and harvesting equipment. And I understand the autonomous farming equipment is down as well. So not the farmers. So who?"

"Follow same process. Ask question. Evaluate answer. Ask all groups. Then ask groups not know about?"

"You think this might be a group we've not seen before?"

"Many groups. More every year. Group well organized. Attack many cities. Sophisticated tactics, weapons. Large mission. Bring down entire sector. Planned many years. Not new group, but maybe group not observe."

"But a group has to recruit members. They leave tracks, traces, and blogs, something that they put out there so people will learn about them and follow a trail to learn more."

"Identify where look."

"But the web has so many places to look. I don't know how anyone could find something like this without knowing where to look." I responded hopelessly.

"Breadcrumbs. Organizer leave breadcrumbs others follow. Look breadcrumbs."

I knew what Xian was saying, but I had absolutely no idea how to find the breadcrumbs because I still didn't know what the motivation was to bring transport down. Was it a tool to force governments to do something? Was it an end in itself? Was someone just looking for attention, or pointing out a flaw in our societal security systems? There were so many possibilities. "How would I recognize such a breadcrumb?"

"Maybe not recognize. Maybe someone else recognize. Not only person looking."

"No, but if I want to keep my job, I better damn well come up with something that breaks this case open."

"Not understand."

"Oh, sorry. The studio is thinking of canceling my show next season unless I do something dramatic."

"You dramatic actor." Xian responded, apparently not understanding.

"I mean I need to do something that will create interest in me or my character so more people will watch if we come back next season."

"Not same dramatic."

"No, not the same, but dramatic has more than one meaning. I just chose one of the lesser known meanings, sorry."

There was a moment of silence as Xian apparently moved past the confusion. "Study blogs. Who wants end society? Who writes affronts not reconcile?"

"You're suggesting I need to look for groups of disgruntled people. People upset with society more than just a politician or a single government."

"People think unfair."

I understood what he wanted me to look for, but it was a tall order. People were disaffected by so much. We never had it so good. More people were out of poverty than in history. And as contradictory as it seemed, there were more poor people than at any time in our history. The more we made things better, the more increasing numbers of people found themselves left out of the prosperity and good times. Unmitigated population growth just made moving the ball forward a near impossibility. We created millions of new jobs, giving graduates their first opportunity for employment. And for each person who found a job there were three who did not. The faster we ran the further behind we fell.

I understood completely why some people were unhappy with the way things were. And the cadre of people who described themselves as thinking the country and the world were moving in the wrong direction steadily grew from year to year. Regardless of who resided at 1600 Pennsylvania Avenue in Washington, the numbers grew. It was inevitable that every few years someone new would appear on the Forbes list of wealthiest men in the world. But most people had long ago given up any thoughts of joining them. An increasing number was hoping to just have food and a comfortable place to stay the night. The situation was becoming more and more precarious. So anyone who proposed a way out for those people would probably have an easy time recruiting. My problem was trying to pick out the one breadcrumb trail from all the others I would encounter.

Chapter Twenty-Eight

Dyllan, my technical production expert from Abu Dhabi really didn't have time for my call. "This is important or I wouldn't call."

"I know, but how does it fit into today's deadlines?" I could tell he was only half listening to me.

"For a lot of folks it will mean the difference between life and death." I thought might catch his attention, but he kept on working from his distracted response.

"Anyone I know?"

"Depends on who dies on your street this week because they can't get enough to eat or medicine they need to fight off disease."

"You're talking in the abstract. None of my friends have anything to worry about."

"When was the last time you tried to buy food?"

"Last Saturday, why?"

"You tried to go anywhere since?"

"Don't need to. All my work is over the net."

"Well, when you run out of food in your apartment and need to go to the store, you're going to find it isn't so easy at the moment."

"Why?"

"You haven't heard the Googlecars have stopped working and nothing's moving?"

"Don't know anything about that."

I was getting angry, "Dyllan. Stop working for a minute and listen to me."

After a moment I could hear he had stopped. "What's your problem?"

"People are dying all around you and you don't even know it."

"Happens all the time. All the guest workers here. Abu Dhabi's full of people from all over the world. They're not my problem."

"You try to leave your house, particularly in your wheelchair, and you're going to find you won't get very far."

"What are you saying?" He was angry now that I'd brought up his handicap. An IED explosion when he was in the Emirates Army had left him without the use of his legs. But for the production work he'd taken up as his occupation, he didn't really need his legs as most of it was done remote from his home in Abu Dhabi.

"Turn on the news and get your head up for at least a few minutes every day."

"Okay, okay. What do you need me to do and when do you need it?"

"I need you to do a search for me."

He was right back at me, "Come on. You could get anyone to do that for you. I don't have the time right now and even if I did, you could get a thousand people who could do that better than me."

"I don't think so. I need someone who can go places on the web that few people venture into."

Now I had his attention. "What kind of places?"

"Hidden places. Ones where you need an invitation to get in."

"But you don't have the invitation." Now I had him.

"No and I doubt you have one either."

"What kind of place is this?"

"A place for people who want something they don't want others to know about."

"Spy agency site?"

"No. More like the people who brought down the Googlecars and blew up a bunch of their repair facilities over the last several weeks."

"Why would they do that?" His surprise confirmed he really hadn't any idea what was going on around him.

"That's what I'm hoping you can help me figure out."

"This for the show or what?" he asked suspiciously.

"Not for the show, at least not directly."

"If I do this are you going to put me on, give me a cameo or something?" He retreated quickly, "Not sure I want one, but just asking."

"This is for real. Someone released a virus that brought all vehicles to a stop. No one can go anywhere at the moment. We've got to find them and figure out a way to get the Googlecars moving again. I wasn't kidding when I said people are dying from lack of food and medicine."

"If this isn't for your show, why are you getting involved? And why me? Why not some cop or the FBI or the secret police? Homeland security??"

"The people investigating asked me to help. I'm not going to blow smoke, if I can help them solve the issue, it will help ratings I'm sure.

You're the only guy I know who could help me find the madmen who have released a virus into the autonomous drive systems that brought them down. The cops, the FBI, your secret police and the various Homeland Security agencies are all working on the problem, but they haven't been able to figure out who or why, at least not yet."

"What makes you think that if all those brilliant minds can't do it I can?"

"Because you've always been able to do anything you set your mind to. You get blown up and lose your legs, you become one of the best media production people in the business in only a couple of years. Most people who spend their whole life doing what you do aren't as good as you are. That's why."

"I can't waste any more time on this right now. What specifically do you need?" he was back looking at the work on his screen, I was sure.

"I need you to figure out how to find the hidden sites where the people responsible for bringing down the Googlecars live on the web."

"You need to give me a little more." I was losing his attention quickly.

"Look for people who are disaffected with the way things are and talk about radical change. They need to be people who've been around for a while because what they've done so far has been very sophisticated. They've used weapons to destroy the Googlecar repair facilities that I'll bet you'd recognize from your days in the Army."

He stopped. I'd caught his attention again at least for a moment.

"Rocket with a fairly large warhead. Enough explosives to blow up a good size building with a range of about a half mile."

"Probably larger." He was engaged with the problem. "And they released a sophisticated virus too?"

"Yes."

"What's the problem the experts can't kill the virus?"

"I don't know, but so far they haven't."

He was finally engaged in the problem. He could see the challenge was worthy of his talents and time.

"When do you need something?"

"More people are dying every day."

"I'll work it in, but don't hold your breath. If the experts aren't tracking them down I don't know what I can do they won't or haven't. But just make sure you tell me when they solve it so I don't continue working the problem when it's already done."

"Deal."

"Now leave me alone so I can make some money here."

"You working for Hollywood or Bollywood today?"

"Bollywood. They're so incredibly behind on this project and they're paying me double to get them what they need by the end of the day, which I won't, by the way, if I keep on talking to you."

"Got it. And Dyllan. Thanks."

The line went dead. At least I'd achieved my objective. I was sure I'd hear from him in the next day or so, whenever he got the Bollywood project done.

Chapter Twenty-Nine

Silmara invited me to join a call with her team. I'd asked if Xian could join. After an awkward silence she'd agreed, reluctantly. I detected some history between them and I wasn't sure I'd be able to discover what it was. Xian was notoriously tight lipped about his dealings with other agencies and so far Silmara was about as transparent as mud.

Bomani and Kalindi joined the call, so for the first time I met some of the other members of Silmara's team. My first thought was they seemed young for the kind of responsibility they evidently had. I knew the best tech folks tended to be young, but I wondered after a few minutes of listening to the discussion whether they were seasoned enough for the magnitude of the task before them.

"A few suspects have been successfully eliminated, but the list remains long." Kalindi briefed Silmara. She seemed guarded in what she had to say, probably a little less specific than she would have been if Xian and I weren't on the call. But then again I could understand why she questioned why we were even invited.

"How have you been able to clear them?" Silmara asked.

"Review of the files. We look at the known expertise, previous events they've been linked to, statements made by the leadership, and so forth."

"Direct contact?" Xian asked.

Kalindi hesitated, probably wondering if she should answer Xian since he wasn't part of the team. Slowly, she did respond. "In a few instances we investigated further. We had contact on more than one occasion, not always with the leadership, sometimes with influential people within or outside the group known to affiliate with them."

"And from that you were able to eliminate them from consideration?" I asked.

"In this instance we have a long list of suspects. We haven't seen these tactics or type of virus previously."

"That why you're having trouble bringing the Googlecars back on line?"

Bomani answered. "The virus logic is not evident. We are reverse engineering, however, the process is slow because we do not understand how the virus interrupts the car software."

"Why is that? I thought you were the best of the best we have at forensic software analysis."

Silmara stepped in. "Bomani is the best of the best. What he is saying is we are looking at something no one has seen before. It is very difficult for us because there are no signatures we would normally follow to find whoever created and released this virus. We are in unexplored territory. That's why we are hopeful you will see something we do not. Something that will lead us in a direction we are not focused on, at least at the moment."

"You still think this didn't originate with a government?" I asked.

"A government that allowed its own people to starve would not long survive." Silmara answered.

"But the governments of all of your countries have failed to take action against poverty that led to mass starvations over the centuries, so I don't entirely accept your premise." I responded.

"Why do you ask?" Bomani inquired even though stung by my comment.

"The people who tend to have the money to create things totally new usually end up being in some classified program in a defense organization. Especially when they appear suddenly. Remember Stuxnet? Most people believe it was a cooperative effort of two countries that were trying to slow the progress of Iranian nuclear research."

"That goes back a ways." Bomani nodded as he responded, apparently having heard of the incident, but then again, I would have expected he probably studied that particular virus.

"We are investigating many possibilities. While every nation has denied any direct involvement or knowledge of the virus, we continue to look for signs someone might not be telling the whole truth." Kalindi informed us.

"Our analysis does not lead to any signatures on the virus we have seen before. The usual suspects in the virus arena all have tendencies and platforms they use which makes it possible for us to narrow down to just a few probable sources. In this case we are not finding any of those signatures. Someone has unleashed something totally new. It is a terribly difficult problem to solve."

"Would you mind if I had my software expert take a look at the virus and tell you what he thinks?" I asked, thinking of Dyllan again. I just knew he'd be thrilled to be given another opportunity to not deliver a project already on his schedule.

Kalindi jumped in first, "I don't think that would be possible. We have to control the virus."

"I could just go out on the street and download the software and virus from one of the thousands of Googlecars sitting in the streets of LA. So much for controlling the virus." I pointed out.

"That won't be necessary." Silmara answered.

"I'm happy to have another expert to collaborate with." Bomani was on board.

"Who is your expert?" Kalindi wanted to know.

"He's an algorithms developer I work with. He's been able to solve some of the most difficult problems I've been associated with. Very imaginative and extremely bright. He'd certainly bring the outside eyes to your problem. I'd also be amazed if he's unable to determine how the virus works."

"Does this expert have a name?" Kalindi still wasn't ready to have us on the inside.

"He does, but it wouldn't mean anything to you as he isn't in law enforcement and anyone outside my industry has never heard about him."

"Why are you reluctant to give us his name?" Kalindi again.

"If you wish to check him out I'll be happy to give you all the information you'll need for a background check. He formerly had a security clearance when he was on military duty and I'm sure he will check out without a problem."

Silmara listened to the conversation, "Please provide the information on your expert. We need to maintain security. We cannot afford to be penetrated just because we rush to solve this mystery."

"Understood." I responded and sent a message with Dyllan's information to Silmara.

"Primary suspect?" Xian wanted to get back to the prime topic.

"We don't have one suspect." Kalindi emphasized the 'one.'

"Don't understand virus architecture?" Xian again.

"The primary suspect must have a strong research background, in our estimation. We think the party probably worked for an internet security firm, someone who worked with virus's and has an encyclopedic understanding of them. So that has been our primary avenue of investigation. What researchers have affiliated with groups of any kind, including just trade groups where they might have met someone with a different agenda." Kalindi responded, apparently wanting to make sure we understood she did know what she was doing, even though she didn't want to tell.

"Military intelligence." Xian added.

"We are looking there as well." Kalindi acknowledged.

"For the same kind of people? Strong security background, threat detection types who might have decided to go a different way?" I added.

"Yes, we look at the files of anyone who might have the required expertise." Kalindi confirmed, but somehow, I thought the task had to be overwhelming given she had to do that analysis for every military cyber security expert. The files on a lot of those folks simply weren't readily available to law enforcement to review.

"Who seems to be the least cooperative in giving you access to files on their people?" I asked.

No one wanted to respond to my question, so I knew I was right about the problem.

"Your question would have to be considered sensitive information. I am electing not to answer you at this time." Silmara responded to make sure we understood there was no appeal.

"But I take it that's exactly the kind of question you're looking for us to ask?"

No hesitation, "Yes." At least from Silmara. Kalindi and Bomani remained quiet.

"Then know questions ask." Xian responded.

Chapter Thirty

Mimi and Alistair joined me for dinner as they did most nights now. Mimi wanted to know how the scripts were coming. Alistair was more focused on how we kept our jobs and he kept his ten percent. I didn't blame Alistair for his more limited view of the situation. I wondered the same thing, although I was less concerned about his ten percent.

"So how would you characterize your role on this task force?" Alistair interrupted Mimi's question about the script.

I wasn't sure how to answer, "Evolving," ended up the only thing I could think of to say.

"Got all that, but are they taking you seriously or just ignoring you?"

"Time will tell. Get the impression I've got to add value every day or I'll soon become a burden they don't want."

Mimi interjected, "So did you add value today?"

"I think so. They refused to answer several questions I asked."

Alistair turned that around, "Meaning they weren't about to give an actor real answers?"

I shook my head, "Think they hadn't thought them all the way through and were reluctant to let anyone know that to be the case."

Mimi again, "What kind of questions?"

"About the nature of innovation. Like what would it take for someone to be able to come up with an entirely new architecture of the code?"

Alistair glazed over, "How would you know anything about code architecture?"

"This goes way back. Episode seventeen. 'The Case of the Video Hacker.' Wherein the subject of our investigation developed a bot that let him see through any webcam without the owner knowing."

Mimi brightened, "I remember that one. Samantha identified the hacker was probably a kid before Rory thought to look for someone like that. One of the episodes where I thought I established Samantha's real value."

Alistair grimaced as he did every time Mimi went off on how her character added value to the series. But then he seemed to remember something. "Was that the one where your ratings jumped and the studio committed to the third season?"

I nodded, remembering it was where we had enough leverage to negotiate an increase in pay for the third season and more say in the script, which I didn't abuse, but most thought Mimi had.

Mimi brought me back out of my recollections, "So they wouldn't answer your questions?"

"They actually answered a lot more than they didn't, but I had to get up to speed. Even though they knew all about what I was asking, putting the questions into a framework for analysis added value to the discussion. I think they recognized that. Well, I think Silmara recognized that, although Kalindi seemed to want us to just go away. Probably thought we were an unnecessary intrusion."

Mimi's antenna were up. "Kalindi? That a man or woman?"

"Woman."

"Thought so." Mimi didn't say more.

I wasn't sure where she was going with her line of inquiry. I decided I needed to challenge her. "Some reason?"

"A woman would feel more threatened than most men, is all."

"That I'm going to take over? I'm only an actor. What kind of threat could I be?"

Alistair put my question into context, "The Mayor offered you the top job in LA."

"That was just a publicity stunt. He never would have given me the job if I'd gone to see him." I was convinced his offer wasn't sincere.

"He just wanted you to be his personal chauffeur. In the Tesla." Mimi observed.

"Probably right." I responded then changed the subject. "We have a draft of the script done, but I'm not comfortable it's what we want to show the first time. Might be a better second script once we've been accepted."

Alistair held out his hand, "Let me read it. I'll give you an opinion."

"I can do better, you know? This is the first time. I really don't know what I don't know. You know Regina much better than I do. What's she looking for in a script? What will drive the audience to either change the channel to watch us or change it because they're bored?"

"Is it formulaic?" Alistair asked in such a way I thought he wanted me to say yes, but I knew I really wanted to say no.

Mimi saved me. "We're looking for something totally new. So we used the formula as a framework to make sure we cover the important story points, but spin it on its head so it seems fresh, modern, unpredictable and totally unexpected."

Alistair looked at me, "You did all that?"

"Tried to." I affirmed.

"Regina will hate it."

"What about Jack and Stan?" Mimi asked before I could.

"Jack will look at the demographics. Which parts will like it and which won't? Stan on the other hand, will want to compare it to Tarrantino. Have you deconstructed the hour mystery action construct? Have you given the audience something they can identify with? Is it a situation they could see themselves surviving were they in your positions? Is it something people will talk about at work the next day?"

Mimi looked from Alistair to me. "You saying people don't talk about our show around the water cooler now?"

"I talk about your show around the water cooler." Alistair responded lamely.

"That's because your senior partner is pushing Johnny Hollywood for my role." I revealed I knew something Alistair would have hoped I didn't.

Alistair tried to respond twice before the words were articulated, "Julio's just doing his job for his clients."

"To the detriment of you and me. Sounds like you need to get a new partner."

"Julio's fine. He's not pushing as hard as you might think."

"Hard enough that Regina's listening, and probably Jack too."

"You think Stan's in your corner?" Alistair seemed surprised.

"Jack looks at each individual decision. Stan looks at the whole line-up of programming to maximize the value. That's why Stan will succeed Regina."

"Jack's a drone." Mimi tossed in to get a reaction.

"I agree with you." Alistair didn't sound genuine. Thought he really liked Jack more than Stan because Jack was more predictable as a numbers guy.

Mimi turned to me, apparently hearing the same thing in Alistair's voice I did, "I want to be on the next call with you."

"Call?" She'd lost me.

"With Kalindi and the others."

Why did she pick out Kalindi? "The task force?"

"Yes. As an Interpol expert I can add some value there."

Alistair looked at her as if she were crazy, "You're no Interpol expert. You read lines. You have no experience or insights to add there."

Mimi came over and stood next to me with her hand on my shoulder. "He pulls lessons out of our shows and solves crimes. Why can't I do the same?"

"You're not him." Alistair laughed, "And thank goodness you're not. Don't think I could handle two of him."

She spoke just to me, "You'll let me join the call, won't you?"

She knew exactly how to get me to do what she wanted. I could see it, and given our current situation I should have been able to resist her charms. "I'll have to ask Silmara. It's her team."

"But you will, won't you?"

"I think it's a bad idea." Alistair warned. "You don't want people to think the whole thing is an attempt to take over the investigation and co-opt it into your show."

"People won't think that." Mimi responded dismissively.

I had to disagree, "Alistair has a point. We'll have to be careful about how we do this."

Chapter Thirty-One

Mimi called her Interpol contacts after Alistair left. It was almost morning in Paris. About eight am. But in Paris that was still the middle of the night for most folks. The early hour probably explained the grumpy responses I interpreted from her end of the conversation.

"Jean, I know you haven't been to Starbucks yet, but this is important." She listened to a response. From the look on her face it apparently wasn't very conciliatory. "But with the autonomous cars out of commission, would you really be getting your morning caffeine anyway?" Another disagreement from what I could tell. "We need to get beyond all that. What can you share about the current shutdown?"

I flipped on the local news and turned the volume down so Mimi could hear. I'd be able to read the breaking news off the bottom tag line and try to interpret the main news stories from the footage and graphics they showed. At the same time I would be able to overhear Mimi's end of the conversation which again, as an actor, would give me a rich set of data points from which I could try to reconstruct the scene that was playing out before me.

"Okay, that's all very useful, but have you been able to zero in on a suspect yet?" A short response and the tone of her voice fell. "Yes, I do understand the confidential nature of the investigation, but I'm working with Silmara's team on this and I volunteered to discuss with you and the Interpol team." Jean's response made her sit back from the phone. "Yes, I understand all about protocol and the need to go through proper channels, but this is me, Jean. How long have I known you? We've been a team for more than ten years. It's not like I'm going to go do a show about what I learn. We're trying to help Silmara's team by performing as an unbiased set of eyes and ears. Frankly we've seen and heard some things that would scare the shit out of the world if it was presented wrongly." Short response at the other end. "Yes. I agree wholeheartedly. If Valery is the official liaison to the task force then everything needs to go through him. But at the moment you're still my official liaison and I need your help to address the problem the world's facing." The person at the other end made a comment she didn't like. "Yes, I know my French accent isn't what it used to be. But what does that have to do with this discussion?" She listened shortly and probably interrupted, "Jean… Jean. This isn't relevant. If you don't know anything, just say so. I'll still love you." Jean evidently said something and Mimi responded, "No, not that way." I could tell Mimi was frustrated her Interpol officer would treat her this way. She thought she was worthy of some deference and consideration given she had been the face of that agency to the world for a decade. She had probably had theoretical discussions like this one on numerous occasions. But then again, in those discussions they weren't dealing with sensitive data.

"Jean. You wouldn't want me to do an episode that indicates all men at Interpol are chauvinists, now would you?" Her jaw dropped, "You are? That can't be right. The fight for equal rights hasn't ended at the borders of France and the rest of the world. I'm serious. I'm writing my own episodes now and it would be very easy for me to…"

Evidently the message got across that she wasn't on the phone just to have a pleasant conversation as the person at the other end suddenly became more serious from what I could tell. "Yes, that is the case. Now what can you tell me about the current situation? I get it you do not want to tell me certain things. I can live with that. But if I am to help you and Silmara's task force to solve this mystery there are certain things I need to know. So do you have a prime suspect?"

Her brow furrowed. "How many?" The number was apparently more than three to five. "And they're all prime suspects? How do you eliminate people from your list? You must have some criteria you use." This was a longer discussion at the other end. I watched her nod to herself several times as she understood what the other person was saying. I couldn't surmise from her response whether she was agreeing that what they were doing was a good way to eliminate suspects or not. As had I, Mimi had been catching crooks on television for more than a decade. She knew what worked and what did not from the scripts we acted. Each scenario and screenplay had to be approved by both the LAPD and Interpol since we represented ourselves as members of those elite squads. So much we had learned was based on reality. Much we had learned was a dramatization of real situations that had occurred, although not all had occurred in LA.

"Where I can be of most assistance to you and to Silmara's team is in evaluating American suspects. I'm here and can access records to accelerate the hunt for these people. I'm sure you have many US suspects." She seemed surprised at the response, "That few. Really? I would have thought you'd have a long list of Americans who'd like to see the world come to an end." A short response at the other end of her call. "Yes, most American's have an unnatural love for their cars. But that doesn't mean their threats aren't real. Someone wrote the code. That person was able to come up with something no one recognizes in terms of the software approach to shutting down a transport control system." A short sharp response on the phone. "No, I am not repeating classified information. Anyone with a half brain could determine the problem with the code." Another short response. "Well, if the leadership of Interpol has not determined the problem, I must interpret they only have less than a half a brain between them." A response which caused Mimi to mouthe a mimic, then, "No, I am not being disrespectful. You were the one who said your leadership has failed to determine the code had to be something experts did not recognize. If it were standard code, the transport system would have been back up within twenty-four hours. How many days has it been now? We are measuring this in weeks now and if we do not act quickly, it will be months. How many will die if this stretches into months, Jean? How many of the sick, elderly and children who are not receiving the proper nutrition? How many people who need critical medications and won't be able to obtain them from their pharmacies? This is already a global disaster. Interpol has to help me stop the people behind this attack before the worst occurs."

Apparently the person at the other end wasn't ready for Mimi's impassioned plea. He apparently made some remark, "I disagree. I have a responsibility to help solve this mystery. I can't simply watch you and others fail to solve the problem where there is something I can do. I'm good at solving mysteries. I'm good at finding clues and tracking them to resolution. I'm good at many things that might help solve this case. I must do what I can and not just sit and wait."

The person at the other end apparently disagreed with Mimi, who cut him off and threw her cellphone across the room. "Men!"

"French men." I corrected.

She looked at me, still reacting to the treatment she had received from someone she had thought to be a friend. "French men do not have all of the world's chauvinists, but they have the worst."

"What got you the most upset?" I asked to get her to talk about the conversation.

"He said I needed to stop wasting his time when Interpol was well along towards solving the question of who was behind the shutdown."

"We both have a certain credibility problem." I noted for her.

"We have no credibility problem with the people who watch our show. They believe we can solve these mysteries. We believe we can solve them. We change the scripts for the better every week by making our characters more believable, more authentic and more inventive in how they go about resolving the crimes. I know we can help solve this, get the Googlecars back on the road. We just need a chance. For whatever reason, my friends at Interpol do not want us involved. Do you think they might be afraid a woman really could solve this mystery without the help of all the many men who are working the case? Is that why they dismiss me?"

I looked at the pain on Mimi's face. She was humiliated. I knew she felt the same way I did. I had to find a way to get her on Silmara's team so she could contribute whatever she could. Maybe between us we would contribute to the final resolution. If not, at least we could say we did what we could. And then the studio would cancel our show and we would go our separate ways. Was that why I was working so hard to find a resolution hoping it would keep us on the air at least a while longer? I'd come to realize we would go our separate ways. I'd no longer see her, talk with her, act with her and write scripts with her. Was I afraid that I'd lose the remaining ties I had with her, now that I'd come to realize just how perfect she was for me?

"What are you thinking?" She challenged me. "Are you thinking I can't possibly help?"

"I know you all too well. You will help resolve the mystery. Of that I have complete confidence."

"Then why aren't you helping me get on this task force? Why aren't you taking on the Interpol big shots who just put me down? Why aren't you fighting for me?"

Was that what she was waiting for? Was she expecting me to fight for her? Had I taken the wrong approach to losing her in the first place? I thought I knew her enough to know she would never believe what I had to say about that night I didn't come home. I'd taken the wait and see if she was curious enough to ask questions and find out for herself. She never had. And I'd not pursued her, always pulling back when I anticipated her response. Maybe she was waiting for me to show her how important she is to me. Maybe now was the time to start fighting for her.

"I need someone sitting beside me in the Tesla as we go about solving this mystery, just like I need Samantha St. Julian helping me solve mysteries every week. Are you up to it?"

Chapter Thirty-Two

Mimi was happier than I'd seen her since that night before I'd not come home. She dug in. She joined the calls with Silmara and took the lead working with Dyllan on the analysis of the code even though she knew less about code development than I did. But I wasn't going to get in her way. She needed to be front and center and she was, now with a little help from me.

She was never shy about voicing what she thought, but on her very first call she came to realize those on the task force knew a whole lot more about what they were doing than we did, from our limited exposure. While on the first call she asked questions incessantly. On the second she backed off and listened more, asking targeted questions hitting at different aspects of the problem. She established her value in the second call and I sensed Silmara and Bomani had accepted her, but Kalindi was still real wary. I wondered if there was more to Kalindi's wariness than I could see. I remembered Mimi had wanted to know if Kalindi was a man or woman the first time we discussed the task force. There seemed to be something behind her question. Now I was seeing the result of what I'd sensed. But I still didn't know what was behind the tension.

I set up a call for our sub team, which was just Xian, Dyllan, Mimi and myself. Because the team was spread over half of the globe, I scheduled the calls early in the morning LA time, which went into evening for Xian. Dyllan was in between.

Dyllan wanted to make a point he'd been thinking about for some time now. "I disagree with your Interpol friends, Mimi. Americans have an unnatural love for their cars, but not for Googlecars. I have not seen Americans washing and waxing a Googlecar on the weekends. I have not seen Americans regarding them as anything more than a service, like a fast food restaurant or an airplane you take to get from one city to another. Americans don't have pet names for their burger joints."

"I understand your premise, but what point are you trying to make?"

"I think Americans are just as likely to be suspects as anyone else. In fact, given all the extreme groups co-existing in your society, I would expect some of them would want to shut down the Googlecars and force people to drive themselves again as they did for so long."

"And call it freedom?" I asked.

"Exactly." Dyllan responded.

"Want society go backwards." Xian observed. "Googlecars symbol. Want symbols go away."

"We see that over and over again. But not just in America. England had the Luddites who wanted to stop progress." Mimi responded. I was proud how she had spent hours and hours researching to try to understand the mindset of those we were confronting.

"Society is divided between the liberals who want everything to change and the conservatives who want to minimize change. And both sides have fringe groups that take those basic tenants and push them as far as possible. We may very well be dealing with an extreme fringe conservative group wanting things to go way back to the way they were." I noted.

"America fertile ground - extremes." Xian noted.

"Are you suggesting we need to focus on fringe groups in the US, Xian?" I asked.

"Yes. Others not put effort America. Good place you start."

"I already have." Dyllan reported. "Have a list of potential suspect organizations. From their websites they seem to have some far right philosophy and a level of activity that could house the masterminds of a plot such as we have seen."

"You willing to share so we can help you?" Mimi asked.

"Absolutely. You should all have it in your mailboxes."

"Any one seem more likely than the others?" I asked.

Dyllan was expecting this question. "Not one or two, but I prioritized the list by the nature of the rhetoric they use in terms of how extreme. Those who want to save the whales are at the end of the list, those who want to do away with death and taxes, well they're near the top."

"Are there really groups that want to do away with death and taxes?" Mimi seemed surprised by Dyllan's characterization.

"Absolutely. And they're not the most extreme. You have the survivalists, who are stocking up on everything you'll need to survive the rapture. And the Free Willies, who want everyone to stop eating fish. Then you have socialists who want the government to seize all private assets and give to everyone according to their need. No one gets more money than anyone else, but those with health conditions get free health care and those who are mentally disadvantaged get less complex work assignments than those with Ph.Ds."

"Soup to nuts?" Mimi asked.

"More nuts than soup if you ask me, but soup is not popular here in Abu Dhabi."

"Good start." Xian added. "Divide list. Each take so many."

"You want to divide up the list for us Mimi?" I asked, hoping she would want to make the assignments.

"I can do that." She readily agreed. "But Dyllan, what can you tell us about the virus?"

"An interesting challenge you accepted for me." Dyllan put his thoughts in kind terms. I could tell by the tone of his voice. "I need more time than I have in a day to give this proper attention, but I understand why the Task Force is struggling with the code. Very dense, very complex, not intuitive at all. Someone deliberately sought to introduce as much complexity as possible so it would be very difficult to defeat."

"I think we all knew that." Mimi responded apparently hoping for some new insights.

"But with that said, I have a feeling about this code. The author went to extremes to mask what he was doing. I think the mechanism itself is probably simple. If he had a complex mechanism within a complex code, I suspect it would have reliability problems. If my premise is correct, what could be happening is most of the researchers working this problem are focused on trying to understand the complexity, looking for a Buckminster Fuller mechanism."

"A what kind of mechanism?" I wasn't familiar with the name he used.

"Buckminster Fuller invented things like the geodesic dome. It's a structure you would think would collapse into itself, but it does not. He once said, 'You never change things by fighting the existing reality. To change something, build a new model that makes the existing model obsolete.' I think people are looking for that new model in the code while all the time I do not think it is a new model at all."

Mimi asked, "And how will you find out if you're right?"

"More time is the problem at the moment, Mimi. I have more deliverables than I have hours in a day. Everyone wants me to do just one more thing for them. I could spend all day working this problem and it still might take me months. But I can't devote all my time, I have other masters waiting for me and once this problem is solved, I will still need them to send projects so I might pay my bills."

"I hear you. But people are dying, Dyllan. Can you accept the death of one more person because you have a film deliverable for a Bollywood epic? People won't die if the film is delayed."

"Mimi, you are a task master. I am only one person. The problem is Bomani's. Why am I the one who must discover the solution?"

"Because you are the one who sees the problem differently. That is precisely what Silmara was looking for when she agreed to have us join her task force."

"You wanted to join the task force, Mimi. I am an unwilling draftee to your team. I never wished to save the world. I have no idea if my theory is correct or not. I could spend a lifetime looking for the simple but elegant solution in the maze of code and never find it."

I interrupted him, "Are there any tools you could build that might automate your search?"

"Not without knowing what I am looking for."

"You do know. A mechanism that kills autonomous car control mechanisms. Go look at the host code and you'll see the answer to your question."

"Easier said than done." Dyllan really didn't want to take on the assignment. "Let someone else do it."

"You're the one with the virgin eyes. You see things others don't. You're the one we need to look over the code and build the tool." Mimi understood what had to be done.

"Only one, Dyllan." Xian had come on board as well with the plan.

"I cannot afford to waste more time on your project. But what I will do is give this conversation some thought. If I come up with something that might be useful I will look into it further."

"I'll send you the host control code from the Googlecar." I volunteered

"What else do you need?" Mimi asked.

"Home baked cookies and twenty-four more hours in a day?"

Chapter Thirty-Three

In the next telcon with Silmara's team, Dyllan did not join. We wanted him working the virus problem and not spending his time discussing who might be involved or why. Silmara opened the discussion asking for the usual reports.

"Bomani, what new have you learned about the code?"

"We continue to trace functionality, but have not yet come across anything we believe could be the control code."

"If you have to continue down this path how much longer until you trace everything?" Silmara's voice was weary.

"A month, maybe two. It depends on the rate of complexity."

"The rate?" Silmara asked before I could.

"Yes. The author has introduced increasing complexity into the functions we are tracing. Each one is longer and more complex than the last. If the author continues to increase the rate of complexity he introduces, it could take longer."

"Then we must find the person responsible immediately. We cannot wait a month or two or three. This is not to say you should lessen your efforts, Bomani. You must do everything in your power to find the mechanism and defeat it. But we cannot wait for you."

"I understand, madam."

"Before you go, have you found anything that could be a signature we could follow?" I asked.

"Unfortunately, no. Nothing we recognize."

"How is it possible we have not seen anything like this code before?" Mimi asked.

Bomani responded, "There are many different programming languages. Each was new when a team developed it specifically to address a desire to have a computer do something differently. Just as teams innovated to create a new programming language, someone has taken an existing language and innovated on the functionality the code represents. I am actually quite surprised in hindsight that we have not seen this before."

"Thank you." Mimi sounded even more discouraged than Silmara. "So who are your top five suspects? If we are to find the person or persons responsible we need to focus on the top suspects and work our way down the list."

Kalindi responded, "We do not know individual names of persons, but believe we have narrowed the probable groups to nationals from China, Iran, North Korea, Yemen and Syria."

"The usual suspects." I observed. "You've gone back to the old Axis of Evil plus two."

"This is not guess work, Mister Jensen. We have traced communications pointing to these groups as working projects that could be this one. We know all have been following the events more closely than others. All have been hacking sites related to the Googlecars. All have experienced coders who have released viruses, Trojans and phishing schemes. These appear to be the best of the best at what they do and what they do is release terror in the world." Kalindi defended her estimate.

"But are any innovators?" Mimi asked. "Have any released anything that was different than a copy of something someone else had already done? You haven't named anyone who I would have expected to see on your list. Those countries don't want to fundamentally change anything other than punish the US and push us out of their homelands.

Whoever is behind this attack wants something fundamentally different. The US is not the only target here. This is some group or someone who fundamentally wants things to change."

Kalindi came right back at her. "Not necessarily. The Googlecar shutdown could be a means of accomplishing a political objective. Look at America. One of the highest obesity rates and urban concentration rates in the world. No wonder the starvation levels are so high there."

"Granted, but…" I acknowledged. "Have there been any demands at all?"

"Silmara apparently wanted to change the direction of the discussion. "There have not and we do not expect any at this time. Our belief is that if someone was holding out for a specific political objective we would have heard by now."

Kalindi wasn't listening anymore. "A general societal shutdown? Not a likely scenario. There may be individuals or small groups who would hold out for such a result, but they are not in a position to have carried out such a software virus development program or be in a position to have carried out the shutdown. It has to have a short term political objective."

"One opinion, Kalindi. We must not blind ourselves to other possibilities by holding onto a notion that does not square with the facts as we know them." Silmara scolded Kalindi, but I wasn't sure that Kalindi took it as a scold.

"Exactly why it must be political. Nothing else squares with the facts." Kalindi continued.

"You have dedicated teams working your top five suspects?" I tried to refocus the discussion.

"Actually many more than the top twenty-five." Silmara conceded. "But most of the resources are working those top five, yes. Do you have some particular insight you would like to share?"

"Just what Mimi was alluding to." I started. "We think there may be extremist groups in the US that might be behind the shutdown. We have a list we are working and will share with you. We would like your teams to validate what they know about the groups on our list and provide that information to us so we can build complete profiles."

"Where did you get your list?" Kalindi asked harshly.

"Developed it ourselves. We're trying to be objective about the various extremist groups in our country. We don't want to just respond to those who law enforcement have been observing. We're trying to open the aperture. Think outside the box. Consider the unconsiderable. Do all the things your team doesn't have time for so that we can be an appropriate adjunct to your efforts."

Silmara was quiet and so was Kalindi. After a short silence Silmara answered. "Our resources are stretched thin. To give you the attention you request will take them off the tracks we are following and slow our efforts. Is there any other way you might obtain the information you seek?"

"We can develop it ourselves." Mimi responded before I could. I hadn't planned to respond the way she did, but with the hostility from Kalindi, I thought Mimi probably had a better understanding of the situation. The only thing I could think of was Kalindi was being criticized for not making faster progress. She simply didn't want to divert resources to what she thought wasn't a promising approach. At least I wanted to believe that of Kalindi, but from the way Mimi was acting I had to consider she thought something else might be going on.

"Thank you." Silmara responded, sounding relieved. I wondered if she picked up on the tension between Kalindi and Mimi. As a woman I had to believe she did. Since Kalindi was her person, I was sure she would back her as necessary. She knew Kalindi, she trusted her and had a long standing relationship where Kalindi had evidently delivered results. She didn't know Mimi at all.

Xian spoke up for the first time during this call, "Suspect virus come western country. May have sponsor elsewhere."

"Why do you think that?" Kalindi again, but not so hostile, as if she wanted to understand Xian's reasoning or what evidence he had.

"No signature." Xian answered. "Only western developers hide."

"We have people in India who could hide the signature." Kalindi responded as if to counter Xian's argument.

"On suspect list?" Xian came right back at her.

"No. They are trusted."

"All?" Xian was clearly skeptical.

"Yes, all." Kalindi wasn't going to be trapped.

"None leave, go private security firms?"

"No one from India would do this." Kalindi tried to end the discussion.

"I hear what you're saying, but we've just made a decision we have to find the person or persons responsible immediately because it's going to take too long to unravel the code." I began. "We've agreed to expand the search into groups you're not currently looking at. I'm not as certain about the innocence of everyone in my nation and that's why I'm working this hard. I'll be happy to be wrong, but if I'm right we'll get the situation back to normal much quicker. I suggest you need to do the same with the people you know to be capable of working without signatures as a minimum."

Silmara clearly didn't like the tension on her task force. I forgot my own observation. "Kalindi is in charge of her resources. She will deploy them as she judges most appropriate."

Chapter Thirty-Four

Mimi came to my trailer late afternoon of the next day. I was planning to go out with the LA detectives again and had argued long and hard to convince the LA police department to reduce their crew by one. They would not agree and insisted we could be more effective if I agreed to do the show live, no editing, and no script. It was going to be raw and uncensored. It was going to be up to the detectives to make sure it was fast moving.

"You have a power bar?" Mimi asked as she went to the drawer where I kept what remained of my food stash.

"Help yourself." I responded, knowing there were only a few left and I would have difficulty finding more.

The television was on. The anchor was reporting on the food situation in LA. "We have no reliable information about how many deaths there have been from starvation, since aid workers can't get out to visit the sick and the elderly who are most at risk."

Mimi looked up as she opened the foil wrapper on the power bar. She looked thinner to me. I always saw it in her face first. The color of her skin had also lost the glow I so loved. Even her hair looked to have less of a sheen to me. It had to be diet. We hadn't had a reasonable meal now in over two weeks. We would catch a few calories here and there, but the power bars were the last we would probably see for a while. At least we still had water, and I still had a few herbal tea bags I would brew up when I got really hungry. The tea didn't replace the calories I needed, but at least it helped me cope with the hunger.

"People are dying and not receiving a proper burial." Mimi observed.

"We have no way to transport the bodies to the funeral homes or cemeteries."

"It must be awful for the family members who have to stay in the houses with those who have died."

"Particularly since they have no idea how long the bodies will remain, or whether other family members will join the deceased."

Mimi looked at the open power bar, "How can we stand here talking about people who have died as if it were an abstract unreality? It's not. People are dying all around us. We just accept that horrible truth and go on about what we would normally be doing anyway. How can we?"

I went to Mimi and folded her into my arms. "We must go on so humanity goes on. Death and life coexist and have throughout our history. Those who die are remembered by those who knew them. Those who live go on about the life they have yet to live. Are you and I responsible for those who are dying?"

She pulled back, "To the extent we haven't solved this mystery, yes, we are responsible."

"But we're not the ones society looks to for solving anything. We're entertainers. We take their minds off their daily lives for a few minutes each week for a defined season. We may portray those who solve these mysteries, but we aren't them."

"Maybe we should be. Throw the scripts away. Let us go solve this. We know more about how to go do that than most people. It's a matter of deciding to. That's all. If we decide we are going to solve the mystery we will."

I didn't want to burst her balloon, but I did anyway, "Unless Silmara's team solves it first."

"I hope she does. Then people will stop dying."

Mimi took a bite and brought her power bar with her as we went to the Tesla, which was just outside my trailer. She ate quickly so she would be done before Walt Simmons joined us. But Walt was coming across the lot with his camera, so she folded the foil around the remaining bar and put it into her jacket pocket.

A few minutes later we picked up Pete and Kareem at the police station. "Where to tonight, gents?" I asked as they settled in to the back seat with Walt in the jump seat behind them, camera rolling live.

Kareem started out right away, "I thought you were going to wear your chauffer's hat for us."

"It's at the dry cleaners. Can't wear a dusty cap. You know how that is." I responded having had a taste of where the discussion was going to go this evening.

Pete Jefferies, the other detective responded to my original question. "Crenshaw."

I pulled out into the street and people were coming out of their apartments and houses to line the street. I wondered why until I remembered we were on live. Viewers could see where we were and where we were going. It seemed to me like we were in the Batmobile or something. People were coming out just to get a glimpse of us, knowing we were on television at that moment. I needed to give them more information about what we were doing and what they could expect. "Whereabouts in Crenshaw and why there?"

"Just above Rosecrans, but before you get to 139th Street." Kareem answered.

"What are we going to find there?" Mimi asked. I had to make sure she had an opportunity to express herself and ask the right questions. I was finding it real hard to script and direct on the fly in my head when I didn't even know what the story was going to be about yet.

"Report of a shooting." Pete responded before Kareem could. I guess he wanted to make sure he got in his lines tonight as well since the broadcast was live.

"Anyone we know?" I asked to keep things moving.

"Shooter or victim?" Kareem answered.

"Either or both? Husband wife? Domestic? In the course of a robbery?" I asked but noticed Mimi was getting ready to ask a question, so I let her.

"Why don't you just run down what you do know, detective."

Kareem apparently was good with Mimi's request. "We took the call on the shooting as we were getting ready to come meet you. Had another event planned for tonight but this one just happened so witnesses and victims still on site. Apparently a drug bust that went bad. Report is the dealers met the buyers in Bolger Park. Buyers were undercover and when the transaction went down, undercover tried to make the bust, only the dealers suspected something and had a shooter watching from nearby. One of our guys was shot in the dust up and the dealers ran for the Dominguez Channel which is dry because of the draught. Our guys followed up the channel and caught up to them just north of Rosecrans, where it crosses Crenshaw Boulevard. Another dust up in the channel there. The shooter apparently tracked our guys north and attacked them from behind, killing two. But our remaining guy was able to take the two dealers into custody because the shooter melted into the crowd on Crenshaw."

"So they're waiting for us?"

"Only way we can put them behind bars is if you ferry them to the station."

We discussed the situation on the rest of the short drive, passing the many non-functioning Googlecars all along the way. Everyone had a chance to get in a few comments or observations by the time we arrived. Walt was first out of the car so he could photograph the rest of us as we came out.

Kareem and Pete went directly to the undercover officer and two dealers. Walt followed them, but Mimi and I stayed by the Tesla.

"What are you doing?" She asked as I surveyed the crowd that had gathered.

"Looking for the shooter. Follow me." I moved through the crowd with Mimi directly behind. I looked closely at everyone who was watching Kareem and Pete interrogate the dealers on television. Then I spotted him, went right to a short Hispanic man of about thirty, wearing flannel shirt, blue jeans and work boots. I grabbed him, put him into a headlock and took him to the ground.

"Kareem, Pete. We need a little help over here." Mimi called.

The two detectives came over and stood over me and my new friend, who I was holding down on the ground. "What are you doing?"

"Meet your shooter." I responded as I held up the revolver I'd removed from under his shirt in the back.

Kareem had to ask, "What episode do we have to watch to know how you figured him for the shooter?"

"This one. I saw the bulge of the weapon when he leaned forward to talk to her." I pointed to a woman standing next to Pete. "You may want to question her. Anyway, when I got closer I could smell the gunpowder from recent shots on his clothes. His boots were still wet from the small amount of water in the channel down below. He was also hanging back so he could easily slip away. I think he was trying to figure out if he could help his friends escape, but he didn't see me coming.

I stood up and brought the gunman to his feet. "You have handcuffs for our friend?"

Pete handcuffed him and took him over to the other two.

Chapter Thirty-Five

Bomani asked to talk with Dyllan, so I arranged a call between them, only Kalindi insisted she had to be on the videoconference. I suggested she would probably be bored since it was going to be a technical discussion about the virus and the different approaches each were using to try to find a way to render it harmless. Kalindi informed me she had a software background and would not be bored. In fact, she said she would probably get ideas of how to better track down the responsible parties by listening to two experts talking about her or him. I was surprised she thought the person responsible might be a woman.

I decided to listen in, but not participate in the call.

Bomani started things off. "Desmond tells me you have different thoughts about how to trace the functionality."

Dyllan couched his response carefully, "Desmond shares his different thoughts, which he does all the time, and that started me thinking. We have all responded to the complexity with complex plans to understand that complexity. But what if the author was only using the complexity as a cover for a simple but elegant solution? Would that not make it much harder for us to find the solution? If we spend all of our time tracing the functionality of the virus and the author has designed it with increasing complexity, the longer we look the less we look at simple embedded functions within larger functions that could in reality be standalone functionality."

Bomani began to nod during Dyllan's description. "And we get lost trying to understand functionality that may not, in reality, do anything at all. Meanwhile we overlook short embedded codes that combine to create a string of instructions causing the result. Brilliant.

But that makes the task infinitely harder."

"Not necessarily. Desmond challenged me to develop a tool that would automate the search for embedded code strings. I told him I had to know what those code strings needed to look like and what they would do in order to know what to look for."

"Absolutely you would." Kalindi this time.

"So he sent me the host code, and you know what I discovered?"

"No idea." Kalindi was captivated by Dyllan's analysis.

"The control system is relatively simple when you compare it to some of the algorithms I have to create for the movie business. I have friends in the intelligence community and the algorithms they create are monsters. In any event, I've learned a lot from working with them and they made me aware of possibilities that have helped me in the movie work I do."

"What does all that have to do with the Googlecar control systems?" Kalindi asked. The tone wasn't hostile as she had used with Mimi. But at the same time it lacked deference, which I thought she should be showing to Dyllan. He is a lot smarter than she thinks he is.

"Let me back up for a moment. I did develop a tool that is scanning the virus code as we speak. That is ongoing. Using the segmented code theory I defined seventeen approaches to the functionality that would be needed to shut down the Googlecar controls. I don't know if that is the total set of possibilities, but thought it a good start. Anyway, that is on-going."

"Brilliant. You must send me the results you are getting." Bomani seemed to have a new found respect for Dyllan.

"Done. Anyway, back to my thesis. The control system is actually very simple. The Google engineers wanted something that would stand up to an extensive period of use, so they took the simplest approach they could find. When I reviewed the code, I realized my theory was even more plausible than I had originally thought. The code sequences required to render it inoperable were not complex, which again reinforced that the complex virus is probably a screen."

Kalindi jumped in. "Let me understand. You believe the virus is a simple virus. Not complex. Not something that would require extensive experience to create?"

"The functionality required to shut down the Googlecar control systems does not need to be complex to render the system inoperable. That is correct."

"So a country that is not on the bleeding edge of innovation could have designed the virus to shut down the Googlecar fleet?" Bomani now.

"Yes, but the code in which it is embedded is not something that could have been developed in any of the five nations you are examining." Dyllan responded.

"But the actual code segments could have been developed in one of those countries and embedded in something they obtained from someone else as a means of further obscuring the source and slowing our response to the crisis, making everything much worse." Kalindi still wants to defend her position as to who is behind the events.

"Isn't that what Xian suggested in your last call?" Dyllan asked.

Kalindi mumbled something I couldn't decipher.

Bomani wanted to get back into this discussion that Kalindi had hijacked. "If you are correct, my teams will probably overlook the very code that has rendered the systems inoperable."

"Depending on how they are conducting their analysis, I would say it is entirely possible they could overlook embedded code strings." Dyllan confirmed Bomani's observation.

"Because they do not, in and of themselves, result in a fully executed operation."

"If that is a requirement you have put on their analysis." Dyllan again.

"It is. How could I have overlooked this possibility?" Bomani is excited a new direction is clear.

"Easily, my friend. I would not have thought of it either if Desmond hadn't challenged me the way he did. I'm usually someone who takes the non-traditional route to delivering functionality, just because I get tired of the usual approach and want to see if I can do it some other way. But that is a peculiarity I have. Always been that way."

"I am as well." Bomani responded to a kindred soul. "I want to see if I can do it simpler, fewer instruction sets, fewer functions to perform, achieve the same or a better result with less effort."

"Exactly." Dyllan responded.

"You may stop congratulating each other. The perpetrators are still out there. What can you do to accelerate your research? We must find a solution sooner than later." Kalindi was getting impatient.

"Would you send me your tool so my team might modify to extend the analysis of the virus code?" Bomani asked Dyllan.

"On its way. I'll also send the results of the scan when the tool completes. I don't think I'll have a complete hit, but I do think it will identify some bits of the code that will help us understand the approach and shape future scans."

"Brilliant." Bomani responded. "I have been wondering about something. Maybe you have some ideas as to whether I am right or wrong."

"Yes?" Dyllan responded.

"What if the coder is someone amongst us? I mean, what if the person who wrote this code is someone who works for one of our agencies? She or he would be hiding in plain sight and helping us to find him or her. If that person were working to solve this, she or he would be perfectly situated to ensure we do not find the solution until the perpetrator wishes."

"My team has discussed this possibility." Kalindi confirmed. "We have dismissed it, at least for now. That does not mean we will not come back to it if certain clues we uncover lead us back there.

Bomani was still uncomfortable, "Dyllan. Do you know anyone who could have developed this virus? Someone totally unscrupulous and willing to see thousands or millions die for what we don't even know?"

"Do I know people who could have developed the code we are looking at? The answer is yes. Would they have done so? Money can be a powerful motivator."

"But why?" Kalindi asked, mystified. "How could anyone be so callous?"

"People dying from non-functioning Googlecars is a very abstract notion, unless those people are dying in your house. I don't think whoever did this has anyone dying in their house."

Chapter Thirty-Six

Later in the evening Mimi came to visit me in the trailer. It wasn't something we had planned so I was surprised to see her. "May I come in?"

I stood aside without responding, but let her know she was welcome. She went right to the power bar drawer. She was hungry. I didn't blame her and in fact had a cup of tea on my table I'd been sipping and rewarming. The tea bags were nearly gone and I wouldn't be able to keep up not eating much longer. Knowing Mimi was counting on my stash for her only meals I'd stopped eating them to save them for her.

"Eight." Mimi turned to me, "There are eight left. The same number I left last night."

I didn't respond to her, not really sure what I should say anyway.

"You're not eating." She's realized what I'm doing.

"I have my tea."

"But why aren't you eating?" I don't want to answer her.

"I can stand to lose a few more pounds. You can't."

"I'm ravenous. I can't stop thinking about food and you know I never eat."

"You never eat when you can. It's when you can't that things change."

She sat down to eat her power bar. I watched her in silence. She seemed to be feeling guilty as she only nibbled on the bar. But maybe she did so to make it last longer. Maybe her stomach had shrunk as mine had, and she no longer had the ability to eat much or eat quickly. She looked up at me as she took a bite. She tried to smile, but she pulled inward almost immediately, apparently thinking about the food she was consuming and the difficulty in only eating a simple power bar with far fewer calories than were recommended for minimum daily nutritional levels.

"How are you feeling?" I asked.

When she finished chewing her bite, she answered, "Weak. I don't have much energy. It seems to take a lot out of me just to walk over here. I want to sit around or take a nap most of the time."

"We have to finish our script." I reminded her.

"You said it's complete." She pronounced.

"It could be better." I observed. I was never fully satisfied with anything I produced. I always thought it could be better and struggled on when to let something go.

"I am sure da Vinci thought the Mona Lisa could be better." Came as her response.

"It could have." I confirmed. "But it clearly didn't need to be."

She finished eating her power bar, neatly folded the foil wrapping and rose to dispose of it. A tour past the garbage can and she came over and sat down in my lap. I felt her thinness. It wasn't pleasing even though Mimi had a tendency to carry more weight than she needed to from time-to-time. She was like a yo-yo. When things were stressful she put on a few pounds, when things were going well and she was concerned about what the audience thought of her, she was always able to drop those extra pounds in just a few weeks.

I kissed the top of her head and hugged her.

"You're saving them for me, aren't you? How long do you think this will continue?" she hugs me.

"I don't know, but at least we're doing all we can to help resolve it quickly."

"You're doing more than I am."

"I wouldn't say that. You're a major part of the team now. Asking the right questions, doing the research on the extremist groups and funneling your findings back in. You were out on the last LA detective tour. You helped us catch the shooter. What more do you need to do?"

"I need to help end this so we all have enough to eat again."

I had to remind her, "Not everyone had enough to eat before this happened. Kids and old folks were going to bed hungry every night. Kids get free lunches at school because that is often the only meal they get. Hunger in America and the world isn't new. We've just had the opportunity to experience it first-hand."

"I don't like it."

"No one likes being hungry. And you hear people say all the time we throw away food at the same time people are going to bed hungry. It's not a matter of there not being enough food, it's always been a matter of getting the food into the hands of those who are hungry. Whether that's through a food bank or now the fact that transport can't get the food from where it's grown to those who need to eat it."

"I'll never take food for granted again."

"Just don't over react and gain a whole bunch of weight when this is all over." I responded to her discomfort.

"You've got to be as hungry as I am. Why aren't you upset?"

"What can I do? Nothing. I've got to help solve the mystery, find the people responsible and help break the code so the Googlecars go back on line. Then the food will get to the stores and restaurants. Medicine will get to the hospitals and pharmacies. People will get stronger and healthier and we will all be able to get back to what we were doing before this all happened."

"But we won't forget." She noted.

"No, we won't forget."

"And we'll never be hungry again."

"I suspect people will be a lot more appreciative than they were before." I replied, holding her against me, stroking her hair, smelling her soapy smells and cologne.

She lay quietly on me. Her breathing seemed to slow so I thought she might be going to sleep, but she asked a question to change my thoughts, "Why do you always come back to me when you know we'll never be together again?"

"I don't know that."

"Sure you do. I'll never forgive you for fucking Allison when we were together."

I thought about her remark about fighting for her. I wasn't sure how I was going to fight for her other than always being there for her. I still didn't believe she would accept anything I'd say in my own defense. She would have to ask Allison as she was the only other person who knew the truth, and I never expected Mimi would. So how could I win her back other than not trying to convince her with words, but through my actions to show her how much she meant to me? "I love you and I always will."

"Doesn't change anything."

"My love for you won't change, ever."

She lifted her head up to look at me. "I don't care about love."

"I know."

"What would you do if I were to die?" Her question caught me completely off-guard.

"I won't let you die."

"How could you prevent me from dying?" She sat up on my lap. I'd spoiled the moment as I had a knack for doing.

"I'd give you my food…"

"Which you're doing."

"I'd take the bullet, I'd give you a blood transfusion, and I'd stay by you in a hospital to make sure you got whatever treatment you needed. I simply won't let you die."

"I know. But that doesn't change a thing. I can't let you hurt me. I can't become dependent upon you for my happiness. I can't do that again."

"I've done exactly that."

"What?"

"Become dependent upon you for my happiness. Just seeing you makes my day. When you give me that perfunctory kiss in the morning I always think of the real kiss you used to give me when we were together. When you straighten my hair on the set, which you still do, I remember when it was a sign of affection and not a gesture to make me aware that I look like hell."

She looked at me quizzically, apparently trying to make up her mind about something. I hoped it was making her want to ask Allison what had really happened that night. I'd suggested in the past that it hadn't been the way she thought. But she never asked me or Allison to give her the details. I looked back at her with the best puppy dog eyes I could pull from my actor repertoire.

She laughed at me. "That won't work." She rose, went to the door, glanced back and was gone.

Chapter Thirty-Seven

The next morning Silmara had her daily videoconference. Everyone was on, including Dyllan in his wheelchair. Apparently Kalindi hadn't noticed the wheelchair in the previous videoconference, probably because Dyllan usually sat close to the videocam.

"Why are you in a wheelchair?" Kalindi asked at the start of the conference call.

"Probably so I can get around." Dyllan responded.

"What happened to you?"

"I was a Captain in the Emirates Special Forces. I was unfortunately very close to my best friend when he stepped on a land mine during a classified mission. I was very lucky my first sergeant organized a team to carry me back to the boat."

"You were a soldier?" Kalindi seemed to be trying to reframe her understanding of Dyllan.

"I am a retired soldier now." He corrected her.

"But that's so different from what you do now."

"I used to protect people through feats of wizardry in combat maneuvers. Now I entertain them through feats of wizardry on the screen. Not so different, really."

"They are totally different. Not even the same universe." Kalindi protested.

"Kalindi, my dear, you think you can protect people by your ability to research and through the process of investigating learn the facts and prosecute someone you believe is responsible."

"I would agree with that assessment." She responded.

"But that's not what you actually do. You research, investigate and gather information which leads you and those you work with in the criminal justice system to build a case against someone. You then turn your evidence over to a judge and jury, who through a prosecutor and defense attorney argue the facts of the case. Whoever is more skillful in bending or shaping the information you all believe to be the facts will prevail. In the end, you never know if you have done justice or an injustice by sending an innocent person to jail. There have been too many instances where people have been exonerated after the fact to show that not to be the case."

"You're devaluing what I do." Kalindi sounded hurt by his analysis.

"Not at all. I'm just putting it into perspective. None of us are right 100% of the time. We all make mistakes. If I was wrong while in the special services, my men died and we did not accomplish our objectives. If I'm wrong today, the movie I'm working on may lose money, but no one dies and maybe the audience is less entertained than they would be otherwise. In either case we can pick up and go on. I may get fewer assignments and have to go find another job. But in the end, no one dies."

"If you feel that way, why do you continue to do what you do?"

"Most people do jobs that are like my job today. Not many do anything that really makes a difference to more than a few people. So if it doesn't work out so well, they move on and find another job. Kalindi, my dear, you have the opportunity to do something that is special. You have the opportunity to overcome a hardship for millions of people around the world and truly make their lives better. Be thankful you're in that position and make sure you deliver. We are all counting on you."

"You did that twice."

"What?"

"Called me Kalindi, my dear. Why did you do that?"

"Because you don't understand you own importance and the power that brings. You are dear to all of us. We are counting on you to lead us from darkness and into the light."

Silmara wanted to change the nature of the discussion. "Desmond tells me you have something you wanted to share, Dyllan. And not your views of Kalindi."

I had to laugh, having not expected his discourse on Kalindi.

"I think I may have discovered something important to our investigation."

Silmara was anxious since I had not given her any details. "Go on."

"A website. Actually a hidden website you have to have special permissions to visit."

"And you have those permissions?" Silmara asked knowing the answer.

"No, but I have friends who have shown me ways to defeat security systems."

"Anyone we need to add to our suspect list?" Bomani asked.

"No, they all work for Uncle Sam, either directly or indirectly."

"What does this site say?" Mimi asked.

"This group wants to return the world to a hunter-gatherer status. Thinks we have given up our birthright to machines who make all the decisions for us. Go back to hunter-gatherer and there are no machines, just tools we need to harvest crops and slaughter animals to eat."

"You're saying it's a societal cause and not a political event." Kalindi responded as if hurt Dyllan would take sides in her dispute with Mimi.

"No, I'm just bringing to everyone's attention there are protected websites for groups whose aims are aligned with the overthrow of society as we know it. Given there have been no demands made of a political nature, we have to consider alternatives. This is clearly one."

"What country are they based in? Can you tell from the website?" Kalindi continued pursuing what she thought was a siding with Mimi.

"No, I can't decipher their homeland. The site discusses things very generically, as if they are deliberately seeking a global audience. Can't tell if they have succeeded from the information I've reviewed, but sure would like to get another set of eyes on it."

Silmara was quick to respond. "Send the access information and I'll have some folks in there while we are on this call."

"Need to be careful. I found multiple levels of security. I think they might be monitoring who is coming onto their site. I'm not entirely sure I got in without revealing more than I wanted to."

"What else can you tell us about the site and whoever is sponsoring it?" Mimi asked.

Dyllan was quiet at first as if gathering his thoughts. "Discussion about shrinking global population. Comments about the world is at a point where global resources can no longer sustain life. That was what caught my attention in the first place. Would seem to be consistent with a group willing to force mass starvation. I could be wrong, but the website was explicit about people needing to die and restricting population growth."

"How did you get into this site?" Mimi asked.

"Like everything I do, I was freelancing, going from topic to topic on blogs and different discussion boards. I found this oblique reference to Malthusian theory and followed it. Originally I was invited into a guest site… really pretty benign. A lot of discussion about Malthus and how the world outstripped the limits he espoused a long time ago. But a lot of discussion about how technology and chemistry has permitted us to do things inconceivable only a few decades ago."

"And I take it those references weren't exactly happy about our ability to change the rules as we went." I suggested.

"No. In fact the site questioned whether such technology was really in the best interests of mankind going forward. And that led me to the site. A link and a question I had to be prepared to answer if I was brave enough to continue on."

"What question?" Xian asked. I knew he would.

"Who should decide mankind's fate?"

"How answer?"

"Those who are willing to defend their choice personally."

"These people sound serious." Mimi now. "Have they tried to contact you since?"

"Not yet. But I expect they will."

"Why?"

"Because of where I live. I suspect they don't have many people involved in the Emirates. We live in a bubble. A privileged few surrounded by thousands of servants."

"A self-sustaining population." Bomani this time.

"An anti-Egypt." Dyllan responded. "You have the population of thousands with a small cadre at the top trying to keep their privileged status."

"The only difference is our servants are the citizens." Bomani observed.

Chapter Thirty-Eight

The next day in our regularly scheduled videoconference Kalindi surprised everyone.

"Did you realize there are multiple levels to your survivalist website?" she asked Dyllan.

"I thought there had to be other sites or something. Didn't recognize multiple levels." He responded as if thinking through what he had observed when on the site. I knew he had been spending a lot more of his time on the code elements project. He had found some of the elements, but not others and had spent much of his time trying to understand the possible architecture used to frame the solution.

"Each level becomes more and more apocalyptic." Kalindi reported.

"Example please." Xian.

"The next level down is focused mostly on survivalist supplies. Where you can buy the kinds of things you would need if there were a nuclear war. Things like canned food for a year, sleeping bags, camp stoves, mass quantities of toilet paper."

"What about the next level?" Silmara asked. I was surprised she didn't seem to know what Kalindi was reporting.

"Seeds for plants resistant to various diseases, information on composting and how to make naturalistic fertilizers, how to tend a woodlot, even how to build a log cabin. Sounds like they're serious about there being no machines, no stores and going back to the land to survive."

"Does this mean you think they might be involved?" Bomani this time.

"I didn't say that. All I'm acknowledging is they seem to have a website that would support Dyllan's observation."

"Track?" Xian asked.

"Are we tracking this website? Yes, I have asked one of my team members to add it to his list of groups to investigate. Not at the top of his list, but we are putting some calories into it."

"Did you find any indication of who or where they are?" I asked.

"The website is in English, probably an indication they are recruiting in the western nations. Who they are? Nothing that gives us direction where to find them. Suspect they do not wish to be found. I think maybe a virtual organization, recruiting members wherever they find them. They want the members to act where they are, not gather for a rally." Kalindi informed us.

"What about technical skills? Anything that might indicate an ability to create a virus and unleash it?" Mimi asked.

I waited to see what kind of response she got from Kalindi, suspecting it to be cryptic or harsh. The answer came quickly. "No."

At least it wasn't hostile like earlier.

"Merits consideration." Xian added to the conversation.

"I agree. If it helps, since Dyllan was invited in, I'll ask him to role play with them and see what more he can learn. Will anyone respond to him personally if he inquires about some aspect of what they're proposing? Can't hurt." I suggested.

"But could warn them someone has developed a sudden interest in what they have proposed doing." Kalindi. She was being protective of her investigation now that the amateurs were showing some ability to investigate as well. I thought she didn't want to be shown up. Probably explained why she had gone onto the site to see if Dyllan had something or was just blowing smoke.

"I'm sure Dyllan will be discrete and not appear too pushy. Just a casual interest. Right Dyllan?" I responded hoping to be more neutral than Mimi would have been.

"Absolutely. I can be real dense when I want to be."

"Speaking of dense, how's the deciphering going?" I asked.

"I have sections, but not the whole thing. The architecture is what I'm puzzling on. The sections I have do what I would have expected, but they do not go together the way I expected."

Bomani engaged now, "How do you mean?"

"It seems to me I have the standard pieces that would be required to shut things down, but they don't fit together. It seems there are code elements that instruct sequencing or some kind of runtime phasing. I can't really explain, but the main thing is this person is cleverer than even I gave him or her for being. There seems to be layers upon layers upon layers to the code. When you think you have the solution you find there are other pieces you weren't expecting. You continually have to go back and look for yet another piece to the equation."

"I have seen what you are saying." Bomani reflected. "Since the virus works we know all the elements are there. But what we are missing is the question. I am not sure how we solve this last part of the equation other than by brute force. We keep the algorithm explorer combing the code for elements we have not yet found. But as you said before, the problem is defining the code elements we are looking for. No tool can find something we have not specified."

"Exactly."

"Parallel paths." Xian again, refocusing us on the important things we needed to be doing.

"What other resources can we bring to bear to this problem?" I asked after a moment of silence.

Silmara responded as I hoped she would, "Everyone with knowledge of the situation is engaged." But I wasn't with what she said after. "To bring anyone else in at this point would force us to have someone bring the new people up to speed and not accomplish what they would have otherwise."

"You're saying anything other than what we're doing will just slow us down." I summarized what I thought I heard.

"I believe that is correct." Silmara responded. I was curious about her tone of voice. It almost sounded to me like she didn't believe what she was saying. Was she protecting Kalindi? I picked up on something there and would ask Mimi about it after the call to see if I was the only one who caught it.

"We just press on with what we're working and see where we end up tomorrow?" I asked since my question had been relegated to the not important bin.

"Yes." Silmara confirmed.

So I signed off and looked over to Mimi who sat next to me. "What did you just hear?"

"Too busy to do anything more."

"What does your intuition tell you about Silmara and Kalindi?"

Mimi puzzled my question before answering, "Silmara is very protective."

"Anything else?"

"I think they must be friends outside of this assignment."

"Probably why Kalindi's in the position she's in. Seems young and a bit hot headed for the level of responsibility she has."

Mimi considered my observation before disagreeing, "You always have insights I don't about things like this. But I do not see Kalindi as hot headed. She has been given an assignment. She wishes not to fail. She seems to expect Silmara to support anything she wishes to do."

"Does that mean Silmara has less expertise in some facets of this investigation than Kalindi?"

"That's entirely possible." Mimi responded.

"So why is Kalindi suddenly interested in this survivalist group or whatever they are?" I asked. "Nothing on the website indicates they're doing anything other than exercising their constitutional right to free speech and to express belief in the most extreme form of craziness."

"I think its Dyllan."

"What about him?"

"I think she likes him. Just something in her tone of voice when she talks to or about him."

I didn't see at all what she was talking about. I didn't understand why all these subtle signals fly around a room or over a videoconference and men like me never pick up on them, but every woman sees and hears exactly the same thing. Must be like a dog whistle or something.

"I give up. What else are you hearing I'm not?"

"I think Dyllan's site is more significant than even we think it is. They may not be the group we are looking for, but I am convinced they will lead us to whoever is responsible."

"And you have this conviction because…"

"Woman's intuition." There it is again.

Chapter Thirty-Nine

Kareem and Pete were waiting for Mimi, Walt and myself outside the station that evening. When I stopped the Tesla to pick them up they finished a conversation before getting into the car. We weren't broadcasting live tonight, as it wasn't our regular night, and I'd convinced John that we needed an extra episode in the can for a time when we wouldn't be able to do a live broadcast for one reason or another.

"Some problem?" I asked as they slid in behind me.

Kareem answered for them, "Possible lead on the party that blew up the Googlecar repair depot."

"The one here or in one of the other cities?" I responded. I wanted to know if we were going hunting or if this was just a point of information for me.

"Here. We'd like to have a conversation with someone over in Manhattan Beach." Kareem replied. "Works for one of the defense contractors in El Segundo. Received a report some inventory was missing."

"What inventory?" Mimi asked before I could.

Pete also wanted some time on camera. "Shoulder fired missiles."

"You have an address?" I asked. Walt stopped filming since we didn't want to give away an exact address.

"Pacific near nineteenth. I'll point the place out when we get close." Kareem this time.

Walt had the camera back on so everyone was back into roles. "We expecting him to be alone or will there be others?" Mimi was trying to understand the situation we were going into since this wasn't a typical law enforcement call.

"Who said it was a him?" Kareem delighted in catching Mimi off guard.

To her credit, Mimi didn't come back at him, as I'd seen her do with Robert, when he played the gotcha game. "We expecting her to be alone?"

"Our suspect isn't an engineer. Works in logistics and supply chain. Apparently entered erroneous information into receiving dock tracking systems. Someone did an unscheduled physical inventory and discovered they were short units."

"Short how many?" I asked, knowing there had been seven incidents of Googlecar repair depot explosions around the country and the Houston Shipyard refinery.

"Ten." Pete confirmed my suspicions.

"I know what you're thinking." Kareem cut in before either Mimi or I could say anything. "We don't know what happened to the last two units. Could be they tested the systems out before the first attack. You know, make sure they understand how to fire it and all that."
"Or they could have more attacks planned." Mimi voiced what I was thinking and from Pete's reaction, I was pretty confident that Kareem and Pete thought so too, but were playing down what they knew would be public fears.

"Possible, but if we take the source into custody, I'd expect whoever has the last units, if they do still exist, to disappear quickly. No one is going to want to be caught in possession of stolen defense department equipment. That's a federal crime and federal penitentiary. That's hard time."

"A nice way of thinking about it," Mimi began. "But if the persons responsible for these attacks aren't criminals as we commonly think about them, then they might be true believers in something. What, we don't know just yet. But true believers never expect to be caught. They think they're going to come to power and make the rules to ensure they don't have to pay for what they've done."

"She has a good point." I noted. "Look, we're on Pacific. Just where do I need to go, Kareem?"

"Pull over there." He pointed to an open parking spot, just off the street. "We'll walk the rest of the way."

Walt was the first one out the back hatch so he could film us. Kareem looked around as if trying to decide if anyone was watching. Of course people were watching because we were the only vehicle moving on the street, even if the electric drive car made very little noise.

"Which way?" I asked. Kareem apparently satisfied himself as to the situation and headed toward nineteenth. We turned the corner and walked a few houses up, crossed the street and went up to a door. Pete knocked while the rest of us stood down on the sidewalk.

A slender bleach blond, with healthy tan opened the door. She flashed a peroxide smile. Her teeth were so while they probably glowed in the dark. Maybe her tanned skin accentuated her smile, but I couldn't focus on the rest of her face.

"Miss Novak?" Pete asked.

She glanced down at the rest of us on the sidewalk including Walt with the camera running. Her smile disappeared and a question formed. "This some contest give away?"

Pete didn't answer deliberately, I thought. "Are you Sherice Novak?"

She apparently became very wary. Maybe it was something in

Pete's restatement of the question, but she looked down at Walt and the camera and finally nodded, still unsmiling.

"May we come in?" Pete asked, apparently hoping she would simply do so and not ask for identification.

"If you tell me what you want, then I'll decide."

"We'd like to talk to you."

"About?" She had her antenna up. We were going to have to give her what she wanted now.

Pete handed her the court ordered search warrant. She read it slowly then looked up. Didn't think I was going to have to worry about the peroxide smile again. "You want to search my house?"

"And ask a few questions."

"Do I have a choice?"

"Actually you don't." Pete pushed past her into the small cottage and the rest of us followed him in.

"Don't I have to give permission for him to film this?"

No one answered her as we split up and conducted the search of her premises. We looked through everything, opening doors, drawers and underneath everything. I thought it interesting that Pete checked under the carpets for hidden doors since there was no basement and by going outside could look under the floor with a flashlight, which I did.

We found no physical evidence any shoulder fired rockets had passed through her premises. I should not have been surprised. If I was going to steal something like that, I wouldn't bring it home either.

We rejoined Sherice Novak in her kitchen. "Satisfied?" She asked Pete, who she judged to be in charge, since he was the one to serve her the warrant.

"A few questions?"

"I want my lawyer present to answer any questions, but I have one for you. Your warrant says you're looking for stolen property. What are you looking for?"

"Your employer is missing government property." Kareem answered

Sherice Novak evidenced a puzzled look, not the one I would have expected from someone who had stolen ten shoulder fired missiles. "Government property? From the storeroom? Would have to be since I don't hold any of the program GFE."

"GFE?" Kareem asked.

"Government Furnished Equipment." She clarified. "Would have to be finished goods."

"This wasn't something the government gave to you, it was something you built for the government, they did a factory acceptance and you were getting ready to ship." Kareem gave her the rest of the story.

It was like something she'd paid no attention to suddenly made sense. "That son of a bitch."

"Could you explain?" I asked.

"Oliver... what's his name." She had to think a moment. "Wilson, that's it. Son of a bitch's always hanging around me, hustling my ass, telling me he loves me and all that shit. Son of a bitch had me show him how to use the inventory system. Woody said he stopped by when I was out last month."

"And?" I asked.

"Repairs the video systems. Could have shut 'em off, taken something and no one would know."

Chapter Forty

Kareem got the court order to conduct a search of Oliver Wilson's apartment on Coliseum Boulevard. It was getting late by the time we arrived. Again we parked down the street and walked almost a block to the address Pete confirmed before we left. Sherice Novak knew he lived somewhere near Culver City, but she didn't have an exact address, having never visited her friend at home.

It turned out Oliver Wilson worked for a contractor to Sherice's company and wasn't a regular employee. We had someone from Sherice's company call the supplier to get basic information, even though it was well into the evening. Home phones were mandatory on the contact lists government contractors maintained. We learned Oliver Wilson had only been with his company less than a year. His employer had never checked his references and he came with a security clearance, so very little was known about this gentleman. That was about all the information we were able to confirm since all the companies listed on his application were closed and only day-time numbers listed.

We walked through the courtyard to the apartment building and up the stairs to the second floor. The apartment actually had a nice view of the center court pool and tropical foliage. The lights were on in the pool, but no one was in swimming. I thought it a bit cool for a late night dip. Pete went to the door and knocked. No response. Pete knocked again, "Oliver Wilson?" Again, no response.

I went down to the office. After ringing the bell, an older gentleman answered, "You need something right now?"

"Yes." I answered.

"Why?"

"Police matter."

His eyes got wide and his whole demeanor changed. "Who is it this time?"

"Apartment two-twelve."

The man scrunched up his face, "Wilson? He ain't never done nothin'."

"How long he been living here?" I continued as the man gathered his keys.

"Let me think. He moved in about a year ago, maybe. Yeah, about a year ago. Nice enough. Keeps to himself and quiet type, if you know what I mean. Never any trouble. Never see him around. Don't know if he was working all the time or he got a lady somewhere. You know what I mean. He got a lady he probably staying her place. Nicer than his. You'll see what I mean."

"I thought all your apartments were nice." I was hoping he'd explain his comment.

"You'll see what I mean. Nice enough, but that's all. Tiny if you ask me. Too tiny for most people, but he seems okay with it. Some people don't need a lot of room, you know what I mean? All they need is a TV, a pot to crap in, a fridge and a microwave. Had some people who sleep on the floor. Don't even want a bed like you an' me. You know what I mean?"

"You been the super here long?"

"Twenty-eight years I been here. Same apartment all those years. Just herding cats is what I do. Go collect the rent if I have to, throw them out if I have to. They don't bother me, I don't bother them."

"Sounds like a good job." We were going up the stairs now.

"I've had better. More money maybe. More responsibility maybe.

But in the end it ain't worth it for the better pay, you know what I mean? I like it quiet. I like people to do their thing and let me do mine."

We were at the door. "Can I see your warrant?"

Kareem produced the document, the super read it carefully, matched the apartment number against the document and opened the door with his master key.

As soon as the door swung open, I understood his comment about good enough. The apartment was a one-room efficiency. Barely a hundred square feet, not including the bath. It wouldn't take long to search these premises. Oliver Wilson had few possessions. A futon to sleep on, a cardboard box in which he kept his clothes, a board across four cinder blocks for a table and a wireframe kitchen chair.

"The fridge and microwave come with the apartment?" I asked the super.

"Brand new, both of them, when he moved in. The last tenant caused a bunch of damage, you know what I mean? Had to replace them. He wrecked the place, the sonabitch. Skipped out an' never paid. Was late on his rent so ate up his security deposit. Hate people like that. Don't care and just want to take you for all they can get."

"Was Wilson like that?" Kareem asked.

"Wilson? No. First class guy. Never had to collect from him. Always pays a day or two early. No problem with plumbing or electric or any of that. First class guy. Keeps to himself."

"Really? Mimi asked.

When the super saw her, he turned and looked at me. "Holy shit. You're them."

I winked at Mimi and turned to the super, "Cops? Yes, we're cops."

"No. I mean, yes, but you're the cops whose on TV. I watch you all a time. You're ... you're what's his name."

"Rory." Mimi wasn't going to wait for him to finally guess.

"And you're her."

"Samantha." I filled in his blank.

"Yeah, Samantha Gallagher and Rory St. Julian. Right?"

"Close enough."

Kareem came out of the bathroom. "Nothing in there."

"Not even the toilet paper?" The super asked. "We gave him a starter roll. You know he's supposed to replace it when he leaves."

"You think he's not coming back?" Mimi asked.

"How would I know? I didn't even know he wasn't here tonight. Saw him just yesterday. Thought that was strange, you know? I never see him during the day. About eleven-thirty I think. Before lunch anyway. Came in like he was in a hurry. Came up here like a banshee was chasing him."

"You Irish?" I wondered aloud.

"Mother was. Father was a Po-lock. Knocked her up and left town. Never met the guy. Hope I never do. He made it hard on us growing up. No money, going from place to place when we got behind."

"That why you're the super? You never have to worry about making the rent?" Mimi asked the question I was wondering.

"Probably. It suits me. I'm okay with just being a super. Not like you movie stars. So these other guys? They work for you?"

"We're real cops." Pete responded, not wanting to be thought an extra or something.

"So what you want this guy Wilson for?"

"Was he carrying anything when he left?" I didn't answer his question.

The super scratched his chin. "Now that you mention it, thought that was strange too. He was carrying a suitcase, only it was camouflage painted, you know?"

"Was it one of those really big suitcases?" I asked to understand if he was making any connections.

"Naw. Kind of middle sized suitcase. Like one suit, you know. That was funny too. Never saw the guy in a suit. Never anything other than blue jeans and golf shirt with the company name on the left pocket."

"What was the company name?" Kareem asked this time.

"Security Electronics Systems. Big SES, everything else was small so you had to get up close."

"So you were up close to him." Mimi asked.

"When he paid his rent. Regular like crap, you know what I mean?"

I took a final look around, knowing if there had been a shoulder launched missile here Oliver Wilson had removed it and any evidence of it the day before. I thought he was probably gone as well. I wondered who had tipped him off. Someone had. Probably someone at the government contractor who had helped him sneak the weapons out. I didn't think Sherice was his accomplice. She'd identified him and wouldn't have done so if they were in it together. But if not her, who?

I was thinking we'd missed out on catching the guy responsible by a day. At least I would have solid information to pass along to Silmara. I had no idea if the two events were connected, but I couldn't fail to think there might be one.

"So what you want this guy for? Warrant said something about stolen property."

"We think he took something that could be dangerous." Mimi responded.

"Would of thought you'd of found it in his storage shed." The super observed.

Chapter Forty-One

The next morning during the videoconference with Silmara's team I gave a full report of our investigations the night before. The super had the information on Wilson's storage unit, having given him a ride there once in the super's pickup truck when Wilson's car was in the shop for a repair. Wilson told the super he didn't need to stay. Someone was going to meet him there and would give him a ride.

The storage unit had been cleaned out, but I did find a book of matches on the floor. The matches advertised the storage center. Inside was a telephone number. Kareem had it run and discovered it belonged to a production studio individual sound stage in Studio City. The sound stage was used by a lot of different production companies and had thousands of suppliers in and out. So while an important and curious lead, it didn't get us much closer to Oliver Wilson.

The entire team listened politely to my report until Dyllan broke in. "The site we've been looking at. The survivalist one? They've had literally thousands of visitors over the last year or so. I found it's been translated into at least thirty-five languages. I also found references on the site suggesting it's been operational for at least five years."

"Maybe longer?" Kalindi asked, which surprised me.

"Yes, possibly much longer. What has me curious is there seems to be a level I can't get to. Now you know how I am about challenges. This particular one has me stopped. I don't know what else to do in order to obtain access. It's taking time I need for the code work."

"The code is much more important than this one site." Silmara confirmed.

"I wonder if Kalindi could attempt to find a way in. I know she's very busy given the activity in her area, but I think if anyone can figure out how to get inside, she is the one most likely."

Mimi poked me in the ribs. I looked over at her and she mouthed, without vocalizing, "Told you something's going on between them."

I mouthed back, also without vocalizing, "They've never met."

"Doesn't matter." The soundless conversation continued.

On the video screen we saw Kalindi go to work on her system, apparently trying to find the site Dyllan identified.

With Kalindi focused on the site the conversation lagged for a moment, so Silmara decided to reassert herself. "We have looked at millions of websites, conducted search after search using every keyword we could think of, and yet this is the first one that seems to have any potential relevance."

Dyllan picked up, "I see how a survivalist group would not be sympathetic to a society dependent upon modern transport, but I have not seen them call for revolution."

"Example, please." Xian announced he had joined the call.

"The websites are a resource for anyone who wants to learn how to live off the land. Instructions on how to build a log cabin, for instance. Information on how to compost the land to help grow crops naturally, without fertilizer. Where to buy seeds that will grow in extreme weather, advice on how to irrigate crops when in drought conditions. I even found information about how to trap wild animals. I don't know anyone who has ever trapped a wild animal. It seems the people involved are trying to recreate the simple life. But it is a western view of the simple life. Here in the Emirates, we lived a nomadic existence, moving our shelters on camel depending on weather, water and wind. Sometimes we ate our camels to survive. It was just part of life in the desert. But the website does not talk about eating your camel. It talks about growing your own food. That is why I know those responsible are not from the Emirates or the Middle East for that matter."

"Unless that's what's on the webpages you can't access." I pointed out.

"You are correct. We do not know what is on the pages we cannot access." Dyllan agreed.

"Card player never show hand." Xian again.

"So you think what we're seeing is not what they show to the inner circle of their group?" I asked Xian.

"Xian is correct if your hunter gatherers are the people we are looking for. But we have no evidence they are. We should not jump to conclusions." Mimi wanted to refocus us. "These people are only one suspect and not a particularly strong suspect if you just look at their public pages. Your linkage is weak. The evidence we need is non-existent. Unless Kalindi finds something on Dyllan's private pages we are probably wasting our resources on a likely dead end."

I turned away from the video camera and mouthed to Mimi, "I thought you had a feeling about these people."

"I do, but I don't want them to know." She responded sub vocally.

"Devil's advocate?" I responded, also without a sound.

Mimi smiled like a Cheshire cat.

"Do you have something you would like to share with us?" Silmara asked, evidently seeing we were talking about something.

"Desmond was just complimenting me on my choice of perfume. Nothing I can really share on a video conference." Mimi rescued us.

"What is it?" Silmara apparently didn't believe us.

"Obsession. A new old scent for me. Used to wear it but had gone away for a while. I simply decided I liked the old me better than the new me."

"What else you find?" Xian lost patience.

Dyllan had to think for a moment before responding. "I am having a problem with the code logic. I have found and assembled most of the code elements. I string them together in a logical sequence and it seems to be a complete instruction set to shut down the Googlecar control systems. And yet, it does not work. I have not been able to discover what I am missing. So it is very difficult to know how to proceed since I do not know what I am looking for."

"Key." Xian responded emphatically.

"Tell me more." Dyllan responded thinking he understood, but needed to clarify Xian's thinking.

"Look key. Activate code. What missing."

"You think he embedded a key into the code that would activate the instruction set apart from the instruction set itself." Dyllan thought aloud.

"Delay activate. Code set when. Look trigger."

Dyllan became excited, "Can someone tell me when the Googlecars stopped working? I need the exact day and time."

Bomani responded, "I'm sending that to you now."

"Did something happen at that time and day? An event that could have been a conditional trigger, not just a time certain?"

"I will do a search." Bomani again.

"Anything else that could have been the trigger?" Silmara was getting excited as well.

"Someone famous died that day. Who was it?" Mimi now.

"Ray Kurzweil." I responded.

Everyone stopped to look at me on their monitors. Mimi asked the question everyone else wanted to know. "Who is...was Ray Kurzweil?"

"An inventor, scientist, futurist. Wrote a book called <u>The Singularity</u>, which was about when men and robots would have a singular consciousness. Even predicted a date. He was also the Chief Technology Officer at Google for many years."

"How do you know all that?" Bomani asked, "You are correct, but how would you know who he was?"

"I read a lot." Was the poor reason I gave, rather than the long explanation that would have taken too long and revealed much I didn't want to share.

"I can work with that." Dyllan noted. "Sometimes you really surprise me, Desmond."

"What else can we provide Dyllan?" Silmara was signaling that she wanted him back on the code. I was sure she was under just immense pressure to get the Googlecars back up and running. I'd seen some statistics on the estimated number of deaths from starvation alone. The number was staggering. And it was just an estimate because without transport no one was able to go out and check on people, or remove bodies, or provide a burial service. Instant global communications were a means of integrating the world, but you had to be alive to communicate and that was the limitation.

Kalindi looked up at us and unmuted her voice. "I got through."

All eyes turned to Kalindi.

"You won't believe what I found on the next level."

Chapter Forty-Two

Xian called me directly the next day. Mimi was with me in the trailer and I thought I detected some discomfort on Xian's part about her being on the conversation.

"Not comfortable." Xian continued to explain why he'd called me.

"Why, old friend?" I responded.

"Not sure, secure. Person write code stop Googlecars. Write code intercept. Write code break encryption."

I heard what he was saying, but I thought he might also have another concern, particularly given the nature of the government under which he lived. "Are you concerned someone on the team might not be who we think they are?"

"Know very little. Never in person. Sure?"

I knew where he was going and frankly I hadn't considered that maybe Silmara and her whole team weren't who we thought they were. But I'd seen Silmara on the news when the Googlecars stopped working. She was the same person on the videoconferences. Wasn't she?

"Do you know something specific, or are you just being cautious?" Mimi asked. It was evident to me she was as surprised as I was by his question.

"How make contact?"

"Alistair made the arrangements." I responded after only a momentary lapse.

"Trust Alistair?"

Mimi responded before I could, "With my life. He has been a friend and advocate for us for more than a decade. I have absolutely no reason to doubt him or question that he put us in touch with the people he said he did."

"Alistair has always been able to get through to people I never would have expected him to reach. Whether it was studio heads, restaurants that absolutely no one could get into, or police departments when we wanted to talk story plots and investigation techniques. He seems to be connected to everyone in some manner." I affirmed.

"Understand. Proceed with caution."

"You're right, Xian. I never would have questioned whether we're dealing with whom we think we are. So what did you want to discuss?"

"Kalindi find smoking gun on website."

"I would agree."

"Still no who."

"That's true. We have a motive, a call and more secure levels we haven't been able to access. We now have an idea of what they want to do, but not how or why or who."

"Diaoyu Dao."

"Pardon?"

"Island between China and Japan."

"I've never heard of it." I responded.

"Neither have I." Mimi agreed.

"Small island. No people, until recent."

"If there were no people until recently, that means there's probably no electricity or sanitation or running water or any of the conveniences of modern life." I saw where Xian was going.

"Correct."

"So these people are survivalists?"

"Build local materials. Grow food. Collect rainwater. Like website."

"How many of them are there?" I asked next, trying to make sure I asked the right questions.

"Less fifty."

I was surprised. I expected he was going to say a couple hundred at least. "And how long have they been on this island?"

"Two years. China, Japan both want gone. Try many times remove. No luck."

"Why do both China and Japan want them removed?" I thought those countries seldom agreed on anything given the whole history of Japanese comfort brides during the Second World War. I was always amazed at how long issues carried forward between nations over ancient history, or what seemed to be ancient history to me.

"Both claim islands. Think people from other country. Try settle. Make claim."

"So neither knows where these settlers came from?"

"No."

"Then I take it no one has actually talked with the settlers to find out who they are or why they are there?"

"Not true. Governments not speak. Graduate student speak."

"And what did he find out?"

"People 'Changing Wind'."

"That's what they call themselves?" I hadn't heard of them so needed more information. "Why do they call themselves that?"

"Start new civilization. They think."

The term civilization caught me by surprise. I knew Xian's English was very good, even if broken. He knew the meanings of the words he used and he seldom used a work incorrectly. But I still had to be sure of what he was saying. "Civilization? Like the Roman Empire?"

"Like Han Dynasty."

Just like Xian to remind me that China had been around long before the Roman Empire and that I needed to not think of this in western terms. The settlers weren't western. They were Asian. That meant Dyllan's characterization of the site having a strict western focus wasn't entirely correct. At the moment we didn't have any sightings of the survivalists in the western world. That didn't mean they weren't there. They simply hadn't come to our attention yet. And here was an example of the kind of people we were looking for. People trying to start a new civilization on a small island. A small island between China and Japan. And two huge countries hadn't been able to evict them in over two years.

As I thought about Xian's information I had a small voice in the back of my head asking how would these people have been able to shut down the Googlecars of the world if they were working from a small island with no electricity, water or communications systems? Then I realized I was making an assumption again. "Do these people have any means of having brought down the Googlecars?"

"Unknown."

When Xian gave one word answers I knew I always had to probe further to understand what he was trying to tell me. Xian was a man of few words. He did so purposefully, as a means of teaching people patience and thoroughness. People who were impatient weren't thorough and would go off spending most of their time looking in the wrong place.

"Is that because we have no evidence they did it, or because we don't know if they have access to those who might?"

"Latter."

"How did the graduate student talk with them?"

"Cellphone."

"With a cellphone they have batteries, battery chargers and some source of electricity."

"Solar."

"So they're not going caveman on us."

"No. Not cavemen. Indication plans. Communicate with others. Unknown who."

"Or where they are for that matter." Every time I spoke with Xian, I learned something new about conducting an investigation. He was teaching me I had to examine all assumptions, particularly the assumptions I didn't know I was making.

"Other name."

"They have another name?" I asked, surprised. I couldn't imagine what it would be.

"Hamartia."

Chapter Forty-Three

Kalindi used 'Hamartia' as a password on the survivalist site. It opened another whole layer to the site that gave much more information than the previous layer Dyllan had been unable to penetrate. She reported her findings on the next morning videoconference.

"Hamartia means tragic flaw. It's from Greek tragedy."

"No one ever said our friends weren't literate." Mimi observed.

"They call themselves the Hamartia because they believe mankind has a tragic flaw. That flaw is having unleashed technology upon the world. And that technology is killing the very planet mankind needs to survive."

"Ecoterrorists?" Silmara asked.

"No." Xian responded. "Not terrorists. Moses. Part Red Sea. Walk safety. Drown rest mankind."

"So instead of drowning us, this Moses is letting us starve to death when our own technology no longer serves us." Bomani. Of course he would pick up on the biblical references and the Red Sea since he lived very close to it.

"Who is this Moses?" Silmara now.

Kalindi responded, "Nothing on the website gives any information about a single leader. If anything, the way the site describes their cause, it would appear to be a broad-based grassroots effort. They say they have people in countries all around the world. Anyone can modify their site if they have the right tools. Anyone can blog on the site and talk about anything they want. I found some blogs that were simply incoherent. Others sounded like university professors and still others like they had been living the lifestyle all their lives. Everyone seems to share. Everyone has a tidbit of what to do or how to do something that will help others when they have to survive off the land."

"May not be what appear." Xian cautioned.

"What do you mean?" Kalindi asked.

"How know not just one person?"

"The visitation logs, the different people identified in the blogs, the vast amount of information." Dyllan this time.

"Things seldom what appear." Xian reminded everyone.

"But the security. Having to find the password to get in. I still have no idea how you came up with that one, Xian." Kalindi sounded curious.

"Understand. Not assume."

"Xian has a very important point we shouldn't forget. We really don't know what we're dealing with here. This whole site could be just a decoy. Something to get us looking in one direction while all the time our Moses is actually just a bank robber who wants to loot our central banks." I noted for everyone's benefit.

"But none of you have been on the site." Kalindi wasn't interested in listening to the cautioning voice. "This site has to be the key to this whole event. It talks about how man has brought on his own destruction, poisoning the waters, the air and our climate. We have decimated whole species. We have outstripped the natural resources and food supplies with our unmitigated population growth. We have allowed ourselves to create great economies that are built on houses of cards, always spending more than we take in through taxation, creating fewer jobs than we have people entering the work force. We have created an irresponsible society, where no one must make a hard choice or pay the price of bad decisions. The site just goes on and on."

"I understand why you think this site is linked somehow." I began. "But the simple truth is what you've just recited has been part of the political debate around the world for thousands of years. Our Hamartia friends are just the latest in a long line of people who think mankind has lost its way. Since Xian has started us down the biblical trail with his reference to Moses, we can look at Noah as well. Even God was reported to have lost faith in mankind and gave Noah permission to start over with two of everything and mankind would spring from his loins, or something to that effect."

I thought it curious Silmara wasn't weighing in. I'd used the biblical reference as a means of trying to lure her in, knowing she was a devout Catholic. But she remained silent and seemed to let Kalindi carry the conversation. However, Bomani surprised everyone. "This site is important, but it remains only one explanation of who and why we have experienced this tragedy. Yes, I think it most fitting the Hamartia comes from Greek Tragedy when it may have spawned a massive tragedy unimaginable by the Greeks themselves. But I have listened to this conversation. I hear both sides. We simply cannot believe anything we are reading on survivalist websites. We do not know the provenance of it. Who wrote it? Why is it there? Is it more than one man's fancy? Is it a spoof on all of us? Totally unconnected to the Googlecar crisis? It has as much chance of being a coincidence and obsession as it has of being the explanation of the world events. I cannot endorse us spending any more time trying to understand what it might mean. We have a mystery to solve. Dyllan and I are the only ones on this call who are centrally involved in solving the mystery of the key to our code. Help us to restore the Googlecars to their normal functionality. Focus on that mystery and we will worry about who and why once we have people once again able to get food and medicines."

Silmara finally responded. "Bomani is correct. We simply cannot waste any more time on something that will not help us in the short run. The code is the priority. What might we do to help you solve that mystery?"

"Now that we are focused on a key," Dyllan began. "We have been making good progress. Ray Kurzweil did die on the day the Googlecars stopped operating. However, I have found no reference to him in the code. But we have been successful in turning our search engines to finding either a reference to the day and time or the events that Bomani has been feeding me. We have quite an extensive set of scans going on and while we do not yet have good news to share with you, I believe we are much closer to that day than we were before our last call."

I listened to Dyllan. There was something he wasn't saying. I couldn't imagine what it could be, or why he was withholding something from the group. But I knew him well enough. I heard something in his voice and it was what he wasn't saying. Dyllan wouldn't blow smoke up someone's ass and that was exactly what he was doing. Then Mimi poked me.

"He's doing it again." She said voicelessly. We were back into the silent game.

"What?" I responded likewise.

"Impressing Kalindi."

Was that what was going on? The world was going to hell and Dyllan was trying to figure out how to get laid by a woman thousands of miles away with no public transport available to get him to her? Mimi had been right before. Her woman's intuition was generally correct. I guess I should have felt good I'd at least picked up on the fact something was going on, even though I totally misconstrued what.

"I agree." Kalindi began. "We have to help Dyllan find the solution to the code. It must be our highest priority."

Not Bomani too? I guess that was an indication the attraction went both ways.

"Thanks Kalindi. You have been amazing through this whole event. You cannot imagine how much you have helped us focus in on the important aspects of code elements and sequences." Dyllan wasn't through.

"You could be congratulating each other if Googlecars were back in operation." Silmara was getting impatient. "But at the moment we haven't delivered the results the whole world is waiting for. I suggest we excuse Dyllan and Bomani from the rest of these calls so they can focus on what's important on their end."

"But the calls have been very important to our efforts." Dyllan countered. "The last call helped us decide what path to take when we couldn't decide what was missing and why the code wasn't working. We have a direction now. We are making progress. I am hopeful we will get another suggestion or thought from these calls that will take us to the final solution."

"I agree with Dyllan." Bomani began. "The calls have been helpful, but I would like us to shift the time to talk about our progress first. When we are done, if you wish to discuss other matters that will not slow our progress."

"What else can we help you with?" Mimi, always the practical one.

"We have looked for dates, events and people dying. What else could be the key to the code?" Dyllan sounded like he was completely out of ideas.

"Try Hamartia." I suggested. "And Diaoyu Dao."

Chapter Forty-Four

While Dyllan and Kalindi tried to figure out how to get laid and Bomani set up new code scans, Mimi and I had another date with the LAPD for an evening cruise in the Tesla. Walt was in the back seat as usual, filming as Kareem and Pete joined us.

"What's the destination tonight?" I asked.

"Back to Culver City." Kareem began, "We have a few people we want to talk with."

"About our buddy Oliver Wilson?" Mimi asked, suspicious of the fact they gave so few details.

"Yes." Kareem was real talkative tonight. That made me curious.

"What can you tell us about the people you want to chat with?" I asked.

"The first is John Peobles. Works with Wilson at the security firm. Wilson's supervisor said they were friendly. She thought they had a relationship outside work, although she didn't know any of the details."

"Bowling teammates?" I suggested to try to get a little more information.

"Who knows? Could be nothing. Wilson's supervisor claims she knows practically nothing about him other than he's shown up for work when scheduled, has performed his job without complaint from any customer, and seemed to know what he was doing."

"So what do you expect to learn from Peobles?" Mimi this time.

"Don't know. We'll take whatever we can get at this point." Kareem seemed to have no idea if Wilson had disappeared for good or had gone off to blow up a Googlecar repair depot somewhere and would return. The problem was how would he get wherever he had gone with his camouflage suitcase?

We arrived at the tiny two-bedroom wood-framed home of John Peobles. The house was painted a medium gray with black trim around the door and windows. The one stall garage appeared to be almost the same size as the one-story flat roof dwelling. Desert plants on a drip watering system populated the stone lawn area. He lived at the end of a cul-de-sac just around the corner from the Wal-Mart. We were clearly in the high rent district.

Kareem seemed eager to get this call over with. He was first out of the car, even before Walt with his camera. Pete seemed as surprised as I was about Kareem's aggressiveness. I wondered if the interview would be as aggressive.

John Peobles was a short man. Probably five foot six and all of one-hundred and twenty pounds. He was still wearing his white Security Electronics Systems shirt when he opened his door to Kareem's knock. From the looks of the house, it was probably the only shirt he owned.

"Mister Peobles?" Kareem began.

"You cops?" His voice was rough and raw, as if he'd just come from a close football game the other team had won.

"Why you ask?" Kareem responded.

"Been expecting you. It's about Wilson, right? Julie, my supervisor, called to tell me you'd been by asking about him."

"May we come in?" Kareem didn't want to have this conversation out on the street. But Peobles wasn't happy about Walt and the camera in his face.

"No need. This'll be a short conversation."

Kareem looked at me and then at Walt. If I could have read his mind he was wishing we weren't along so he could get Peobles inside. But that wasn't going to happen.

"Alright. Mrs. Simpson said you were friends with Oliver Wilson."

"We did a lot of jobs together, if that's your definition of friends." Peobles kept his eye on the camera rather than looking at Kareem, which I know bothered Kareem even more.

"What kind of jobs?"

"Installations mostly. If it was a repair or replacement, Julie only sent one of us. Trying to keep costs down, and all that. At least that's what she always said."

Pete scanned the neighborhood standing behind Kareem. That caught Peobles' attention and he glanced around as well. Taking their cue I glanced around and noticed several neighbors had come out on the street to see what was going on. Why were people talking to their neighbor out on the street? Why was a man with a camera filming the whole thing? People were curious and I thought Peobles was probably trying to decide what he would tell us.

"Did you do the installation with him at the defense plant over in El Segundo?"

"He didn't do the installation. I did that about five years ago, before he came on board."

"So you've been with the company a while?"

"About seven years. Probably time to move on. Been there too long, you know?"

I noticed the neighbors were becoming more curious, but were staying out of range, not sure if we were going to take him away or something.

"Were you ever on site with him at the defense plant?"

"Yeah. Couple times Julie sent both of us when they wanted an estimate for some additional equipment and wiring. She likes to get two estimates, so we check each other and she thinks the number will be more likely correct."

"Notice anything unusual about Wilson when he would go there with you?"

"Like what?" Peobles' antenna were up.

"Anything you wouldn't have done if you'd been there alone."

"You talking about what's her name? The broad he always had coffee with?"

"Sherice Novak?" Kareem offered.

"Never knew her name."

"Was he sleeping with her?"

"To hear him tell it, she wanted into his pants bad, but he was saving himself for someone better."

"Saving himself?" Mimi asked as if she couldn't believe Peobles' comment.

Peobles looked around Kareem. He furrowed his brow like he should know Mimi, but couldn't place her. "Yes, saving himself. Wilson told me he was a virgin. Wanted to only do it with the woman who would be the mother of his kids. He wanted kids you know. Bad. But said the woman he married had to want the same kind of life he did."

"Same kind of life?" I asked, hearing words that resonated with the website Kareem wasn't aware of. "Did he ever talk about what that kind of life was like?"

"Just said he didn't intend to do this kind of shit work all his life, just until he could get enough together to have a place and family where he could live a quiet life."

Quiet didn't necessarily mean survivalist. I was hoping he'd said something that would have tied him back to the Hamartia, but quiet didn't make it. "Did he like to go hunting, or fishing, camping, that kind of thing?"

"Never talked about it, but he wasn't around on weekends. Couple rush jobs came up needed to be done on a Saturday or Sunday, I always got stuck with it because Julie could never get him on the phone."

"What about things you noticed about him. Something that struck you as odd?" I asked. Kareem wasn't happy I'd taken over his interrogation, but I had information he didn't and I had questions he wouldn't ask.

"You ask me, everybody's odd." Peobles began, "But I guess if I had to pick out one thing didn't make sense to me? It was lunch."

"What about lunch?" I continued.

"He never ate with me or anyone I talked to. We on a job together... I'd go do fast food. He never went. Never saw him eat anything. Not even chewing gum, you know?"

"Was he on a special diet?" Mimi asked, probably trying to understand if it was a religious or externally imposed restriction he thought someone might recognize.

"I don't know. Like I said, I never saw him eat anything. Like he was a robot or something that didn't need food."

Kareem wanted back in, "Why do you think he was a robot?"

"Don't think he was. Seemed like a regular guy to me. Just saying he didn't eat and the only thing that comes to mind is a robot who wouldn't need to."

Chapter Forty-Five

Kareem was still unhappy. We drove on to the next person Julie Simpson, Oliver Wilson's supervisor, had given us.

"Name's Alice Wheeler. She's the person who schedules the technicians and works as the dispatch operator for Security Electronics Systems. She's not far. Around the corner from Tito's Tacos and I know you know where that is."

Remembering we'd apprehended a shooter there for an earlier episode, he was right. I knew how to get there from John Peobles' humble home.

Alice Wheeler lived in an apartment house. An old apartment house. Must have been fifty or so apartments in this complex. Two story with apartments up and apartments down. Bright area lights illuminated everything and probably for good reason. The yard wasn't particularly well kept with rusty lawn furniture and butt cans for those who smoked outside their apartments. With the building being a wood structure the owners probably didn't let people smoke inside. When we walked up to the door we were surrounded by cats. Seemed like a hundred of them. Black cats, calico cats, striped cats, all kinds of cats. Big cats, little cats, but none looked undernourished. All were on the furniture outside her apartment apparently awaiting their evening meal.

Kareem knocked on the door. I heard the television on inside through the thin wooden structure. I also looked around. No one in this neighborhood came out on the street to see what we were doing there. But I had the distinct feeling people were looking at us from behind the blinds in their windows. People knew we were there, they just didn't want to get involved in whatever was going to happen next.

Alice Wheeler came to the door, opened it so we could see the security chain across from the inside. She peeked out. She looked like one of the seven dwarves, round with loose fitting black clothes and a knit cap on her head with her stringy black hair sticking out in all directions.

"Who are you?"

"LAPD." Kareem answered, "You're not in any trouble. We'd just like to ask you a few questions about someone you work with."

"He in trouble?"

"Who?" Kareem responded, probably expecting Julie had called her too.

"Whoever you're looking for. All the techs at work are guys, so it's gotta be a guy."

"Could we come in?"

"There's not enough room for all of you." The chain was still in place and she didn't look like she intended to remove it to either come out or let us in.

"Why is it no one from your company wants me to come into your home?"

"No offense, but I don't let nobody in. Not in this neighborhood."

"All right. What can you tell me about Oliver Wilson?"

"Ollie? What's he done?" The fact she called him 'Ollie' was encouraging. Meant she was on familiar terms with him. Apparently more so than John Peobles.

"The defense company over in El Segundo. Was he over there recently?"

I noticed she closed the door down, just a bit. The chain was hanging just a bit lower. She also took a half step backwards. She was afraid of something.

Alice's voice was only about half the volume it had been before, "Yes."

"What was he doing there?"

"Bid." Her voice was still small.

"Your company was bidding on some work?"

"Yes."

"How long ago was that?"

"Six weeks, maybe more." At least she was giving more than one word answers.

"He turned that bid in and then what?"

"Other jobs."

"Was that the first time he'd been over there?"

Alice shook her head. It was hard to see through the narrow crack in the door.

"Was he there a lot?"

Alice shrugged, but no words were forthcoming.

"Did he ever mention Sherice Novak?"

"Sherice?" came across loud and clear. "Did he fuck her?" Alice took the chain off the door and came out into the night time air. She was wearing pajamas, which explained why she didn't want us coming in. And Alice in pajamas left little to the imagination, although it also brought a memory I was sure I'd wish I didn't have to keep. Alice wasn't a pretty sight at five foot and well over two hundred pounds. "Well, did he?"

"We don't know, Miss Walker." Kareem also seemed to be wishing he were somewhere else.

"Wheeler, names Alice Wheeler." She was getting angrier. "She charge him with rape?"

"No, Miss Wheeler. She didn't charge him with anything. She just thought he might know about some missing property from her company."

Alice Wheeler seemed astonished, "Missing ..." but then she stopped as apparently something clicked for her.

"You know we did it, me and Ollie." Now it was my turn to be astonished, particularly after John Peobles said Wilson was saving himself.

"So are you saying you have an intimate relationship and we should treat you as hostile?"

"If he fucked her, you'll see hostile like you've never seen it."

"We don't think he did, Miss Wheeler." I wasn't going to get in the middle of this one, at least not until things cooled down a bit more. But then an important question occurred to me.

"I take it you know Sherice Novak." I asked. Kareem looked happy I was picking up the point.

"She's my sister."

"You don't look anything alike." Mimi observed.

"Half-sister. We have different fathers. Our mother got around. Seven kids, seven fathers."

"Did you introduce them?"

"Yeah. I wondered why he ain't been coming around as much recently. Thought it was the yeast infection. He complained about the itch. So I finally told him so he wouldn't think it was the clap. You know some guys get freaked out about STDs. And he was always washing up afterwards, you know like he didn't want to sleep with me on him or something."

"When was the last time you slept with him?" I asked wondering if it would coincide with the last visit to the defense plant.

"About six weeks ago."

"About the time you sent him over for the bid to the defense plant."

"Just figured that out, did ya? So did I, just now. He was using me and he probably used Sherice too. How can you be such a bad judge of character? I thought he was a sweet guy. He was kind and gentle in bed, except when he got hard and then it was like he was drilling for oil. Wham, wham, wham. You know what I mean? And he was hung. I mean the biggest I've ever had."

I couldn't ask the logical follow up question, but realized the super at Wilson's apartment had said something about being out nights probably meant a woman, so changed tact. "Where do you think we might find him?"

"You tried his place, I'm sure. You know he has a storage unit?"

"Been to both." Kareem had stepped back in now that the fun was over.

"He didn't talk about no relatives. You know he really didn't talk much, now that I think about it. He had these eyes. You knew just looking at him he wanted you in bed. That's all it took. He didn't have to say much because you just knew what he was thinking."

"Anything else you can tell us about him, anything that might help us find him?" I asked.

"You think he stole something from the defense plant. Anything I need to be concerned about? Nuclear or anything like that?"

"No, nothing like that." I reassured her.

"Good, because he just left here about an hour ago, on foot with a camouflage suitcase."

Chapter Forty-Six

After checking Alice Wheeler's apartment, we drove around the area until my battery light came on and I knew I had to take the Tesla in for a recharge. Oliver Wilson had disappeared, although we knew he was in the area. LAPD put their beat cops out on foot to go house-to-house in the areas near Alice Wheeler's apartment. It was going to take four hours for the Tesla to fully recharge, so we decided to let the foot patrol do what they could, given Wilson was also on foot.

Mimi went back to her trailer and I got a few hours of sleep, although Walt had asked to stay with Kareem and Pete in case they caught Wilson. We definitely wanted that on film if it happened.

When the morning came I dialed into Silmara's morning call. Mimi didn't make it as she must have either been real tired or Robert was back on the scene. I was never sure with Mimi. I knew she wasn't sleeping with me. And I knew she had needs, just like I did.

The first part of the call was supposed to be a report on the code progress. Dyllan began, "We have found Hamartia and Diaoyu Dao in the code, but that has not been sufficient to unlock the code. There must be something more. Kalindi, have you found anything we should try?"

Kalindi was waiting for this question and I wondered if they'd had a side conversation to arrange it? Mimi would have just rolled her eyes if I'd asked her, like how stupid could I be, of course they talked off line.

"This site is like a rose pedal. You may keep peeling away layers and find something even more exciting every layer you go down." Now her speech was getting all flowery. I wasn't sure how much longer we were going to be able to keep her away from Dyllan even without transport. "What is most exciting is I think I may have found them."

That got everyone's attention.

"Those of you who have visited my wonderful country know we have many beautiful places, much rich architecture and gardens... indescribable. But we also have some places very remote and harsh climates. Places where people would not want to live. One such place is along our border with Pakistan in the Kashmir. Both of our countries have claimed this land since Independence. We have had many clashes between our armies in this region. But at the northern most border there is an area very high in altitude. Because of the altitude, we find very cold temperatures. It is like the Eskimo lands but without the sea life."

"Are you saying people are living there?" Bomani asked.

"Yes. People who would embrace the Hamartia lifestyle. People who want to be left alone. People who do not need electricity and transport and Macy's."

"What specifically do you know?" I asked.

"I have found a reference to Amit Shah. He was the Governor of Uttar Pradesh, one of the northern Indian provinces, not so far from the Kashmir."

"What was the reference?" Silmara this time.

"The reference was not clear, but could be interpreted that he was the leader of these people, living high up in the mountains above the Kashmir."

"How could he be the leader if he was the Governor somewhere else?" I was confused.

Kalindi's voice sounded impatient, like she had already gone through the whole story once and now had to go through it again. But then I realized she probably had done just that with Dyllan before the call. "He resigned from office about five years ago, before his term in office was over. He then disappeared until just recently. No one knows where he went. But in his recent pronouncements he said he was on a pilgrimage to find himself and the way for his people. It is a very Indian thing to do, go into the wilderness, get in touch with your soul and then return to lead the unenlightened to Nirvana."

"Should we look for Nirvana?" Dyllan asked. Since he had already talked with her I was sure he was just posturing so we wouldn't think he had already had this discussion with Kalindi.

"No, I'd use the term Shivaists. That's what the mountain people call themselves. They could be Hamartia, but not wanting to go by a Greek name. I think we will find every group we encounter will have adopted a locally recognizable name."

"So who are the Shivaists?" Bomani asked now.

"Shiva is the destroyer among the Trimurti, the Hindu Trinity of the primary aspects of the divine." Dyllan recited.

"How did you know that?" Kalindi challenged Dyllan although she seemed more surprised than I would have expected if they'd coordinated this call, but it could be Dyllan did some research to come up with this factoid between the calls.

"I'm fascinated by Hinduism and Indian mythology."

Kalindi sounded affronted, "Hinduism is not mythology." Guess Dyllan wasn't going to be crawling into her bed anytime soon. That made me think he was still a ways away from finding the key to the code and had time to recover.

"I did not say Hinduism is mythology, I said Hinduism and mythology. I was saying Indian mythology as separate and distinct from the Hindu religion. Every civilization has mythology. Every civilization has beliefs that are separate and distinct from those mythological stories passed down from generation to generation. I am fascinated by the stories societies tell about themselves. That's part of the reason I love to be part of movies. We build new stories on the foundations of myths and religious beliefs. Putting them together in new and yet illustrative ways ensures future generations embrace the traditions and beliefs of their parents and ancestors."

"You are making fun of me and my country." Kalindi sounded insulted.

"No. I am very respectful of you and your country. India has a very old civilization, a great civilization. One most people have very little awareness of. And yet we can learn much from you and all your country brings to any discussion. You have wisdom and insights guiding us through the troubled times in which we live. You have resources helping us address the needs of the world in which we live. The more I read about India, the more in awe I am."

"On the last call..." Silmara decided to refocus everyone, "Dyllan, you were the one who asked for time to talk about the code and keys to help you bring the Googlecars back into service. You were the one who didn't want to waste time on whether the Hamartia are the people behind our crisis. So why are you wasting everyone's time waxing eloquently about Indian civilization's contribution to world peace and understanding?"

"Oh, sorry." Dyllan was now embarrassed.

"And Kalindi. You are no better. What has gotten into you both?"

Kalindi tried to address the question, "I fear our colleagues do not take us seriously because we are not from the US or China or any of the other major powers. But we are the ones in charge of this investigation. We are the ones who will accept the blame for how long it has taken us to solve this mystery. We are the ones who will be accused of ineptitude if we are not successful in turning around the situation quickly. The stoppage has already gone on much longer than we can tolerate. Too many have died already. And we have no estimate as to when we will solve the riddle of the software virus. What has gotten into me is a fear. A fear we are failing the world and a fear I shall be disgraced in front of not just my family, but the whole world." Kalindi let her head drop. I couldn't tell if she was crying, but she was visibly upset.

I looked at Dyllan on the screen. His face told the whole story. He was feeling Kalindi's pain. He wanted to do whatever he could to erase her self-doubts. But since Silmara had asked the question of what was going on, he apparently felt he couldn't answer for her.

Everyone gave Kalindi a minute to gather herself. Then Silmara asked a simple question. "What can we do right now to fix this?"

"More keys." Bomani responded immediately.

"I'd look for Amit Shah, Uttar Pradish, Kashmir, Shivaists, and the Hindu Trinity. Which one did Kalindi mention?" I suggested as a neutral person in the recent discussion.

"Trimurti." Dyllan and Kalindi both said at the same time. They smiled at each other over the monitors.

Mimi arrived at my trailer. "What did I miss?" She asked in a low voice.

"Kalindi found more of the Hamartia, we think." I responded as she came in and sat next to me. She didn't glow like she normally did after sex, so apparently Robert hadn't been over. That meant she simply slept in. Probably needed the sleep. She clearly wasn't getting enough to eat as she was looking thinner and thinner.

"Where?"

"Kashmir."

"Is that like a sweater?"

Chapter Forty-Seven

I decided after the call I needed to get Mimi out of LA, find a farm and get her some real food. I knew I could use something to eat as well since all the restaurants were now closed, the canteen had nothing to serve, and the groceries shelves were bare.

"You up for a ride?"

"Tonight?"

"Now."

She looked confused, then at the clock and finally back to me. "Where we going?"

"To find a farm. I need to get you some real food."

"I doubt I could eat much. My stomach has shrunk." She protested, but it was a weak protest.

I found Walt without his camera and picked up Alistair on the way.

"This is a marvelous idea." Alistair commented as soon as we left the curb outside his house.

"Don't get too excited. We have limited mileage so we need to explore farm areas that aren't too far out, but still have food left on the trees and gardens." I wanted to set the ground rules.

"We can't bring back enough to even begin to feed just the people we work with, let alone everyone else we know." Mimi was feeling

269

guilty.

"This is like an airplane that's in trouble. They always tell you to put the mask over your own face first to get the air going before you try to put the mask over anyone else. We'll eat, and then bring back as much as we can. I need at least four hours to recharge before tonight's ride so we don't have a whole lot of time."

"We probably can't get all the way to Bakersfield, but if you head up in that direction you should reach the Central Valley where they grow everything." Walt suggested.

So I headed north out of LA, up the 405, expecting I would cut inland at a major highway to be determined as we went. If I came across a suitable place before having to go inland, so much the better.

"What do you think of your ratings?" Alistair asked. I wondered why he would ask until I realized I had no idea what they were.

"What should I think?" I asked.

"You're the highest rated show on television at the moment. Didn't you know that? You have almost a 60 market share."

"In LA?"

"No, globally. More people are watching what you're doing than watch the World Cup or the Olympics. They can't possibly drop you for next season."

I was stunned. I had absolutely no idea how many people were watching us, however, the big BUT formed in my mind. "But what happens when we get the Googlecars operating and people are going out again? We'll drop like a rock and be right back where we were. The Studio will be looking to better deal us with Johnny Hollywood. Besides how much of our audience will survive what's going on? I'm not even sure we will."

"The mayor asked you on television to take the job as top cop detective for the whole city. You turned him down. I'm sure we can work a deal with the LAPD once things settle back for you to continue your reality show since you've been doing that at no cost to the city as a public service."

"Nice spin Alistair." Mimi was going to nail him. I could hear it coming. "We're making a television show. You tell us it's the top rated show in the world using the LAPD as props. Sure it's great publicity for them, but how long do you think they are going to want to be props on a television show?"

"You got this all wrong. LAPD loves the show. You're showing them taking down bad guys. You're showing them working important cases, like this whole show about what's his name? You know. The guy who stole the missiles. That was huge. That was the one that put your international audience on top. People are seeing this isn't just a parochial show. You're not just solving local crimes. You're doing big stuff, since people realize this guy, what's his name, Mimi?"

"Wilson." Walt filled in Alistair's blank.

"Wilson. Thanks, Mimi." Alistair poked Walt in the side. "Since people know this guy Wilson stole the missiles that were used on the Googlecar repair depots. People made that connection without you having to say it on television. You couldn't, I know. But people got it. They want to see you nail the bastard. They hope to God he's tied in with the people who released the virus and that you'll nail them too. Everyone is focused on your show because you're giving them hope. And that's something that's in short supply at the moment."

Mimi touched my arm, "You think we can bottle that up and play it back when Alistair goes into the studio to negotiate for us?"

"You won't have to play it back because I've already started negotiations for both of you. Package deal so don't go getting any ideas about going your separate ways. Of course the studio says they can't reopen Mimi and they are absolutely against doing a package deal, but I've got all the cards and they know it."

"So who are you talking to?" I asked, wondering how high he was.

"Got Jack and Stan together. Of course they won't let me go any higher because they need someone who can make the deal when they get stalled."

"Where are you at?" Mimi asked as if she didn't believe what he was saying.

"We've exchanged opening positions." Alistair seemed very happy with himself.

"You asked for the moon, I assume." I responded.

"And a few minor stars, but the good news is they didn't throw me out. That means they know they got to come way up to keep you under contract."

"Or it could mean they're stalling to see if we flame out. Draw out the negotiations until things go back to normal and see where we are." Walt suggested. Alistair looked at Walt, like where did you come up with that? "That's the same tactic they used with the cameramen last round. We asked for a decent wage, they came back with a ridiculous wage, then they waited until the last minute and stared down a strike before giving us a modest increase."

Alistair tapped me on the shoulder, "You bring him along to make sure I could still wear a hat?"

"No, I brought him along because if I don't feed my cameraman, we won't be on the air much longer. As Walt said, we got to stay in there with fresh material and keep the audience glued to their sets when we're on."

"He didn't say that." Alistair corrected me.

"No, but he was thinking it. That's the thing about a good actor and his and her cameraman. We all gotta eat."

"Speaking of gotta eat, look at those strawberry fields." Walt pointed out the red berries under the bright green leaves covering the ground on the farm up ahead.

I pulled into the drive and drove up to the well-kept white board sided farmhouse. A young man came out followed by his mother and then father.

"Hi. Any chance we could buy some food from you?" I asked as I walked towards them.

"You're Rory Gallagher." The young man said. "Sure. You can have all you want."

I nodded, "This is Mimi, also known as Samantha, Walt, our cameraman and Alistair our agent.

"This is my wife Rosemarie, my son Jeff and I'm Barton Fox. Welcome. What made you chose us to visit of all the people out this way?"

"Things are getting bad in the city."

"We see that on the television. They're bad here too, because without transport we can't get our crops into the markets. We're losing our shirts."

Jeff went over to the Tesla, "This the car you drive in your series?"

I nodded.

"Why don't you come in and we'll visit while Rosemarie feeds you. Looks like you all could use a good meal."

I looked out over the farm. He had several large autodrive tractors just sitting. The laws prohibiting driving your own vehicles had been extended to farm equipment as well.

Rosemarie brought out her pots and pans and Jeff brought in vegetables from the garden. Mimi went to the kitchen and talked with Rosemarie while Walt, Alistair and I sat with Barton Fox.

"How long you been a farmer?" I asked.

"Born a farmer and I'll die a farmer. Now, Jeff on the other hand, I keep telling him to go get a good job up in Silicon Valley. He's real good with a lot of them tools and things they use to make money out of nothing. I can't do that. I got to create it with my hands, till the soil, plant the seeds and tend the crops until it's time to harvest and deliver to market. It's all a cycle. I can understand that. I can deal with the weather and the drought and the heat and all that Mother Nature wants to send my way. But use the tools to make something that makes money appear out of thin air? I can't do that."

"If we get the transport back up soon, will you be able to save much of your crops?" I asked after a moment of quiet.

"Depends on what you mean by soon. This week, yes, I should be able to save enough to get by. Next week, it will be a whole lot less and it will be touch and go as to whether we'll be around next year."

"I didn't realize it was that bad for you out here."

"Don't say anything to Rosemarie or Jeff. They suspect what the situation is. They watch me like a hawk and when I stop talking about things, they know how bad it is. But I just don't want to confirm things for them. You know what I'm saying? Sometimes it's just better to leave things unsaid. This is one of those times."

"What's your take on what you're seeing on television?" Walt asked.

"I'm just totally amazed it's taking us this long to figure out what the problem is. Why that Elon Musk guy over in Freemont, I would have thought he'd have come up with a fix in a week. But I don't hear anything about him fixing anything. He's supposed to be the wizard, don't you know. He built a car company when everyone said you couldn't do that anymore. Not only did he build a car company, he built an electric car company and now all the cars are electric. Then he goes and builds a rocket company and delivers crews and supplies to the space station. He decides we need solar electricity and he builds the biggest solar company in the world. He's the guy I would have thought would have had this all figured out in a week. But it hasn't happened."

"From what I know, his company didn't write the software for the autonomous cars. That was mostly Google and I'm sure they have every programmer and software developer in their company working this problem." Alistair responded.

"It's mostly in the hands of law enforcement. They believe someone did this for political reasons. What those reasons are, I don't think anyone knows for sure other than the people responsible." I summarized.

"Sounds like you know more about what's going on than most people." Barton Fox observed.

"I'm helping out as I can."

"Are you close? To finding those responsible?" I could see the hope on his face.

"Those working the problem have made a lot of headway, but this has been a particularly difficult event for them to track and solve. I don't think we have ever seen those responsible in any other law enforcement situation."

"You mean this is the first time they've broken a law?" Barton seemed incredulous.

"The first time they've done something that would have brought them to the attention of the authorities, yes. I think that's the case. And because they aren't in some 'persons of interest' database, we're not really sure who we're looking for."

"Do you at least have some ideas? I mean I got a week and things go downhill really quickly from there." Barton looks like he is losing hope.

Rosemarie called us to the dining room. The room was small, wood furniture and lace curtains. Pictures of Jeff in high school sports, wearing baseball and football uniforms.

The lunch was a fresh garden salad, a big bowl of strawberries and egg salad sandwiches made from fresh eggs and bread Rosemarie made herself.

"This is just incredible. Everything is so fresh." Mimi noted for everyone.

"It is," I noted. "We're doing everything we can to help get transport back. Barton was telling us how important that is to you. So thank you for feeding us today and hopefully we can repay your kindness with transport quickly."

Rosemarie seemed almost embarrassed to ask a question. "Do you think you could drop a package of food off to my sister in Santa Monica? She's been telling me she's been out of some of the things we have plenty of here for weeks now."

"Absolutely." I responded. I could feel her helplessness. She had family not so far away, but too far to be able to get food to them when they needed it. We were a godsend. A means of getting a limited amount to them. It wouldn't carry them long. But it was something to help them out.

"Why would someone do this to us?" Rosemarie asked simply hoping I'd have some answer that would make sense.

"I think whoever's responsible has no idea what he or she is doing to you or any of the others who are affected by this so severely. That person or those people must be so detached from the world they don't see any of what's happening. But we will find him or her or them. And we will get your transport back." I answered as honestly as I could. I just didn't know when.

Chapter Forty-Eight

The box of food we delivered to Rosemarie Fox's sister took up much of the room in the back. We had some room, but not as much as I'd imagined when we drove up. Alistair and Walt took two thirds of the food as they had families to feed. That didn't leave much for Mimi and I, and I deliberately gave her almost three quarters of what was left. I could afford to lose a few more pounds. She really couldn't. I tried to hide what I was doing the best I could. I think she knew, but she didn't say anything when I helped her carry it to her trailer.

"Four hours and we're out for another episode of the highest rated show on television. Could you even in your wildest dreams think we would ever achieve that?" I asked her as I was about to leave.

She leaned over to me as I stepped down from her door and kissed me the way she used to kiss me, back before Allison Andress, before I was untrustworthy, before I knew what it was to miss her. She didn't linger as she wanted me to know the limits of her gratitude. I was still all those things, but she at least knew I was trying to be the person I'd been before.

I returned to the Tesla and carried my portion of the food back to my trailer. I wasn't hungry even though I had an urge to eat at least a piece of Rosemarie Fox's loaf of bread. I resisted the urge as I knew I would need that piece of bread in the next few days more than I needed it right now. Knowing the people I worked with were hungrier than I was made it tough to put it away. It would be so welcomed by any and all. I was going to need to go back and visit the Fox's again in the next few days. We were going to need more to eat. As we continued to lose weight our desperation would grow and our thoughts would become more obsessive. We couldn't let that happen. I also knew each time we returned to the Fox farm without having solved the transport mystery the harder it was going to be to face them, since they only had a week to be able to recover to life the way it had been.

I went to find Mimi when it was time to head off for the evening ride with the LAPD. When I got to her trailer I found her on the floor unconscious. I picked her up and took her to her bed, laying her out. She came around and looked at me with wild eyes at first, then settling back down.

"What happened?" I asked when she seemed focused again.

"The food. Someone saw us bring it in. They came and took everything. I was going to just let them take it, but one of them thought I'd call security as soon as they left and knocked me out."

"Did you recognize anyone?"

"I recognized how desperate they were. But that's about all. Probably day laborers or something. No one we work with daily."

I felt so badly for Mimi. I'd tried to give her a little more to help her and it had only made her a target. I expected I'd find my trailer broken into as well when I returned from the evening ride. "How do you feel?"

"You don't think you're going out alone tonight do you?"

"Are you sure you're up to it?"

"You're going to get your fondest wish, I'm moving in with you tonight. Don't think it's safe for me to stay here alone."

"You can have the bedroom."

"Glad you know your place." She winked at me, but there was no smile. She was serious and I was still in the doghouse, so the couch and I would become good friends until we got the transport back up. Now I had a real incentive to solve the mystery, namely my bed back and a good night's sleep, but the downside to that is Mimi will be gone back to her place and my loneliness will come back to visit.

We picked up Walt, Kareem and Pete at the usual times. Pete noticed Mimi kept rubbing her neck. "You sleep wrong?" he asked her.

"It's nothing. Just a crick."

"Too much necking, my wife always says." Pete responded.

"I didn't realize you were married." Mimi responded.

"Two kids, seven and nine."

"They must keep you busy."

"Just trying to feed them, keeps me busy." And his comment took on a whole new meaning beyond what it normally would have.

"No sign of Oliver Wilson, even though he only had an hour head start." I summarized what I understood from an earlier conversation with Kareem.

"No. I'm not entirely sure Alice Wheeler was telling the truth about him being there."

"She described his suitcase. Not sure she would have known about that if he hadn't been there with it at some point." I responded.

"But what if she's in it with him? She set the whole thing up with her sister to get the weapons and he was just the courier?" Mimi was free associating.

"Wilson brought a missile over the day before and left town. Someone else came and took the weapon that same day. Both had more than a twenty-four hour head start. That would certainly explain why we weren't able to find him in the area." I built upon Mimi's thoughts.

"That certainly could be one scenario." Kareem had to admit.

"I vote for picking up both Alice and Sherice, taking them in and doing separate, but equal interrogations. Meanwhile, I'll bring a few investigators out and we'll canvass their neighbors. Find out what anyone might have seen. You never know. Might even get a description of the second man if in fact there was one." I suggested as one possible course of action.

"I'm agreeable, since we don't have any better idea where he might have gone. I was going to interview one more person his supervisor Julie Simpson mentioned. Someone who had called looking for him and left a number for him to call. It was fortunate Julie wrote the number down in her work log and was able to retrieve it."

"Do you know who the person is?" Mimi asked.

"A personal trainer to the stars. Jake Goodbody." Kareem responded with disdain.

I couldn't believe my trainer had called Oliver Wilson at work. "I know Jake. I'll go see him while your guys do the neighborhoods."

We went by, picked up Alice and Sherice and delivered them with Kareem and Pete to the station. Walt made arrangements to get the videos of the interrogations and came along with us. I then took two investigators out and dropped one each in Alice and Sherice's neighborhoods. Mimi and I then took Walt with us to visit with Jake.

When we arrived at Jake's studio he was just finishing up with none other than a shirtless Johnny Hollywood. I noted the kid's six pack and thought of my own beer bong in the same place. I still thought I could take the kid out with one good punch if push came to shove, but I didn't have any reason to be worried about him at the minute so I simply said, "Hey kid. Understand you want my show. Forget it."

Johnny Hollywood flipped me the bird, so I did what any other threatened species would do, I punched him in the mouth. He went down like a sack of potatoes.

"What the fuck?" Jake pushed me back and hustled Johnny Hollywood out.

Jake was pissed, "You'll be lucky if you don't get sued."

"How do you know Oliver Wilson" I asked directly. There was no other way to get the answer I needed.

Jake looked dumbfounded. "He's a client."

"You work him out like you work me out under contract? Who's the contract with?"

"Cash customer."

"You called him at work once, spoke to his boss. Why?"

"He missed an appointment. He's not under contract so he doesn't show I don't get paid. I called to find out why he missed the appointment."

"What did he say?"

"Left a message never to call him there again. Haven't seen him since."

"Why did he leave that number if he didn't want you to call it?"

"He didn't give it to me, I saw the name of his company on his shirt, looked it up and asked for him. Reception gave me to his boss. She relayed the message to call me."

His story was plausible. But was Jake was hiding something? What? Did he pass along information to Wilson? I needed to better understand this link.

Chapter Forty-Nine

Mimi and I picked up the investigators about ten o'clock and returned them to the station. We checked in with Kareem and Pete. I asked them how things had gone.

"Tough nuts," was all Pete would say.

"Tomorrow is another day." Kareem offered.

"Thank you Scarlet O'Hara." Mimi replied.

"A night in a cell often works miraculously, when they realize that they'll be staying in that cell until after a hearing and bail is set."

"That's usually the next day." I responded.

"They don't know that, and we don't bother telling them." Kareem had a wicked smile. "What did our investigators find?"

"They're working their reports. From what they said in the car, Sherice had a guy over regular. When the investigators compared notes, he matched the description of a guy seen coming out of Alice's apartment carrying the camouflage suitcase. Said he definitely wasn't the same one who brought it."

"Can we get a sketch artist on the second guy?" Mimi asked.

Kareem motioned for Pete to arrange it. "You take the sketch artist out to get the sketch?"

I nodded.

"So your theory has legs. We got two bad guys. One has a probable weapon and he's the one we know the least about. He has a two day head start. We draw a circle around Alice's apartment we should be able to know how far he got, but not in which direction. We can send the sketch out, as soon as you can bring it in, to see if we get lucky."

"Don't forget the camouflage suitcase. That's more a giveaway than anything else." I noted.

"Right."

The investigator called the neighbor who had seen the man leave Alice Wheeler's apartment and she agreed to meet us, even though it was late at night. But only when the investigator told her I'd be coming along and she'd be filmed for the show.

It was two am when Mimi and I entered my trailer. It had not been ransacked, but I was lucky. I'd called security from Mimi's trailer and alerted them as to the fact some people had broken into Mimi's trailer and assaulted her. Two armed guards had been assigned and watched over the trailer.

She got the bed and I got the couch until eight when the video phone rang. It was time for Silmara's call. I threw on a Dodger's T-shirt and waddled over to answer the call, being careful to sit such that the camera would not show my boxer shorts and bare legs.

"You look like you've had an active night." Silmara greeted me.

"Out with a sketch artist until two." I mumbled.

"I hope she was worth it." Silmara's rejoinder made my day.

"She was doing a sketch of someone we think may know the whereabouts of the same kind of weapon that was used to take down the Googlecar repair depots."

"There's still more out there?"

"One or two, we think. Watch the show next week."

"I do watch it. That's why you're on this team." Silmara's response surprised me. "Okay. Kalindi has another report for us. I know Dyllan and Bomani you wanted to talk about the code first, but just listen to this part and then we'll go on to the code."

"We have another potential Hamartia sighting. This one is in the Amazon River basin in Brazil."

"That makes sense. Kind of the prototypical place for survivalists." I noted.

"Much more so than the Kashmir." Bomani added.

"What can you tell us about this one?" I asked.

"They have established a colony actively trading with the native populations, but only the fresh fruit and vegetables they grow. All work is done manually. No tractors, plows or machinery of any kind. They had been regarded by the locals as eccentric, but now they have been more active in trying to recruit others to join their 'cult'."

"So they were thought to be a cult. Makes sense if you think about it. Wouldn't want anyone to be suspicious of them. How many are there?" I inquired.

"It's a larger settlement. Over one-hundred and fifty from the reports we were able to study. They've been there for at least seven years. Started out small, ten or fifteen people initially. They grow a few dozen each year. Nothing dramatic. Just a steady influx of new people."

"What brought them to the attention of the authorities?" I asked again. It seemed Bomani and Dyllan were doing something else and not paying attention.

"They brought in solar photovoltaic cells to create electricity. Until then they were completely survivalist. Suddenly, a satellite dish appeared and the natives they are trading with have seen the cult members using computer workstations. Seems like they were trying to link up with others."

"I take it until then, the cult members had shown no interest in dealing with anyone other than for trading fruit and vegetables or to get seeds for new crops?" I was on a roll and it seemed to be just a conversation between Kalindi and me anyway.

"Correct. But the solar cells and computers just suddenly showed up. The locals had never seen anything like them. The government investigated, but the cult people wouldn't discuss them, just said they were only doing things within the law and that was all the government investigators needed to know. The investigators did confirm in their reports. They did see the solar cells, quite a few as a matter of fact. Probably cover an acre or so."

"Name?" Xian had joined.

"Good evening, Xian." I called out.

"Underwear?" Xian asked. He always had a good eye for details.

I stood up and revealed my entire wardrobe for the day to hoots and hollers from Dyllan and Bomani. I took a bow and sat back down.

Kalindi scanned her monitor, "Yes, they had a name. It was in the report. Give me a minute."

"Have you learned anything more about the Changing Wind on Diaoyu Dao?" I asked to give Kalindi a little more time.

"Government try remove again."

"Chinese or Japanese?" I asked.

"Japanese. Broadcast live pictures." I wasn't sure I heard him right.

"Broadcast? Does that mean they have electricity and satellite dish hookup? On that tiny island?"

"See connections. Kashmir too."

"So if they are the Hamartia, they're getting ready for something." I noted just as Mimi came out of the bedroom. At least they couldn't see where she came from and she was a whole lot more put together than I was, although she hadn't showered yet, so I knew it was all a temporary fix up of her appearance.

"What's the Hamartia getting ready for?" she asked.

"Three sites, with electricity and communications. Looks like they're trying to hook up."

"Does that mean they think they've won?" Mimi asked.

"It means there may be a second trigger in the Googlecar code. Something else we haven't even considered." I suggested.

"Short the batteries to cause fires?" Dyllan suggested.

"Start them up to crash into anything in the way?" Bomani riffed on Dyllan's suggestion.

"Erase the code all together." I suggested.

"But that would allow us to go out and install new code." Silmara proposed.

"If we went back to an earlier version, before the virus code was uploaded. But at the moment we don't know how far back it goes. Has anyone asked Google to check the code versions?" I asked.

"They've confirmed these code elements were in the earliest versions." Bomani informed us.

"That would mean someone got to the code almost at the

beginning. You would almost have to assume it was a member of the original development team." Dyllan suggested.

"Dormant for decades." Xian observed.

Chapter Fifty

Mimi and I went to the station to pick up Kareem and Pete. They weren't waiting for us, so we went inside to find them. They were in the interrogation rooms. Pete talked with a handcuffed and chained Alice Wheeler and Kareem had Sherice in the next interrogation room, where she was not cuffed and smoked a cigarette.

We listened in to Alice and Pete first.

"Why are you trying to protect Sherice's boyfriend? We should be picking him up any time now. What's he going to tell us about you? You tell us it won't go so hard on you in court."

"I'm not going to court you asshole."

"If Sherice's boyfriend blows up something you're an accomplice. We got people who saw him come out of your apartment carrying the weapon you arranged to steal from the defense plant in El Segundo. You won't never get out of jail if you're carrying all those convictions."

"You mocking me? You're talking just like I do. This some kind of psychological warfare you're trying on me? Well it won't work. You know why it won't work? 'Cause I'm a whole lot smarter than you give me credit for. And not only that, you take these here cuffs off me and I'll whip your ass, right here, right now."

"Threatening a police officer. That's another one to add to your ever increasing list of offenses."

"I won't talk no more until I have a lawyer present."

"You said you don't have a lawyer."

"I don't. But I know my rights. You got to provide one for me. Public expense."

"No, public defender. Pimply faced kid just out of law school on his or her first job. You know I'm right about that. So what kind of defense you think you're going to get from a wet behind the ears recent law school grad?"

"I just need him here to talk to you. I ain't never going to trial anyway."

"You keep saying you're not going to trial. Why are you saying that when we have enough to lock you up and throw away the key right now, even if you don't threaten me a second time?"

"I'm not going to waste my time. Get me a lawyer. Then I'll answer your questions through my mouthpiece. You understand me?"

I could see a night in jail had done wonders to break down Alice's resistance. I turned the switch to listen in on Kareem and Sherice.

"You and Alice, sisters. I mean I just can't get over that. You two couldn't be more different."

"Her genes didn't like her much."

"You know anything about her daddy?"

"My mother said he was around until I was about three, but I honestly don't remember him at all. None of my mother's lovers were in it for anything other than a good time, for a short time. When responsibility showed up, it was time to hit the highway. Every last one of them."

"Is that why Alice is so nasty and you're so agreeable?"

"I really don't have any idea how genes work."

"So getting back to Oliver Wilson and James Finch."

"I'd rather not."

"I know, but we're going to hold both of you until you tell us what you know. Our time is nearly up and that means the other detective is going to come back to talk with you again. Now he's been with Alice for the last hour. Do you think he's going to be cordial and respectful like I am, or do you think he's going to be nasty and unpleasant after an hour of Alice's shit?"

Sherice butted out the cigarette. "I can handle him."

"You don't have to if you just tell us what we need to know."

"Look detective. I've told you all I know about James Finch. You say that probably isn't his real name. Well it's the only one I have. I mean I never asked to look at his driver's license. And even if I had, it was probably, if you're right, fake anyway."

"You admit you slept with him. Did he have any distinguishing marks? Birth marks, scars, skin conditions, anything that would positively identify him?"

"A big dick. Bigger than yours."

"That wasn't nice."

"Why should I give a shit? You don't think I'm a nice girl anyway."

"I'm sure you'd like to get home and go back to work."

"You think the defense plant's going to let me come back to work after you file your reports? Not gonna happen. I'm toast. I'll be doing nails for all the Vietnamese immigrants who sold out their nail salons and moved up to working in Trader Joes."

"You have a license for that?"

She looked concerned, "No, do I need one?"

I turned off the volume. The interrogation wasn't close to giving us anything of value. I didn't want to wait around for Kareem and Pete to wear them down, so Mimi, Walt and I went down to the break room and sat down. The snack machines and coffee machines were empty. No one else was in the room since there wasn't anything to eat anyway.

"If you were on foot carrying a shoulder launched missile where would you go?" I asked both Mimi and Walt.

"I think they have a target and it's got to be local." Mimi started

"I would agree, but they already took out the Googlecar repair depot. So what other target would they be after?"

"Television station, broadcast tower, telephone exchange building, electric substation, gas pipeline, a bridge, city hall, police station, train station, airport, it's really hard to tell." Walt rattled off his list of possible targets.

"Okay, so which one would people notice most? Which one would cause you to lose hope?"

"The television station," Mimi offered. "If people really are watching our show and it's giving them hope." I was in agreement with her, but then had second thoughts.

"That was Alistair's perspective. Not sure our friends share that. What do you think, Walt?"

"Everyone's sitting at home, but they're calling everyone they know. I'd go after the telephone exchange building. Cut off the communications."

Walt's thoughts just made a lot of sense to me. "Mimi, I love you, but I'll have to go with Walt on this one. Let's head over there."

"You going to tell Kareem where we're going and why?" Mimi

worried.

"What's he going to do?"

Mimi didn't like my answer, but didn't protest further.

We drove over to the exchange building in downtown. The building had been there since the 1950s and was the central exchange for all of Los Angeles. I tried to remember what I'd read about the range of the weapons. Seemed to me it was about a half mile, so I started to drive through the neighborhoods about a half mile from the building. My headlights lit up places where someone could be hiding, setting up a weapon to launch at the building that was taller than anything else in the distance.

We drove in circles around the exchange building, coming a block in closer with the completion of each circle around. Walt had the camera on straight ahead through the windshield. Mimi watched out her side and I scanned back and forth for any movement.

Suddenly there was a shadow. Movement. Someone, in an alley with something on his shoulder. I turned the wheel sharply and floored the Tesla right at the figure, now down on one knee. My LED lights blinded him. I saw him put his trigger hand up to his eyes in an attempt to see. I intended to run him down right there to prevent him launching the missile. The man evidently got the message as he jumped up and ran away from us down the alley, missile still on his shoulder. The Tesla was quick and in a moment I was right on top of him. I thought of Uncle Jim as I ran into the man, knocking him to the ground. Uncle Jim would forgive a dent or two, wouldn't he? For a good cause?

The man got up as I backed away and made a mad dash for it, leaving the missile behind. Walt jumped out of the car and retrieved the missile so I could follow the man. In only a moment I knocked him down again from behind. I backed off him and got out of the Tesla. Once I was out of the car, Finch evidently thought he had a better chance of escape and made another attempt to run away from me. But

Jake had made sure I was fit and able to keep up. What was it? Something about being able to do whatever a man of similar age and fitness could do? That wouldn't have been enough as Finch, or whatever his name was, seemed to be younger than me and he was literally running for his life. But I wasn't going to let him get away. Natalie was right, when I was determined, nothing would stop me and James Finch wasn't going to stop me tonight.

Catching the running man, I got my arm around his neck and pulled him backwards and down to the ground on top of me. He tried to break my grip around his neck, but I tightened it, choking him.

Rolling over, I pushed his head down and tied his wrists behind his back with a handkerchief.

"Who the fuck do you think you are?"

"I know who I am and who you are, James Finch. Oh, Sherice sends her love."

"Sherice? What's she got to do with this?"

"She told us where to find you. Amazing what starvation and interrogation will do to a person. Oh, and Alice? She says 'Fuck you.'"

Finch didn't know what to make of my little conversation so he clammed up.

"I find it hard to believe they're sisters and somehow you convinced Wilson to take Alice and make him think he was getting the better end of the deal." I said as I brought Finch to his feet.

I escorted Finch back to the Tesla and into the back seat. Walt had packaged up the missile and put it in the trunk where he usually sat, then slid into the back beside our guest.

"Man, I don't see what Sherice sees in this bozo." Walt decided to help me with the psychological preparation for the interrogation.

THE TRAGIC FLAW

When Mimi and I brought Finch into the interrogation room, where Pete was shouting at Sherice, both stopped talking at once. Sherice leapt to help Finch, who was now wearing handcuffs.

"Baby, did they hurt you?"

Chapter Fifty-One

On the videoconference call the next morning I was surprised when Silmara made an announcement to the team. "We made a breakthrough last night. Desmond and Mimi apprehended some of those responsible for the Googlecar repair depot bombings."

Everyone looked at their screens with big smiles. That was one of the strange things about a videoconference, you never saw people looking at you as they would if in the room with you. I gave a small hand wave in acknowledgement.

"What can you tell us about the man you took into custody, Desmond?" Kalindi asked.

I had to think on my feet for a moment, not something I had to do often as actor, but I'd been getting a lot of practice since the show had become in essence a reality show. I thought that odd. I'd become most successful as a reality television star who were the people I usually disparaged. But everyone was waiting for me to speak. "Male, late thirties, Caucasian, goes by the name of James Finch, but we suspect that's not his real name. Apprehended in the act of attempting to fire a shoulder launched missile at the central telephone exchange in Los Angeles."

"You even sound like a cop. Did Robert script that for you?" Dyllan was giving me shit, but he was laughing with me and not at me.

I shook my head and waited for Silmara to move the meeting along. "Have you made any connection between your perpetrator and the Hamartia?"

"No. Not at the present time. He's being less than cooperative. But we have his girlfriend and girlfriend's sister also in custody. So between them we think we can find a weak link."

"Since they only had one missile," Kalindi began. "Was the exchange on their primary list of targets or was it just a target of opportunity?"

"We don't know for sure, but it appeared to be a target of opportunity. For some reason the missile had been held back and not sent to another city. Could be they saw it as a spare. Don't really know. Anyway, they were probably warned by an accomplice at the defense plant, who probably told them the theft had been discovered. We believe that was the reason they tried to employ it."

"Do you know who the accomplice is?" Bomani asked.

"We think it was Sherice, the girlfriend, who worked there in finished goods inventory. She was aware of the discovery because we questioned her about it."

"So until someone talks you have no more suspects." Kalindi summarized.

"That's the situation, yes."

"Bomani?" Silmara asked for his report.

"Unfortunately no progress on the software front. We continue scanning for key elements, we have tried removing the identified code, but that has some redundant mechanism which also shuts down the system. We are running out of ideas. So if anyone has any suggestions, please make them."

No one responded. Silmara moved on, "Kalindi?"

"Nothing new."

"Xian?"

"Changing Winds televise documentary."

"On what?" I couldn't help asking.

"Recruiting. Want more people join on Diaoyu Dao."

"Is that what the communications systems are all about?" I asked aloud. "Looking for converts? Maybe they realized they'll need more people to grow and produce enough food to survive."

"Something we will have to consider." Silmara summarized. "I think that is all we have for now. Need to work the code issues and continue to look for other possible cells of the Hamartia."

I signed off and knocked on the bedroom door. Mimi had slept in late again. Even though she'd eaten the day before, she was getting weaker and sleeping more. Not a good sign. I was becoming increasingly worried about her. She was strong emotionally but not physically and I had to remember that. "Mimi?"

"Yes?" she responded, although she didn't come to the door.

"I'm going over to get Alistair. He wanted to talk with us today."

"Fine. I'll be showered by the time you get back."

"Eat something when you get up."

"Did you?"

"Yes." I lied.

It only took about twenty minutes to get Alistair and bring him back to the trailer.

"What do you think will happen when Jack and Stan take it to Regina?" I asked him as we entered the trailer. Mimi was up, drinking a cup of hot water. The coffee and tea were gone, but the habit remained. Her hair was still wet from her shower and she just pulled a white lounging sheath on. No underwear, I detected. That brought memories of Sunday mornings and her lying in bed naked, looking at me with contentment when we were together. I quickly set those thoughts aside.

"If they're smart they'll counter, but close enough we'll accept the counter. But then no one ever said they were smart."

"Wishful thinking Alistair." Mimi said by way of greeting.

"No. I really think we have a chance to get a deal done before things change back. I can tell Stan is working everyone. He's afraid I'm going to go shop you as the Tesla Cop. Different title, different series. We'd have to give your character a different name, but you rarely use it in the current show. Everyone remembers your names from before, but it would be an easy transition."

"Has anyone else approached you about a deal?" I asked.

"As a matter of fact, I have taken a number of calls. Fishing expeditions, I'd call them. People don't expect you'd want to move when you're in the stratosphere like you are at the moment. But people are also watching, hoping, really, that things will go back to normal quickly. In a period of readjustment who knows what might happen?"

"Yeah, we readjust back to the unemployment line. Yesterday's fifteen minutes." Mimi was not in an upbeat mood. I needed to find out why.

Alistair sat down in my chair, as he always did. I stood next to Mimi as I was feeling restless. Alistair began, "So tell me what's going on with the Task Force?"

"We made real progress for a period of time. Think we have a handle on a group that may be responsible, but all our efforts to crack the autonomous car virus code have gone to a point and not beyond. We find bits and pieces, but we can't find a way to restore the systems and delete the virus."

"Not good. What do you think's going to happen now?"

"We don't know. We might get lucky and James Finch might lead us to their leader and or the person who wrote the code. But that's not going to be quick. They know things become more and more untenable every day."

"Tell me about the people you suspect?"

"We've found a website that sets out a lifestyle focused on living without technology. The more we've burrowed into it we've discovered someone has been recruiting people for at least a decade. That doesn't match up with the virus, since that was planted several decades ago. But someone has been very patient. Waiting for a day to release the virus. We don't know why now, but I'm sure the person responsible had this all planned out."

"I'm overwhelmed."

"If we have the right people, that's what it looks like."

"You said a lifestyle focused on living without technology. What do you mean?"

"Survivalist. We've actually found sects of them in Japan, India and Brazil so far. We don't really know how many of them there are, but there have been thousands of visitors to the website."

"Survivalist? Like people who go live in the woods without toilets, tools or the internet?"

"Yes."

"I know someone like that. Hugh Aguirre. He was a producer and director of sophomoric sitcoms. Made a bundle. Had a big house up in the hills. One day he just vanished into the Sierra Nevada hills with only a sleeping bag and canteen. Or at least that's what I've been told. But you know, I think I know where to find him. He might know something about your cult. He was always a bit strange that way."

Chapter Fifty-Two

Dyllan called Kalindi that same day. They had been chatting off-line from the main calls every day. At first the calls were strictly business, but more recently they had ventured away from the common problem.

"What is it like living in a desert?" Kalindi changed the topic.

"Abu Dhabi is a modern city. It is not an oasis, if that is what you are thinking. We have all the conveniences of any western city, you would not feel like you were in a strange land if you came to visit, other than there are a lot fewer people and the signs are in Arabic and English."

"Tall buildings to leap in a single bound?"

"I do very little leaping now, but yes, we have tall buildings that are both offices and residences. We have large shopping centers, western style hotels, restaurants and streets filled with Googlecars sitting there waiting for us to find a way to restore them to their prior functionality."

"But the Emirates are mostly desert." Kalindi was looking for Dyllan to confirm what she thought she knew, since he was trying to convince her that Abu Dhabi was not a backwards country. That was an impression Dyllan often encountered in people who had never been there.

"Outside the cities, yes, you are correct. We still have nomadic tribes moving around the county in the traditional ways, but there are fewer and fewer every year."

"Would you tell me about your accident?" She was probing something to which she didn't know how Dyllan would respond. Was he sensitive about it? Would he talk about it or was it a taboo subject. She wanted to better understand him, but was fearful he wouldn't discuss the events.

"I was an officer in the Emirates Special Forces. I had several very important assignments including protection of the crown prince. That is an honor accorded to very few. When I finished that assignment, in order to be promoted again I needed a combat billet. Most of the time when in the combat brigades, all you do is train and drill. Very seldom does anyone experience live combat. So when given command of the elite brigade it was a recognition that I would be promoted to a general officer. There are only ten in the entire Emirates military. All I had to do was train up my brigade to a very high level of readiness, expecting that nothing significant would transpire during my tour."

"Obviously you were wrong."

"Obviously. A secret mission was approved by the Crown Prince to support our allies against a particularly nasty group of people. It was supposed to be a single lightning raid, to capture or kill the leadership of this group of terrorists. We knew they had sophisticated weapons. We knew they were well trained. We knew they were prepared for us as they had been on high alert from what inside sources told us. What we learned afterwards is our inside sources were double agents, posing as agents for us while secretly gathering information for their real masters, those who were our target."

"You were betrayed." Kalindi offered.

"Yes, betrayed my people we had paid very well to tell us what we needed to know."

"You did screen them, did you not?"

"Screened them and obtained recommendations from people we worked with in the past who know them well. They had been

302

undercover for years, observing and sending information back to this particular sect. But they gave us very sensitive information about their real masters. Information that proved useful to us and our allies. It amazes me how patient people can be in pursuit of their goals. In a world of instantaneous gratification I seldom meet people who can wait patiently for anything."

"How did it happen?"

"I decided to go ashore with my teams. I wanted to be in the midst of things to shorten the communications chain. In special operations speed is essential. The faster I respond, the greater chance we will prevail. So I was there. On the ground. In the midst of a ferocious fire fight we didn't see coming. One of my Captains stepped on a delay fuse land mine. They are particularly nasty because people step on them and nothing happens. Several people step on them and still nothing. So people believe the way is clear and the mine goes off deep in the formation that is moving across, taking out the leaders who are not up front, which is usually the higher ranked individuals."

"The Captain was killed?" Kalindi still waited for what happened to Dyllan specifically.

"Yes, and the shrapnel peppered my legs and severed my spinal cord in my lower back. Left me with my upper body, arms and head movements as normal, but nothing below the waist."

Kalindi thought about Dyllan's story for a long moment before asking the next question, "So how did you go from being an almost general to movies and becoming a tech guru?"

"You know the story of Siddhartha?"

"Of course. It is an Indian legend."

"Siddhartha spent his life seeking enlightenment and had many adventures as he sought his goal, not realizing the journey was more important than the goal. I was going to take a new journey whether I wanted to or not. That journey could either be a self-limiting passage through life or I could reinvent myself. A cousin is a professor of digital technology. He offered to have me attend any class he taught for free. At first I was overwhelmed by what I was learning. All too much. I resolved to find another path and told my cousin of my decision. He understood how I felt. Said he had felt the same way once. So he asked me to take just one more course. If after that course I was still resolved to find another path, he would help me make that transition."

"What happened in that course?" Kalindi couldn't wait to know.

"My cousin had the class read a book by Ray Kurzweil, entitled, The Singularity."

"The book Desmond spoke of?"

"Yes, the same book. It foretold that there would be a time when man and technology would become a single entity, with consciousness moving to a machine. That book gave me hope someday my limitations would no longer hold me back. I realized I had to learn everything I could about technology and particularly biotechnology. I could have gone into medical research and help lead that revolution. But I realized I would need to study medicine to truly understand the human body before I could be insightful about how the two will someday merge."

"And you were not willing to spend most of your life preparing to contribute."

"I wanted to see results sooner than I would have been able to if I'd gone to medical school, done a residency and practiced long enough to validate my knowledge. I did not want to be theoretical doctor. I would need to be an experienced doctor. My cousin introduced me to a colleague in the cinema department. He talked about how they were applying technology. I knew I could contribute immediately in filmmaking. I'd always loved movies, but never thought I'd one day end up helping to make them."

Kalindi was quiet for a bit, thinking about Dyllan's story. Then he asked her, "What about your journey? Did you always wish to be a police person?"

"I never wished to be a police person. My father worked for the Foreign Ministry as the person who made arrangements for visits to the Prime Minister from dignitaries of other nations. It was an important position. He met all the heads of state on their visits. But he was never the person they came to see. He was never in the room when important matters were discussed. He was an arranger. And while important in his position, no one remembered his name the day after their visit ended unless some arrangement went awry."

"So you wished to be the person in the room."

"I wished to be the Ambassador to America."

"A noble ambition, but you are a police person. What happened?"

"I went to University and studied International Relations and Diplomacy, but also software development as a backstop. I studied very hard and made good grades. When I graduated the Foreign Ministry did not offer me a position, even with my father talking to the Prime Minister on my behalf."

"Was he told he should not bother the Prime Minister with such matters?" Dyllan guessed.

"Yes and was transferred to a much less important function, reviewing contracts for purchases of goods and services for the Foreign Ministry, where he retired after only a few years."

"So, police?"

"The Ministry of Justice offered me a position in a training role. Lowest level entry position. But once given an opportunity I showed initiative and learned all I could. I came to the attention of the Deputy Minister for Internal Investigations, who offered me a position working directly for him. He became my mentor and from there I rose rapidly.

All I needed was a chance. The rest was up to me."

"Accidental people."

"Would you explain your comment?"

"Neither of us are who we wished or expected to be, and yet here we are, saving the world."

Chapter Fifty-Three

Alistair assured me we'd be able to drive the distance to Hugh Aguirre's camp and return on a single charge. While the camp was remote, it was really only about fifty miles from LA. What he didn't tell me was it was fifty miles by roads and then another ten miles of mountainous paths. Those paths were nearly impassable under the best of conditions. We had to drive very slowly so as not to damage the Tesla. As we drove, I thought the way more suited to a jeep. The last mile was impossible. We had to walk in. There was no way the Tesla was going to traverse the heavy underbrush of a nearly vertical dense pine forest.

Luckily I'd convinced Mimi she shouldn't wear heals. She'd intended to, wanting to look her best for a former producer/director. She'd worn tennis shoes under much protest as long as she could carry flats to change into once we arrived. And guess who got to carry the flats for her as we hiked through the woods?

When we came out into a forest glen, a small log cabin lay on the other side of a mirror-calm lake. Smoke came out of a chimney next to two arrays of solar panels that covered the entire roof of the cabin and a significant area behind it. The cabin faced east so the panels were arranged to gather sunlight in the morning and afternoon, with more panels providing power in the afternoon. I also noticed a satellite dish, although not exactly like the ones I'd seen in my neighborhood. The dish had a peculiar shape and three receivers set to pick up the reflected signals. Why three? Don't think I'd ever seen one with three before.

"This is amazing." A tired Mimi gushed as she stepped into the sunshine and felt the warmth on her face. "I could live here."

"Three hours each way?" I inquired as to whether the distance was a problem for her.

"Well, not live here like every day. But weekends definitely."

"I'd give you a month. Then you'd never return." I called her bluff.

"I might surprise you Mister Jensen." She was playing with me, which meant she knew I was right, but wouldn't admit it.

"I'll admit you're full of surprises."

We walked slowly across the tall grassy field, still tired from the hike up. It took a good fifteen minutes to hike around the lake to arrive at the cabin, which looked larger up close than it had from across the glen. I noticed a stream ran through the back yard, in fact, it ran right through the solar array. Curious.

Alistair knocked on the door.

In a moment we heard rustling inside and then the door opened. At first Hugh Aguirre looked puzzled and curious at the same time. He was unshaven, although did not sport a beard.

"Hugh? It's Alistair. Do you remember me?"

"You're wasting your time. I'm not returning." Hugh responded to Alistair, then looked at Mimi for a long moment, and then me. "What are you thinking? I'm not the right person for anything you might have in mind. I'm strictly comedy, not the genre of interest to you. At least not from what I've seen you do in the past. You trying to make some kind of transition? Whatever it is, I don't think it will work."

"May we come in?" Alistair asked.

"You've come a long way, both figuratively and literally." I couldn't tell if he was agreeing or not.

"So you've seen our show?" I asked wondering about his reaction to us being there.

"Everyone's seen your show." He stepped back to let us in.

We entered into another world. The single room had a wooden floor, fireplace, with an andiron to cook over the fire, and rough-hewn shelves upon which Hugh Aguirre displayed his many Hollywood awards. At one end was a row of doors. One was open and we could see it was his pantry. In front of the fireplace was a futon, rolled up and tied, standing on end. Nothing in this space would use the electricity he was generating from his solar panels. I had to assume his television and any other communications devices he had were behind another set of the doors. The other three sets could have been anything. A bathroom maybe? But there was no sign of running water in this part of the house.

Hugh Aguirre lived simply, as Alistair had mentioned. But still, the solar and satellite dish didn't seem to add up in the context of his simple life.

Hugh motioned and we sat down on roughly sewn cushions on the floor in front of the fire. "Why've you've come to find me after all this time?"

"Five years?" I sought confirmation.

"Over seven." Hugh corrected. "It was seven last December."

"You built this yourself?" I estimated he could have, but with all the money he made wondered if he was living the life, or living a carefully orchestrated Hollywood lie.

"I did. First thing when I came up here. Took me nearly a year. Lived in a tent during that time. Every day went quickly then as I was busy every single day. But enough about me, why are you here?"

"Desmond thought you might know something about others who've chosen to live like this." Alistair began for us.

Hugh looked at me, "So you're the one. You're responsible for dragging Alistair and Mimi up here looking for an old man. I'm not the guru of the mountain. I have no unique knowledge or insights I can share. I hope you aren't here searching for enlightenment. I'm just an old man who wants to live quietly and enjoy what nature's remaining bounty affords me."

I picked up on 'remaining' bounty. I'd have to see if he provided any other clues as to why he gave up the good life for a simple one. "We're not here to study with you for a film, or ask you to come back with us to make one. We're really just looking to know if you have any insight into a group or confederation or loose affiliation of people who are living much like you. Survivalists, really. People who have sought to live a simpler life than those of us down in the valley."

"There are many people who live like I do. Are you asking if we have an annual convention, hire lobbyists to influence legislation and seek to change laws to favor causes we believe in?"

I was surprised how he equated his life to the many interest groups that had warped society and political life. "Not exactly. More like are you aware of websites trying to interest people in living a simpler life? One not dependent upon technology."

"There have been websites like that for decades. I may have researched them when I was preparing to come up here, but I can't give you any details about any of them. It's been a while."

"Have you ever heard of a group, "Mimi started, "that calls themselves the Hamartia?" I wasn't ready to ask that question yet, but now that it was out on the table, I was curious what Hugh Aguirre would do with it.

"The protagonist's tragic flaw? I know the concept from Greek tragedy. Are you suggesting a group of people are calling themselves that?"

"Yes," was all I'd give him.

"A curious choice. What are these people advocating?"

Now he seized on advocating. There's something here, I thought.

"We're not sure yet." Alistair wanted to make sure everyone kept him in the conversation.

Hugh didn't look at Alistair, seeming to process this information. I wondered what he was really thinking, not sure his response was genuine. "I'm certainly glad you made the trek up here. This has been a stimulating discussion. You know I don't get visitors. None at all. You're the first to visit me in probably four years. As a reward for your adventures, I'd like to offer to make you dinner. Now what I eat probably doesn't resemble what you do, but I guarantee it's healthier than anything you're normally eating. No genetically modified foods. No pesticides in your water. No chemicals, no added sugars, trans fats, monosaturated fats, or any kind of fats. No animal protein. No dairy. Just good healthy foods that won't make you fat, keep you awake at night or cause you to gain unhealthy unneeded weight."

"So you grow all of your own food?" Mimi asked.

"Every bit of it. I haven't bought a thing in seven years."

"Can I help you prepare the meal? I love to cook." Mimi volunteered, although I had no idea how long it had been since Mimi cooked anything. She hadn't the whole time we'd been together.

"You can all help. Alistair, please take the pot next to the fireplace out to the stream and fill the pot two-thirds full of water so we can heat it on the fire. Desmond, if you'd pick some vegetables from the garden, which is also out back, I'll make us a nice salad. Just make sure you pick enough for four. Mimi and I'll visit the root cellar and select the ingredients for a nice meatless stew. I hope you don't mind. I've gone completely away from meat. Incredibly I feel so much better and I've lost weight. But only in the right places. Lean muscle and all that."

I wondered what Hugh intended to say to Mimi in the root cellar.

Chapter Fifty-Four

Hugh Aguirre knew how to entertain. His Malibu home parties were Gatsbyesque as I remembered. I'd attended the last two and maybe that was why seeing him in this setting was so jarring. The Malibu home was right on the beach. Many millions had been spent to construct it. But the one thing I'd never realized at the time was the house really was an outgrowth of its surroundings. The stone walls were the same color as the beach sand. The wood wrap around porch was unstained and reminded me of driftwood. The roof was Mediterranean tiles, although green rather than the traditional terra cotta. The house was at least ten thousand square feet on two levels with a penthouse atop that reminded me of New England homes I'd seen with a Widow's Walk. The Widow's Walk is a tiny room from which the wife could walk the roof to watch for her returning husband, whether out hunting or fighting in the revolutionary or civil wars. Hugh's Widow's Walk, was much larger than what I remembered on those New England houses. It seemed out of place on his modernistic home. One person had said it looked like the bridge of a ship. The interior furniture was mostly built in and incorporated into the flow of the rooms. The fabrics were the same color as the stone walls with accent pillows of bright colors. At the time I'd thought of his house like the pictures I'd seen of a bright red rose in an all-white room. The color just explodes in your eye. I'd thought the style Danish or Norwegian, but I now realized, the furnishings weren't a style so much as few in number and generally built-into the house.

Seeing Hugh in this rustic setting gave me pause. He'd demonstrated tendencies in that Malibu house he realized in the simplicity of his log cabin. The house had been perfect for a person who didn't buy into the whole Hollywood excess lifestyle, but used it to his advantage. As I said, his parties were legendary and anyone in Hollywood not invited wasn't anyone. I'd attended the last two, but only because, I'm sure, I was then the star of a new show with a growing audience.

"You're wondering why, aren't you?" Hugh asked as he ladled vegetable stew into a bowl and passed it to me.

"You were kind to invite me."

Hugh smiled in remembrance. "My Gatsby nights. That's what I called them."

I was amazed we both connected his parties to F. Scott Fitzgerald's novel. "Everyone you invited attended." I noted.

"Everyone in Hollywood loved for me to spend my money on them," he laughed. "If you remember I greeted everyone and disappeared until people started to leave."

"Where did you go?" Mimi inquired. She'd never been invited.

"I had a hide-a-way. I was there. I watched, but I wasn't a part of the revelry."

Yes, very Gatsby, I thought. *What was his Daisy?*

"Why not?" Alistair inquired, evidently as curious as I.

"I never wanted to be a part of all the Hollywood glitz. Didn't believe in it. But it was what was expected if you wanted to work in that town. You know I didn't live in my Malibu house. I had a very simple apartment in Culver City. That's all I needed, but everyone had to believe I lived in the lap of luxury. So as someone who created illusions for mass consumption, I created one about myself so I'd be accepted and permitted to work."

"What drove you to produce sitcoms?" Mimi showed her curiosity as well.

"I wasn't driven, I was kind of dropped off at the curb. If you go back to my earliest work it was all serious stories. Tales of danger and redemption. But nobody watched. And then I met Jeremy Stewart and he changed my life and my fortunes."

Jeremy Stewart was the star of his sitcom series. "So Jeremy had the ideas for your shows?"

"Jeremy had great ideas, but couldn't translate them into producible scripts or shows. We were introduced by a mutual friend at a party. We started talking and I told him I'd seen his standup routine and thought him very funny. He asked how I'd stage his sense of humor. I gave him some flippant response and thought it was time to go talk to someone important. He resonated with my concept and wouldn't let me leave. We ended up talking the rest of the evening. That's how it all happened. A casual conversation at someone else's party."

"Is that why you gave the parties?" Mimi asked, guessing. "Give others an opportunity to make the same kind of connections?"

Hugh looked at Mimi as if looking through her. "Maybe subconsciously. But they started out as something to create buzz about me. Jeremy and I wanted to start our own production company. We were going to need a lot of help and financial backing to get started. So the first party was more something to draw attention to us and give us a chance to pitch our idea to a whole bunch of possible backers. When word got out about how lavish it had been, everyone wanted to be invited the next time we did it. So we did, invite nearly everyone. From there it just got out of hand."

"People talked about it for weeks before and after." Alistair noted.

"Funny, how things like a party are what people most remember about someone, not the things I produced, or the people for whom I created jobs, or the impact of helping millions of people to laugh at themselves." Hugh reflected and shared with us.

"What are you most proud of?" I asked trying to get a sense of the contradictions he displayed.

Hugh raised the glass of homemade wine, inhaled the aroma and gave the glass a slight swirl considering his answer before speaking. "Ask me when I'm on my deathbed."

"Are you not proud of your many accomplishments?" Mimi tried to interpret Hugh's response.

He looked at her as he answered, "I hope I'm not looking back at a career and all my accomplishments are behind me."

"Are you working on a new project?" Alistair asked, trying to follow Hugh's point.

"Always. Many projects. Everyday."

"Would you be willing to share what they are?" Alistair again.

Hugh pushed his half empty bowl of stew away and dropped his spoon in it with a clang. "Am I working on another show? No. Am I doing anything with Hollywood? No."

"What about Bollywood? A number of Hollywood people have been working projects there recently." Alistair commented.

Hugh laughed a slight laugh. "People from Hollywood who work in Bollywood are only doing it because they can't get work here. No. I'm not doing anything you'd recognize from my previous career. And that's why I don't think you'd be interested."

What's he trying to tell us? Why won't he say? I wondered. "Are you keeping track of what's going on in the wider world these days?"

"I came up here to get away from the wider world."

"So you're not curious?" I continued.

"The world can take care of itself without any further contributions to the sitcom genre from me."

Another response that avoided the question and steered me away. "Is that how you define yourself? A contributor to the sitcom genre? You practically reinvented it with Jeremy's show."

"People move through phases. I was a contributor. I was an innovator. I was successful beyond anything I could have imagined when I went to Hollywood. But I chose to move beyond that phase of my life. That isn't me anymore. I don't have any desire to return to Hollywood, my former life or make any further contributions to that art form."

"How would you describe your new phase?" Mimi bailed me out.

"Exciting. I'm living on my terms. I'm not beholding to anyone else. I'm not living my life according to their expectations. I'm perfectly content to be alone with Mother Nature providing for my needs. There aren't many who can say that. From what I remember, it seemed the race was on to see who could be the first to buy out an entire shopping mall of material goods, whether needed or not. One of the things I remember was walking through the Santa Monica mall, looking at all the stuff in one shopping center and then realizing there were tens of thousands of such shopping centers across the world. Just how much stuff that represented was inconceivable to me. We didn't need it, but we wanted it. Why? Not because it was essential to our lives, but because we had been sold an image of ourselves with those 'things' we really didn't need. I couldn't be a part of a consumer society. I needed to get back to nature, to simplicity. To healthy living, free from want and free from another's imposed definition of need."

"No hints about what we can look forward to from your place here high upon a mountain?" Mimi asked. Better her than me.

"My hope is you won't hear from me again." He raised his glass, to toast his concept.

We raised ours and clinked glasses. "To peace and understanding." I said.

Hugh didn't drink to that, but said instead, "To freedom." He then raised his glass again and finally took a sip when we had clinked glasses again.

Chapter Fifty-Five

We left Hugh Aguirre's camp about four o'clock. The walk down was much easier than the walk up. The Tesla waited for us right where we'd left it. I had no doubt it would be there as we'd seen no one else since we left the highway some nine miles down the mountain.

Once in the car Alistair vented. "That ungrateful son-of-a-bitch. After all Hollywood did for him, to just walk away from it all, taking his talent and experience. That just frosts me. You know? Jeremy disappeared when Hugh did. Not in the literal sense. He tried to get another show going, but without Hugh's sensibilities, Jeremy just couldn't find anyone else who could translate his humor the way Hugh did. So Jeremy's done. He has no place to go now."

"He should go back to standup." I suggested.

"I've talked with him. He would, you know. Do standup. But he thinks he should do it in a football stadium with tens of thousands watching. It doesn't work. I've tried to explain to him a big piece of his humor is physical. People have to see his face. They have to understand the joke's on Jeremy and not the person Jeremy's character thinks it's on. You don't get that if you can't see his face. Television was perfect for him. Close up on Jeremy. But when you go to a stadium, even with a Jumbo Tron, you lose the intimacy needed for the humor to work."

"Did Jeremy come to you?" Mimi asked, surprised Alistair would have been talking with him, knowing his agent was much higher in their partnership.

"He did. Jackson told him to retire. Suggested Jeremy had a great ride, had more money than God and should just go and enjoy all his money. Jeremy didn't agree and came to see me."

"Why you? No disrespect, but you don't handle clients like him."

"With your current numbers I'm number one in the agency." Alistair beamed.

"Do I hear a private Lamborghini coming when we get the code working?" I kidded him.

"I'm more of a Porsche Panamera kind of guy." Alistair pushed back at my comment.

"So what did you tell Jeremy?" I came back to the original question Alistair hadn't answered.

"That he needed to reinvent himself. Much like what you and Mimi have done. You've become the reality stars of the century. Not something I ever thought would happen."

"Nor me." I responded.

"What's he doing?" Mimi asked.

"He's taking pitches from directors who want to work with him. Somebody comes up with a concept he can buy into, and a relationship he thinks will work, he'll go sell it. People are still receptive because his series was tops for so long, but he's only got two, maybe three chances before people will stop listening."

Typical Alistair. He knew Hollywood. He knew no matter how successful you were, today's audience is not yesterdays. What people want to see today is different than what they wanted to see last year. Everything has to continually be new or no one will care to watch. Jeremy was on top of the world for a decade, and now no one cared. He'd had his run. What could he do to make money for me today? And it was all about the money. A great series that didn't attract sponsor advertising would never be seen. And what sponsors would pay for changed almost weekly. Everyone wanted to ride the hot horse, but no one knew from one season to the next what series that might be. Once the series made it, the sponsors that helped them get there were in. Those that had stayed on the sidelines were out, unless they ponied up a whole lot more money than most people would just to get their message in front of that many eyeballs.

"Wasn't that just a great meal." Mimi was done discussing Jeremy Stewart.

"One of the best meals I can remember." I responded.

"Any meal is unforgettable at the moment." Alistair tried to put our discussion back into context, but that wasn't what Mimi was trying to say.

"Would have been regardless of the current situation, Alistair." She sniped back.

"Probably. But we really didn't learn anything helpful." Alistair saw the meeting as a failure. Hugh hadn't talked about survivalists as a group. Didn't react to the Hamartia comment. But the simple fact he didn't react was significant as far as I was concerned. He didn't dismiss them. He simply didn't respond other than to show he knew the reference in Greek tragedy.

"Did you expect he was going to give us the cell number of the leader of the Hamartia?" I asked.

"No. But I didn't hear anything other than he was happy living alone on the top of a mountain. Did you?"

"It's not what we heard, so much as it's what he didn't say." I responded.

"Like why he has solar panels and a satellite dish when he never showed anything they'd be used for." Mimi knew where I was going.

Alistair raised his eyebrows. "You're right. He never did. I guess I just assumed he was watching sitcoms to see where things had gone."

"That may be what he's doing, although he was pretty emphatic about not going back." Mimi noted.

"He said he wasn't watching the news." Alistair responded.

"Not how I remember his response. He said the world can take care of itself and then tied it to further contributions to the sitcom genre. He didn't answer the question. He has access." I pointed out.

"The satellite dish?" Alistair wanted to confirm.

I nodded. "I'm with Mimi. He could have shown us what he's doing with his solar panels and satellite dish, but he kept talking about how he was living off the grid, when he's actually still plugged in to what's going on."

"What do you make of the day with him, then?" Mimi asked.

"I'm reserving judgment. He may be what he tried to communicate to us. A guy disaffected with what it takes to make it in Hollywood. But on the other hand, the fact he didn't show us what he's doing with his communications systems leaves questions on the table." I responded.

"But you didn't learn what we all went up there to learn." Alistair continued.

"About the Hamartia? No. We didn't learn anything. But I'm also not about to write off the trip. I wouldn't be surprised your friend knows something about what's going on in the world. Even though he professes not to. Is he involved in any way? I can't tell. Not enough information to this point. But he could clearly communicate with folks if he chose to do so with the equipment he's deployed."

"But is he?" Mimi asked.

Alistair dissented, "I think the electric cells and satellite dish are to let him interact with the people who are looking for a mentor. You know, the new directors and producers coming up. I think he's communicating with them about what worked for him and what didn't. I think he's giving them the same advice he's offered to us."

"Which is?" Mimi wasn't going to let Alistair generalize.

"That he's not coming back. That today's audience doesn't want to see what they did in the last five years. Today's audience want's something new and they expect to be served just that."

"Alistair, if this were only a Hollywood conversation, I wouldn't disagree with you. You know how the town works much better than I do. But in this case, we're not dealing with a Hollywood story. We're dealing with someone who's fucked with the whole world." Mimi was getting angry.

"Hollywood has established the agenda for liberalization over the past fifty years. We're much more influential than any other media." Alistair said proudly.

"What has Hollywood's liberalization bought us? Genetically modified foods that are killing us? Every time government pushes an agenda it's exactly the wrong one for the county." Mimi noted. "The only ones pushing legislation through Congress are the special interests who stand to make millions off the taxpayer." Mimi wasn't about to let him off the hook.

"The exact people liberals want out of government." Alistair responded.

"And the same people who contribute to the liberal's re-election campaigns, to ensure they get the rewards they're looking for. The liberals and the conservatives have been bought by the same interests, only they drive to the same point from the opposite ends of the spectrum. The only thing that results is those special interests continue to feed at the public's expense. It doesn't end, Alistair. It just goes on and on, regardless of who we elect. That's the conundrum of the modern political state."

Alistair wasn't prepared for Mimi's tirade, thinking she must be a good democrat since she works in Hollywood.

"Ronald Reagan worked here too, Alistair." I reminded him.

"Wasn't he a democrat?"

"Hugh Aguirre may be just what he seems. A disaffected man who left what was repulsive to him behind. But on the other hand, he may know more than he shared. We must keep looking and if something comes back this way, we pay another visit." I summarized.

Chapter Fifty-Six

Silmara's standup call started off slower than usual. Everyone seemed at a low energy level. Dyllan and Bomani sounded discouraged about making progress on cracking the virus code. They'd tried everything they could think of and much more. Nothing seemed to be getting them any closer to breaking it.

"I have nothing." Kalindi responded.

"Nothing?" I responded. "You've not learned anything about anyone? Nothing that could eliminate someone from consideration. Nothing that could further implicate someone we've been looking closely at, like the three Hamartia groups?"

"We still don't even know if they're related to each other, let alone the Hamartia." She responded to me, sounding defensive.

"What do we need to do to answer the question?" I challenged her.

"Dyllan and I have been asking ourselves that very question." She responded.

"Dyllan?" I went right to the source.

"She is right. I do not know what will link them. The website does not. We have not been able to trace the communications they have established because they are on a private virtual network and the carriers have no records of who they are in touch with. All the privacy legislation in the last two decades has made it much harder to gather information."

"Xian?" I asked.

"China not participate. True. But hard get information."

"But you will." I challenged my old friend, knowing he would find a way.

"Try. No guarantee."

Classic Xian. Always leaving a way out. But he'd never failed to get sensitive information in the past to help us understand a situation we were creating an episode around.

"What's the situation with the virus, Bomani? You sounded frustrated, but where have you gone off the rails?"

"The key is elusive."

"Are you spending too much time on the key?" I asked.

"What do you mean?"

"Have you looked at alternative software approaches? Something that might replace the control systems rather than find a way to reopen the existing software?"

"Are you suggesting we simply delete the control systems and wholesale replace it with something else?" Dyllan sounded angry, like I was suggesting heresy.

"If closing out the virus is a problem, what's the next shortest route to resuming Googlecar operations? A new control system might solve the problem quicker. You seem to have come to a stonewall you've not been able to get over. So move on. Find another way."

"I seem to remember a software system developed by a competitor company that was never used." Dyllan had more knowledge about the history than I expected.

"Who developed it?"

"Microsoft."

"I'd go take a look and see what the issues would be to delete the existing systems altogether and reboot with the Microsoft software."

Dyllan seemed resistant to the idea. "What?" I asked.

"Microsoft and Google were like oil and water when the software was being developed. They took entirely different paths to get there. Not sure the Microsoft software would work with the hardware configurations deployed and evolved over the years."

"Test it." Was my challenge.

"Can do that, but I'll predict it won't work. Google was very thorough. I can't see them developing a system that would work with a competitive software."

"Test it." I insisted.

"What else? How are we doing with the other alternative groups we've been looking at?"

Kalindi saw I wasn't going to take no progress as an answer and apparently Silmara wasn't going to protect anyone from my tirade. "Each party we examine has a political motive and agenda. But when we dive into their capabilities, we come up blank on virus development."

"You could say the same for the Hamartia." I observed.

"We are saying the same for the Hamartia. But they have resources we've not been able to penetrate so far. The other groups are more transparent in terms of their capabilities."

"Who would you say are you top five suspects?" I asked.

Silmara answered for her team. "The Russians are the top suspects. They have very highly developed software capabilities, but we have been studying them for decades. We know their signatures. Nothing they have ever done in the past comes remotely close to the approach of this virus. It is so atypical we have difficulty believing they are responsible."

"Next?"

"The Chinese."

Xian answered, "Not come from China. Confirmed."

"Who next?"

"North Korea."

"Maybe the most probable, except they do not have a history of successfully planting such a virus on a global scale. So far they have had one off successes. But I would be amazed if they have been able to take such a leap." Silmara summarized.

"After them, Iran?" I suggested remembering the earlier brief. Always nation states and I doubted any nation state was responsible, although I could definitely be wrong, after all, I was only an actor and not a seasoned diplomat. But I read the media. I formed opinions based on what the experts wrote in the various media. Could I really be that wrong?

"Yes. Probably more capable of planting a virus than North Korea, but they have had limited success outside of hacking. They have only seemed interested in learning what we know, not in trying to bring down the global order."

"Have you listened to the Ayatollah recently?" I asked not agreeing.

"Our analysts have been studying his pronouncements, if that's what you mean." Kalindi jumped in. "The Ayatollah is an expert at deception. He says one thing in public and something very different when behind closed doors."

Kalindi's comment made me reflect on the visit with Hugh Aguirre. He'd said he became an expert at illusion. I wondered. "What would Iran's motivation be to release such a virus when it had nearly as severe an effect on their own country as ours?" I asked.

"Their motivation is to bring the west to its knees. To once and for all time rid themselves of our media, or multinationals and our foreign policy in their neighborhood. I think of all the candidates Iran is the one most likely to have unleashed this virus, not understanding the effect it was going to have on their own people." Kalindi summarized.

I couldn't argue with Kalindi on her observation, but I still doubted a nation state was behind the event. "If so, why aren't they number one on your list rather than Russia?"

Silmara answered, which surprised me since she never overrode Kalindi, "We are aware of restraining forces in the government that do not exist in Russia. While the public leadership of Iran is bellicose, we are working with moderates who have been able to restrain the vocal elements of their society, at least to this point. Those moderate elements assure us their government is as worried about the current events as we and are working to discover who and why, just as we are."

"So who's left?" I asked pondering Silmara's summary.

"Syria." She answered. The same five as before we joined the team. We'd not changed a thing other than to get them to look at the Hamartia. But behind closed doors they were still carrying out the whole response aimed at finding the country responsible. Was that so the President could send in cruise missiles and hope that caused the Googlecars to suddenly start working? A flawed strategy from my vantage point.

"And what's your analysis there?" I asked.

"Syrians rely on Iran and the Russians. They are not as disciplined about their efforts, but that also means they are more likely to do something the others would not. If anything, the Syrians are the wild card. They would like to make a statement about being able to bring down the American nation without setting foot on your soil. But on the other hand, they have both the Russians and Iranians telling them what and what not to do. I believe they may have been responsible just to show the Russians and Iranians they can do something on this scale. But at the moment, I can't say it's them."

Chapter Fifty-Seven

Kareem and Pete waited for us outside the station house. That told me they were finished with their interrogations of James Finch, Sherice Novak and Alice Wheeler. If they were finished they had apparently come to the conclusion they'd be obtaining no further information from them in the short run. They needed time behind bars to let their discomfort age a bit.

"Evening. You have a nice day?" I asked.

"Alice sends her regards." Kareem responded as he closed the door on the Tesla.

"And how is Miss Alice?" I responded.

"Screaming entrapment. Insists we set her up and her neighbors couldn't possibly have positively identified Finch as having come out of her apartment with a suitcase. She's convinced we told them about the suitcase and they just agreed."

"Wait." I responded, "She told us Ollie Wilson left like an hour before we got there carrying the suitcase."

"Neighbors say it wasn't him. They knew him by sight. Finch, they'd not seen before and the description is real close for all the witnesses." Pete explained and Kareem nodded agreement.

"Glad you had a great day. Miss Sherice. She more cooperative?"

"Completely, although she insists you planted that missile on James Finch. No possible way could he have done what you said he did."

"You show her the video Walt took?" I asked.

"She insists you had that modified. Some other person you caught, but now you're trying to frame James. She insists she told you Oliver Wilson is the guy you need to find. He took all the missiles. She has no idea what he did with them, but he's the guy who had them last."

"Glad these stand up law abiding characters want us to get this arrest right."

"Really." Kareem agreed.

"So where we off to tonight?" I asked.

"Report that someone matching Oliver Wilson's appearance was seen over on Wilshire near MacArthur Park Lake. Need to cruise the area and see what we find. As we check out the area, we'll stop by and chat with the woman who called in the sighting."

"Saw his mug shot on Television?" I asked.

"Looked him up on the web after a broadcast. Insists it has to be the same guy."

We headed for Wilshire and we slowly drove the area all the way over to LaBrea and the Tar Pits. Nothing.

"Okay, where is this upstanding citizen we're trying to find?"

"Lives on South Park View Street. Said she was walking in the park when she saw him."

I drove to the house of Britney Sommes. We exited the Tesla about a block away and walked back up, not wanting to call any more attention to our visit than necessary.

"Miss Sommes?" Kareem asked as a slender woman in her early

thirties answered the door. She had long black hair and a nice top and slacks. Not someone who I'd have imagined would turn in a police report.

"Yes. You LAPD?"

Kareem showed her his identification. "May we come in?"

"Of course."

I scanned the neighborhood as we all entered her well-kept single story home. Everything inside was picked up and neat. Not much for decorations, she showed us into her living room. Kareem and Pete sat down, but Walt, Mimi and I stood near the door as Walt recorded everything.

"What did you see, Miss Sommes?" Kareem started the questioning.

"Your Mister Wilson. No question about it. He was in a hurry, walking through the park along the north side of the lake. Heading towards South Alvarado Street."

"What were you doing?" Kareem continued.

"I was on my way home. I often go over on that side of the park to walk along the lake. It's just a peaceful walk on a nice day like today."

"What do you do?"

"I'm in the department of Forensic Psychology at UCLA."

"Professor?" Kareem made an assumption.

"Graduate assistant. I'm finishing up my degree this semester, finally."

"How did you know it was Oliver Wilson?" Kareem continued.

"I saw the news story he was wanted and googled him. I have an excellent memory and when he passed me I looked up. Recognized him immediately. He looked right at me, but kept on going.

"Where did you lose sight of him?" Pete this time.

"When he crossed South Alvarado. A car stopped and picked him up."

"What kind of car?" Pete continued. Seemed to want to change up the questioning.

"Old beat up white Toyota pickup. The real small one, don't know the model name."

"Did you get a license plate?" Kareem now.

She shook her head. "Too far away."

"He head north or south?" Kareem continued.

"Went up and turned south on Wilshire."

I had to ask a question, "What was he wearing?"

"White shirt with some kind of logo on it, he didn't turn enough for me to be able to read it. Blue jeans and work boots. Oh yeah, a brown belt."

"Clean shaven?" I continued.

"No. Not a beard or anything, but maybe a couple day's growth. Reddish tinge."

"Hair color?" From Mimi now. We all had to get into this since it was going out tonight.

"Brown but the facial hair had a red tinge. Didn't match. Made me think he'd dyed his hair."

Kareem nodded to Pete, "Call that in. See if anything pops up."

"Is there anything else you can tell us about Mister Wilson?" Mimi asked.

"Nothing other than he was in a big hurry to get somewhere. A real fast walker."

"Thank you Miss Sommes." Kareem concluded.

We walked back to the Tesla. "What do you think?" I asked Kareem.

"Sounds like the dude. Glad you asked about what he was wearing, matched what we know."

"And she wouldn't have known that as it hadn't been released. So he had an accomplice who picked him up." I noted.

"What kind of vehicle did Finch have?" Mimi asked.

"None that we found, but the Super at his apartment said he took him to his storage unit in his pickup. Think we need to go pay him a return visit." I suggested.

We drove back to Wilson's apartment house and I found the super right where I'd found him the first time.

"You find Wilson?" the super inquired as I walked into his office.

"No, but you gave him a ride about three hours ago."

"You outta your mind? I ain't seen him since I told ya when."

"Witness saw you pick him up by MacArthur Lake, corner South Alvarado and Wilshire."

"Wasn't me. Been here all day."

"Lock up. You're coming downtown with us." I motioned to him to come along.

The super looked behind himself and then gave me a thumb gesture towards his apartment directly behind him.

Kareem and Pete followed me, with Walt trailing, catching everything on film.

Wilson sat at the small breakfast table next to the back door. He was wearing the white shirt with Security Electronics Systems logo, Blue jeans and work shoes, just as Britney Sommes had described him. When I came in, he broke for the door.

I instantly reacted, launching myself into the door to keep him from getting out. Wilson turned into me, grabbing my shirt and trying to throw me back into the room, but I jammed my shoulder into his midsection and drove him back against the kitchen sink. He pounded on my back, but Kareem and Pete were on him, showing their ID and reading his rights.

"Oliver Wilson. You have the right to remain silent…" but Ollie wasn't interested in his rights.

"I been framed." Was his opening defense.

Chapter Fifty-Eight

Silmara began the videoconference with a question: "Now that you have both James Finch and Oliver Wilson in custody, what have you been able to learn about the Googlecar Repair Depot bombings?"

"Wilson didn't know we had Finch." I began. "That was helpful because when we told him Finch gave him up and helped us find him he seemed more amenable to talking. He's answered some questions, but adamantly insists he didn't take the weapons. His story is that Finch did and Sherice Novak is covering for Finch."

"What do you think? That a plausible story?" Silmara responded.

"Plausible from the perspective that Sherice was living with Finch and we have witnesses saying they saw Finch carrying the suitcase containing the missile from Alice Wheeler's apartment."

"Any motive yet?" Silmara was driving this part of the discussion.

"No." I responded. "I'm convinced someone else set the whole thing up and they were just the people recruited to carry it out. Don't think they fired the weapons in the other cities. Probably shipped the weapons by bus. Less likely to be detected."

"If they give you anything, we need to know right away." She finished with me. "Bomani, what's happening with the code?"

"We have the Microsoft code and are experimenting with it. As we thought it wasn't a plug and play, but early indications are the conversion may not be as difficult as thought. We have engineers from both Microsoft and Googlecars working it."

"Estimated time to completion?"

"No more than a week."

"And how long to bring the Googlecar fleet back up?"

"That is the hard part." Dyllan answered. "Right now we would have to go do a manual deletion and uploading from a thumb drive on each vehicle individually. We have another team from the Defense Department working on a bulk load approach. We hope, if their technology works, to be able to do it all at once, remotely. The delicate part of all this is the tool they would use does not technically exist. If they use it no one can know how we did it or that the Defense Department was involved. It will be a bit tricky, we have a team from the US Transportation Department working on it. I think we will be able to work it out."

"No further progress on the existing code?"

"Nothing significant." Bomani answered. "Another strand, but it still has no effect in overcoming the shutdown messaging."

"Kalindi?"

"I have a report that Desmond and Mimi met with a retired producer/director named Hugh Aguirre."

"That's right." I answered, not wanting to go into any detail. "A friend said he might know something about the psychology of the Hamartia."

"Why would this man have knowledge of the Hamartia?" Silmara wasn't pleased I hadn't mentioned the meeting.

"Mr. Aguirre retired to a log cabin in the mountains near Los Angeles after a successful career. My agent knew where the cabin was, although few do. My agent thought Mr. Aguirre might be able to give us some insight into..."

"Did he?" Kalindi interrupted.

"Aguirre know Deng." Xian broke in.

"Deng?" I repeated having no idea who Xian was talking about.

"Deng Lo Minh."

Xian providing the full name sparked my recollection. "A Chinese Director. I've heard of him."

"What's the significance?" Silmara again.

"Deng disappear same time Aguirre." Xian put pieces together.

"Disappear?" Silmara didn't like the sound of this and I had to explain.

"Deng retired about seven or eight years ago. At least he hasn't made any films since then. But I hadn't heard he 'disappeared.' I think he's still in Beijing, isn't he Xian?"

"Disappear. No one talk."

"I didn't know that." I clarified.

"That's the same time Raj Thyagaraj moved to Tibet or Mongolia, I forget which." Kalindi added to the fire.

"Three movie directors all retired about the same time and moved away from where they made their films. What's so unusual about that?" I asked too soon.

"Genre." Xian pointed out.

Then it hit me. "I understand, Xian. I'm sorry, I didn't put two and two together. Deng produced apocalyptic stories of unsustainable technology. Thyagaraj made films about ecoterrorism."

"What about your Mister Aguirre?"

"He did sitcoms on television. Ever watch Jeremy Stewart?" Mimi answered.

"He doesn't seem to fit in with the others." Silmara responded.

"They were all friends. I continued. Aguirre said he knew nothing about the Hamartia and that a lot of people have chosen to move away from the cities. He gave us nothing specific we could use. No insights, no gossip of plots amongst the survivalists. No reason why someone might attempt to bring down society. That's why I didn't bother to report it. There was nothing of value that came out of the conversation."

"Do you still feel that way in light of the Deng and Thyagaraj information?" Kalindi saw an opportunity to bring me down in Silmara's eyes.

"For the moment, yes. However, in light of this additional information I'm sure we'll go back and take a longer look at Hugh Aguirre, Deng and Thyagaraj together."

"Not a high priority." Silmara began. "But please advise us of other people you are going to question. As you see there are sometimes networks we might be aware of your person of interest might belong to. We might be able to give you some questions you should ask. I'm sure Kalindi will review what our threat databases can tell us about these three men, although I doubt we will learn anything of significance."

The call ended shortly thereafter. Silmara gave us the usual admonitions about needing to push hard to solutions. We can't wait another week as the death toll kept mounting exponentially from starvation and lack of medicines to fight disease and infections.

Mimi wouldn't look at me when I turned to her. "What's the matter?"

"I just remembered something and don't know how to tell you."

"What?" I responded.

"I was young then."

"What are you talking about?"

"Raj and I slept together when I made Desperation. He was the director. First major film with a big budget. He interviewed me for the part I got as Desdemona."

"I really liked you in that film."

"But Raj said I had to sleep with him. It was the only way he could capture a sense of my spirit and know if I was right for the part."

"I understand. Your first major role. You did what you had to." What's the big deal?

"Not the point. Raj talked a lot when asleep." Mimi really didn't want to tell me this.

"You stayed the night?" I was surprised knowing how when Mimi and I first got together she never would stay with me.

"He insisted. In his sleep he said people had approached him. They had the key to 'changing the world'. I didn't think much about it then. Nothing happened. Thought it was a dream."

"And the men who approached him were…"

"I didn't put it together until just now, but Hugh Aguirre and Deng Lo Minh were two of the names, I'm sure."

"There were others." I realized.

Chapter Fifty-Nine

Silmara called only Kalindi, as she did every day. "I need to know about the relationship between Desmond and Mimi."

Kalindi thought it a strange request. "Why?"

"Something doesn't add up," was all Silmara would say.

"And you wish not to tell me of your concerns? It would certainly help me to ask the right questions." Kalindi had little use for Mimi. Couldn't understand why she was permitted to join the team. But at the same time an internal affairs type of investigation meant something had come to Silmara's attention. The fact that several members of the team were not law enforcement officers meant the usual investigations organizations didn't have authority to conduct one. But Kalindi's real concern was Silmara might want to investigate Dyllan since Desmond brought him to the team. Being an Emirati she had no idea what might turn up in an investigation. She also didn't want to be asked to investigate him, afraid he would never understand if it came to light.

"I need to understand the dynamics of my team. If there is a weak link, or someone with a different agenda, I need to know what it is. I cannot be effective if someone is deliberately blocking, slowing or attempting to thwart our work."

"And you think Desmond or Mimi is a mole?"

"Not necessarily a mole, but someone who might have been influenced to support a different agenda and working behind the scenes to make it reality."

"That makes no sense. No one could have predicted Desmond or Mimi would have been in a position to join this team. They're actors." Kalindi wanted to make Silmara understand her fears were remote possibilities. She never thought she'd defend Desmond.

"But they did not tell me about meeting with Aguirre. And then Xian brought up Deng and you identified Thyagaraj. Are they trying to hide something from us? How did you learn of the meeting?"

Kalindi didn't want to tell her, but felt she had no choice. "Dyllan mentioned it."

"Have you been able to help him with the code segments?"

Kalindi knew Silmara noted she was having separate conversations with Dyllan when there didn't appear to be a reason for her to do so. Dyllan was working the code, not the perpetrators. Kalindi expected to start getting comments about staying focused on her task, but knew Silmara wouldn't comment further on it today. "We've exchanged ideas both ways."

"How are you feeling about Desmond and Mimi finding the bombers?"

"Proximity. The perpetrators are in Los Angeles. Desmond and Mimi are in Los Angeles. If I lived in Los Angeles I might have been more involved."

"But they didn't coordinate with you, did they? Did you know what they were doing? Did you guide them? Did they give you intelligence before taking action, or get help from you at all?"

Kalindi understood Silmara was holding her responsible. "No. I had no idea they were working the bombing angle. We still don't know if there is a relationship between the bombings and the virus. None of the individuals apprehended have a background in virus or software development. They do not appear to have connections with anyone who would. So while you may see the seeds of a conspiracy, I am not ready to make that connection. Not yet anyway. But I hear what you are suggesting and will look into it."

"It is important you do. So what is your fascination with Dyllan?"

Kalindi couldn't believe Silmara had come right out and asked about Dyllan. She was never direct about anything. *She must be under enormous pressure to be chasing phantoms.* Kalindi noted to herself before responding. "We seem to see the world through a similar set of eyes."

"He's an Emirati, for God's sake."

Silmara never swore and to take the Lord's name in vein, a good Catholic like her, that was just unheard of. A lot more pressure than Kalindi realized. "A very intelligent Emirati."

"He will never be able to satisfy you." Silmara came right to the point. *What is going on? She is never like this.*

"That depends on what I want him to satisfy. He can be soulful in a way I've never seen in a man before. Maybe his situation is the reason. I do not know. But we seem to relate on many levels. We share a way of looking at things. We are not exactly the same, but our values are aligned, as strange as that seems for a Muslim and a Hindu. Maybe we have grown up in a secular world and we bridge our world views there. I do not know. But we value the same things. We are both concerned more for family than ourselves. We have both overcome handicaps of very different kinds, but we have overcome them nonetheless. I don't know the answer to your question. I don't want to know it. I only know that I can't get enough time with him, talking, laughing and sharing what we know of the world."

"I see what you have described." Silmara began. "And it is good you have found someone with whom you can share what is important to you. But I must remind you that you are an officer of the law. Dyllan is not. You must not reveal what you know of the situation to him carte blanc. He could be the one who is working with the perpetrators. That would explain why our team has failed to achieve a solution…"

Kalindi found herself exactly where she didn't want to be. "Bomani would know if Dyllan was an obstacle. Have you asked him?"

"Every day."

"And the answer you get back is?"

"No. Bomani believes Dyllan is brilliant, as you say. He seems to take personally the failure of the team to solve the problem. He has worked through the night on a promising approach and never becomes discouraged. Although Bomani says he is not working as quickly as before. It seems to Bomani that while not discouraged, Dyllan has slowed down to make sure he explores the right possibilities, rather than charging headlong down a rabbit hole."

"Rabbit hole?" Kalindi asked not sure where that comparison came from.

"That was what Bomani said. I asked him and he admitted he heard it from Desmond and thought it an interesting visual when Desmond referred him to 'Through the Looking Glass.'"

"Did Bomani read the book?"

"He hasn't had time, but said he intends to when our crisis is over." Silmara confirmed.

Kalindi wasn't sure what she needed to do at this point. Silmara knew she liked Dyllan and had tried to warn her off. Kalindi wasn't quite sure why Silmara was concerned other than the differences in culture and religion. But Kalindi knew Silmara was aware her comment wouldn't change a thing. Kalindi would continue to talk with Dyllan and hope they would find a way to meet in person when the current crisis was over, which they were both dedicated to making happen soon. Silmara was on a witch hunt, to use another curious western expression. She had read all about witches. Thought westerners were superstitious in a way she could not appreciate. But it was something she constantly came back to when dealing with them. Now Dyllan, on the other hand, was closer to her belief structure, but still, as a non-Hindu, not quite there. Could she ever want a relationship with a westerner like Desmond? She was curious, but she knew the answer would be no. From what she had seen, Desmond viewed the world very differently than she did. He was an actor, trying to be something he wasn't. What he wanted to be was what she was. She thought the situation ironic. Everyone knew who Desmond was. He was probably the most famous policeman in the world. And yet he wasn't a policeman at all. She on the other hand, was a policeman, and few would ever know she even existed. She would solve the mystery, but Desmond would get the credit because he was on television. He had name recognition. But the more she thought about the situation, she had to admit that Desmond was earning any recognition that would follow. He had taken the Googlecar Repair Depot suspects into custody, even capturing and thwarting one in the act. He wasn't a cop, but he was walking in their shoes.

"So what is the problem we need to focus on today?" Kalindi finally asked after what had become a long silence between them. It was the longest she could remember.

"I don't want you to get hurt when Dyllan disappears once this ends." Silmara answered.

"He won't." Kalindi was confident.

"I hope you are right, but I have seen too many romances forged by the heat of a crisis that fail when the cold light of day finally casts its shadows on the daily life we all lead."

"Are you speaking from experience?" Kalindi finally understood the interest in Desmond, Dyllan and Kalindi's relationship.

"I only want the best for you." Silmara wouldn't comment on her own situation.

"So tell me, why do you really want to know what's going on between Desmond and Mimi?"

345

"I read they used to be a couple, but broke up more than a year ago."

Chapter Sixty

Xian's call came early. He knew my schedule started late, and yet what he wanted to talk about apparently couldn't wait. "Desmond."

"Yes, Xian. I'm here." I said groggily, not quite awake, still lying on my couch, which I'd not yet been able to find a comfortable way of sleeping upon.

"Late in day. You engage. Bad guys not wait."

"The Hamartia?" I responded.

"Not Hamartia. Much closer home."

Xian got my attention. I shook my head to clear my thoughts. "Not the Hamartia?"

"Watch back."

Mimi came out of the bedroom, wearing the same white shift that showed everything I remembered when she wasn't wearing anything. That part of me that often thought for itself began to stir. I didn't want her to see it at full attention. Not the message I wanted to send as I knew how she would respond. And it wouldn't be favorable. So I turned my back to her, which I knew also wasn't a good idea, but it had to be the lesser of two not so good situations.

Mimi didn't seem to notice as she went straight for the pot of hot water I'd brewed for her in my coffee maker. Since I had no coffee, it was the best I could do, knowing her addiction to early morning caffeine.

Mimi poured herself a cup and came over to sit on the couch across from me, warming herself both inside from sipping and her hands from the cup itself. I'm sure she noticed my erection, but she said nothing and listened as Xian and I continued the conversation.

"Why should I be watching my back, Xian?"

"Heads of state not happy."

"About the lack of results? We caught the bombers."

"People dying."

"Yes, there's that too." I admitted. But the heads of state had to have been briefed on just how difficult this problem had proven to be.

"Silmara on short rope."

"Have they given her a deadline? That's what I've been expecting."

"Unknown."

"Your concern is they might pull the plug and put someone else in charge."

"Probable now."

I didn't want to see Silmara replaced. She'd been the victim of bad luck. I was sure she'd been successful in the past. Had to have been to be in her role. The top dogs only put people into place who they have confidence can succeed. Silmara had that confidence. But she'd not been able to deliver what everyone wanted. A quick end of the crisis. Silmara had been unfortunate to be given the opportunity to succeed against an opponent who'd changed the rules of the game. That is if we even understood the nature of the game that was being played. Silmara would be remembered as a trail blazer in law enforcement circles and as someone who failed to quickly restore order in the Great Googlecar Crisis amongst the general public.

"Any idea who?" I had to ask, although convinced I wouldn't recognize the name just as I hadn't recognized Silmara's name at first.

"You trending moment."

"Me?" I was appalled. I couldn't do what Silmara did. I didn't have the relationships in the law enforcement community. I wasn't trained for counter espionage or counter terrorism work, or whatever this situation really was.

"Expect Silmara blame."

"Who?"

"You. Only non cop."

I saw where Xian was going. If Silmara was dismissed, which he was saying looked inevitable, the world leaders may put my name forward as the head of the investigation. But I had to expect that Silmara would try to shift the blame onto me. I was the non-professional forced upon the team who insisted that it focus on dead ends. Xian wouldn't even be surprised if Silmara accused me of being a double, planted on the team to make sure it couldn't possibly succeed. All that really needed to happen was for the world leaders to remove me from the task force and reinstate Silmara and she would have the Googlecars back up and running in practically no time.

"What are my options?" I had to ask.

"No options."

"What do you mean none? There has to be more than one course of action."

"Accept Silmara accusations. Offer resign."

"And do what?"

"Show. Continue show. Solve mystery television. No need task force."

Xian was telling me not to sweat whatever came out of Silmara being replaced. What he was asking me to do was so unlike me. But maybe that was the brilliance of what Xian was recommending. People had apparently calculated what my response would be. As a self-centered actor I'd be in screaming about the equity I'd created in my character and series. I'd need to be adequately compensated for that structure and content. Of course the studio was in no position to make such an equity pay-out. I'd have to find another way to monetize my art-form. But that was part of the deal. The series itself wasn't worth what would be owed me. They, meaning Regina, Jack and Stan would be looking for an excuse to reduce my ownership of the series. But that was a problem. They'd tried this same tactic the last round of negotiations. I'd turned the table telling them I was willing to accept the rights to reruns and sequels in return for the arbitrator's difference calculation between what I'd been paid and what I was owed. Funny how those who stood to gain from a decision were always happy to render it and soon disappear right afterwards. Since I was personally in charge of most of the value going forward, I was sure Jack was charged by Regina to find a way to recoup some of what they'd given up in earlier negotiations. I'd seen that reruns and sequels ownership as my pension. Some people would want to see the reruns. I'd get paid each and every time an episode aired. The studio had calculated the value of such rights were going to be small in relation to what they would owe me in cash if they were going to negotiate a compensation package similar to what other studios had paid to the stars of similarly popular shows. It was a big gamble for me at the time. The studio had thought they'd kept me on the air for a pittance in comparison to what they'd expected they'd have to pay me. I was glad to let them think that. But no one could see the series would become the most popular reality show ever during the worst crisis in modern times. Even worse than the many wars and plagues that had hit man kind. The death toll of all of those events combined, was far less than what we were experiencing now due to the Googlecar shutdown.

The record was thirty million deaths estimated globally in the 1918-19 Spanish Flu Epidemic. No one had any idea how many had succumbed to malnutrition in the past few weeks. But experts on the media were starting to proclaim this was far worse. I didn't know. No one did. The experts were guessing since no one was out knocking on doors and tallying the deaths.

"You're right. I have to be ready to walk away."

"What?" Mimi didn't like the sound of that. "What about me? Don't I get a say in your negotiations here. I'm part of this team you know. I have as much stake in the outcome as you. We are creating something that has never been seen before. A truly global franchise. We can't just walk away."

I realized she'd been only half listening. "We're not talking about walking away from the show, only the task force."

"Oh. Those people couldn't get out of their own way." Mimi summarized her feelings. I'd not realized she felt that way.

"They're in a tough spot. They have the responsibility to get the Googlecars back up and running and at the same time find who's responsible. They have a huge global team working on different parts of the problem."

"Maybe that is the issue. Maybe they have too many people working parts and consequently no one really sees the whole problem."

"Or maybe the person in charge sympathizes with the devil." I mused.

Chapter Sixty-One

I'd picked up Alistair in the Tesla and brought him over to my trailer. He had called earlier in the day to say there'd been progress in the discussions with Jack and Stan and he wanted to discuss in person rather than over the phone. Mimi joined us.

Before we got started with our discussions, a news flash came on the video. The scene was in Compton. People were in the streets rioting, looting and burning nearly everything in sight. The newscaster spoke over the scene we watched, "What you see seems to have broken out in major cities everywhere. We have crossed the point of no return. So many are now dying or dead that people no longer care about law and order."

Alistair shook his head, "I was afraid things would come to this sooner or later. I was hopeful it would be much later."

"This is awful. What are we going to do?" Mimi responded as she took a sip of scotch from the glass I'd presented her when she arrived. The food we brought back from the farm was gone. We were now subsisting on calories from alcohol and that would run out soon as well.

The newscaster continued as the scene shifted to London, "Even the very disciplined Brits are having difficulty containing the rampage throughout their city." The scene shifted to Paris, "The same could be said for the French, however, riots are nothing new there, with the continued problems of Algerian and Muslim integration into society." The scene shifted to Istanbul. "In Turkey even the Muslim residents of this storied city have taken to the streets, with people eating what little grass remains and leaves off of trees. The last cats and dogs disappeared here more than a week ago. It is hard to understand how order will be restored when transport of government officials to deal with the riots is still not operational. In fact, it appears most governments have abandoned the quest to restore order. Policemen have returned to their families to protect them from neighbors and friends who attack them to obtain any scraps of food or medicine that may remain. Few find anything to help."

"My God. What have we become?" Alistair was appalled.

"We've moved beyond resignation to desperation." I noted. "And no one is safe anymore."

"Is cannibalism an option?" Alistair remarked more to himself than to us.

I tried to answer him anyway. "In some parts of the world I could see that as a real possibility. But hopefully not here."

"Are we supposed to just lie down and wait for the end?" Mimi asked me directly.

"No. We will go on as long as possible. We still have a bit more scotch."

Mimi checked out my liquor cabinet, "A full bottle of Bourbon. Too bad I don't like it."

"I suspect we will develop a taste for it if it's all we have left." I replied, not trying to be too light nor too down.

"Do you think," Alistair began, "That we could take another trip out into the country?

I now understood why Alistair wanted to meet face-to-face. He was hoping I'd take him back out to the Fox farm and bring back another carload of food for him and his family. "It would be dangerous."

"More dangerous than doing nothing?" Alistair was angry. "Desmond, my family is starving to death before my very eyes. I can't sit by and do nothing and watch that. Not when you have the means to prevent it."

"Do you know why Mimi is staying here now?" I knew he didn't.

"I'm assuming you two are back together."

Mimi snorted her sip of scotch. "No. We're not back together."

"When we returned last time with the food three men broke into Mimi's trailer, beat her unconscious and stole all the food. The only reason they didn't do the same to me was I alerted security and have the trailer under surveillance with armed guards ever since."

Alistair looked at Mimi, "You poor thing. Why didn't you tell me?"

"We didn't want to call attention to it." I answered for her. "We've been out of food longer than you have. That's why we're drinking scotch at two o'clock in the afternoon."

Alistair shifted uncomfortably in his chair, glanced at the riots on the video, then turned back to look at us.

"What do you think will happen if your neighbors see you bringing food into your house?" I challenged him.

"I wondered why you didn't offer to go back up. I thought it was going to be every few days. We ate everything in three days, Desmond. My wife and kids are starving. I'm starving. I'm sure you see it. I've lost weight. I never lose weight. My weight has been the same for twenty years. This can't be happening. You absolutely must do something. Help me. Help my family."

"Are you prepared to fight off your neighbors and friends?"

"Yes."

"Kill them if it comes to that?" I had to put it out there.

"Anything. I must save them." Alistair was almost in tears

"I won't let you bring food back, Alistair. What I will do is drive you up there, if they are agreeable and leave you and your family there. You won't be able to return until this is over. Are you willing to do that?

"Yes, yes, anything." Alistair broke down crying.

I called Barton Fox. After I explained the situation, he agreed his family would take in Alistair, his wife and three kids, all of whom were young.

Alistair called his wife and they were ready when we picked them up. There wasn't room for suitcases so they went with only things they could carry and hold in their lap, which was mostly clothing.

"You need to say good-bye to your home. It'll probably be ransacked by the time you get back." I said as we pulled away. Alistair's wife was wide eyed.

The ride was quiet. Going to the farm would save their lives, but it would forever fundamentally change them as people. They'd been able to escape what was coming, but only because my Uncle Jim had bequeathed something to me that I'd never wanted. I'd been able to find a way to keep his kids from taking it from me. And it had been the vehicle of my success and survival. Now it was their ticket out of LA and an end to their hunger.

Barton greeted us upon our arrival, introduced his wife and son to Alistair's family and his wife took them inside. "Stay with us, at least overnight."

I glanced at Mimi who gave a slight shake of her head. She didn't want to take advantage of the Fox family. They were doing more than they needed to and I expected if we stayed his wife would ask me to bring her sister's family up. I didn't want to be the arbiter of those who survived and those who did not. "I really appreciate your kind offer, Barton, and I appreciate you taking in Alistair and his family. But we need to stay in LA. We have to stay close to those who are trying to end this tragedy, help where we can. Do whatever we can to get the transport moving again.

"I thought you'd say that. Would you drop another box of food at my wife's sister's house?"

Barton loaded another large box into the Tesla and a smaller one for Mimi and myself. I tried to pay him, but he wouldn't take my money. We drove slowly back to LA. Mimi was silent for nearly the first hour.

"You're going to replace Alistair when this is all over, aren't you?" She asked.

"Yes."

"It was his family. You can't blame him for doing anything he could to save them."

"I know." I answered quietly.

"Then why replace him?"

"He gave up. How do I know he won't give up on us if the contract negotiations get protracted or someone comes up with something that puts him into a bad light? Don't get me wrong, Alistair has always been there for us. Until now. In the next few days I expect we will come to know who our true friends are."

Mimi listened to my explanation. I knew she didn't agree with me. Maybe she would keep Alistair as her agent, but I would not. "If I got to the point it was clear I would die if you didn't take me up to the Fox's farm, would you take me?"

"I would try, but you wouldn't let me." I responded, looking at her out of the corner of my eye.

"You would let me die, rather than forcing me to go where I could survive?"

"I would follow your wishes, even if we both died in the process." I responded.

Chapter Sixty-Two

Dyllan was excited. There was no mistaking his excitement. Silmara noticed and opened the call with, "Have you made a breakthrough, Dyllan?"

"An unexpected breakthrough." He responded.

"You have the Googlecars operating again?" Silmara inquired, surprised she hadn't heard anything.

"We will speak of that in a minute. I went back to the website we've been tracking. There was one portal I'd not been able to get through. I used 'Aguirre' as the password and suddenly I found myself in what I think is the communications channel for the various groups, just now."

"How do you know?" Kalindi was surprised she hadn't heard of this from him before the call. I could tell she was hurt. Mimi poked me to call my attention to Kalindi.

"I think I've identified Diaoyu Dao, Kashmir and Amazon nodes."

"Just three sites?" Mimi asked.

"I've counted at least thirty. Maybe more."

"Are they communicating with each other or is there a hierarchy to what you're seeing?" I asked.

"Looks to be both. One site seems to be a focal point. Not sure where it is. Seems to be the most active from what I can tell."

"What time is the highest activity? Should tell us approximately where it's located." I suggested.

"Minus eight." Xian said.

"Minus eight?" Mimi asked, "What does that mean?"

"Eight hours earlier than Greenwich Mean Time. In London." I responded.

"Where is that?" Bomani asked.

"California." I replied, "Why do you think California, Xian?"

"Guess, my part."

"Dyllan?"

"I haven't had an opportunity to look at that."

"I will do it." Kalindi volunteered. "The code is the most important thing we are doing."

"Agree." Silmara took back control of the meeting. "This is an important finding, but it is Kalindi's area of responsibility and she needs to take it from here. Thanks Dyllan. So what can you tell us about the code work?"

"We are real close on the Microsoft control system. Still working out bugs, but we have a car working in the lab again. Shouldn't be more than another day or two at most."

"Great news." Silmara sounded as if the weight of the world had been lifted off her shoulders. And Dyllan was the one who had come through, not the members of her own team. I sensed that was an issue, but expected Silmara would find a way to not call attention to the fact. The one I was most worried about was Kalindi. She had to be embarrassed. Maybe that was why she was so eager to check out Dyllan's new communications portal. I wondered how the budding romance was going to survive this little hiccup.

"Minus eight more California." Xian brought our attention back to his statement.

"What are you thinking?" I asked.

"Pitcairn Islands, Canada, Oregon, Washington."

"What's in Pitcairn?" Bomani asked.

"Stamps." Dyllan responded.

"That all?" Mimi seemed puzzled.

"It is known for stamps and honey. Not much else. Was the original home of sailors from the Royal Naval Ship Bounty." Dyllan continued.

"As in the famous mutiny?" Kalindi asked. *Being from India, it made sense she would know of a British mutiny*, I thought.

"How do you know so much about Pitcairn Island?" Bomani wanted to know.

"Curiosity." Dyllan responded. "When I was in the Emirates Army I read extensively of military history. Sometimes I would read about great military failures to learn the lessons. The mutiny on the Bounty was one of those failures I read with interest, wondering what Captain Bligh did wrong that brought his men to seize the ship and put him off."

"I forgot you were in the Army." Bomani confessed. "How did you come to be a software wizard?"

"Another time. We have much work to do. We cannot relax now. We must restore the Googlecars to operation and we must find the perpetrators." Silmara cut the discussion. "What is the primary issue we must solve with the Software?"

"The app." Bomani explained. "The Googlecar app is different from the Microsoft app for calling and scheduling. We have the Googlecar engineers working the problem with consultants from Microsoft, but that is the current major issue. We must be able to keep the app the same. Converting every device would be a logistical nightmare and would simply take much too long."

"I see your point. Do you need any further resources or are you confident?" Silmara challenged Bomani and Dyllan. "If I report you will have the transport restored in the next two days, we must deliver on that promise. We must stop the rioting and that will only happen when the Googlecars begin operating. Too many believe we have been ineffectual. We cannot raise false hopes. All are depending upon us, hoping for the miracle that will save their lives."

"Can we stage the return of service?" I asked. Everyone stopped and turned to look at me on their video screens.

"Why?" Silmara asked.

"If the service returns before there's food in the stores there'll be worse riots." I suggested. "I think we need to find a way to get the merchandise transport working first so we can stock the groceries. We want people to find the shelves full. How would we do that?" I was worried. As I thought through the problem I didn't see an easy way to stage the return of service so it would be smooth.

"You raise a serious problem." Silmara observed. "Bomani? What do you think?"

"Technically it is not a problem." I could tell Bomani was thinking the question through as he answered. "It is a policy question and that is your domain."

"We need to coordinate the transport," Mimi began. "For farmers to bring their goods to market during the night and have the Googlecars return to service mid-morning in a staged roll out. Certain neighborhoods first and then others to funnel people into the stores in manageable numbers." She continued thinking through the problem.

"Not every country same." Xian observed. "Need contact governments. They decide how."

"Xian is right." I noted. "We aren't the right people to decide how the restoration of transport should work. But it is important we identify the issue and give the responsibility to the people who can best make it work."

Silmara was hesitant. "Once I let the genie out of the bottle, to use a Dyllan metaphor, we can't turn back. We have to deliver on time. So you are all absolutely sure we will be able to restore service the day after tomorrow?"

"Give us one extra day." Dyllan replied. "It will probably take the governments that long to make arrangements. So one extra day will increase our probability of success."

"But more will die in the meantime. We must deliver tomorrow." Bomani dissented.

"Then I will so advise the council. However, we must provide an update on the perpetrators. What should I report?"

"Bombers." Xian suggested.

"The whole world saw Desmond and Mimi take them down." Dyllan responded. "Nothing new there."

"You could report we believe we have identified the perpetrators and are in the process of verifying what we believe we know." I suggested.

"Real weak." Mimi shook her head at me. "Too many believes."

"We are closing in on the primary suspects." Kalindi suggested. "Simple, strong and yet it doesn't say anything."

"Exactly what we need to say." Silmara agreed.

"Now all we need to do is exactly that." I observed and winked at Mimi.

Chapter Sixty-Three

Kalindi went right to the portal Dyllan had cited and entered the password, 'Aguirre.' The page opened up into a live chat format with a dropdown pick list of sites in code names. Tabs also opened to ongoing discussions and notices posted. Kalindi started reading one discussion between two sites. It started recounting recruitment techniques and confirming five new members had arrived just that week. One of the more successful campaigns. The other site noted they had not been as successful, not having a university to recruit from. People with homes and families continued to resist the lure of what was often characterized as a primitive lifestyle, even though free from want for the most part.

The first site discussed success with new seeds that seemed to have a much higher yield in their drought conditions. The second site responded they had experimented with those same seeds the prior season and found they didn't respond well to cold.

Kalindi thought *this might be a communications channel, but those who were communicating were not discussing anything useful in their investigation.*

She moved on to another tab. The first thing she saw was a notice. Required training for all members had concluded as scheduled. Everyone was now ready to perform to the standards agreed. Kalindi read that statement twice, tried to read anything she could into it, and then tried to examine the site to find any further clues as to its potential meaning. The discussion amongst several sites with names like BIRD1 and SEABREAM could be interpreted to mean just about anything she wanted to read into it. In both cases, however, she was able to identify at least one possible conspiracy meaning. Required training to standards agreed could easily mean that everyone had been trained in passive resistance or armed conflict. It could also mean that everyone now understood how to milk cows or sheer goats, or whatever kind of animals they might have in their enclaves. The discussions around improved morale could easily have been to address desire to return to the larger world by members of the group who were becoming disillusioned about life without cell phones, internet access and social media.

Kalindi needed to read more, but was feeling pressured for time. Silmara was not happy she had not found even one indisputable link between the Hamartia and the virus. The site was amazingly intricate. Each protected level they discovered enabled more and more potential. The problem was potential for what? Kalindi thought the site had been very effective in serving as both a recruiting tool and handbook for those who embraced an ideology. Particularly if there were more than thirty such colonies or groups or whatever had been established.

She tabbed several more discussions, reading superficially at each stop, hoping to find some kind of smoking gun. However, each one proved to be more boring and predictable than the last. She had difficulty believing people were concerned about the insemination rates of the hogs, or whether the rate of egg laying by the chickens would be sufficient to permit a weekly ration of chicken meat to everyone. It was so much easier to live in a city and go to the store to buy what you need. Why would anyone want to move their existence back to a state that was so much less convenient? But from what she saw on the site, apparently there were quite a few who were willing to do just that and new members were coming to join them every week. What did the state of affairs say about society? Why were people becoming more disillusioned with convenience to the point they would give it up? But then she considered many of the recruits could be poor people who were finding a dependable source of food and self-worth. No particular skills were needed to live in such a society, other than the ability to work hard in the fields growing crops or raising animals. She wondered what else these groups might use to attract people, to convince them to give up what they had in favor of the unknown, unknowable but purported simple life. The exchanges she read sounded like people who were literate. Spelling was correct, and always in English. She wondered about that given two of the sites they knew of were in countries where English would not have been the native language. Xian surmised the leaders were on the West Coast of America or maybe an island, which one was it? Pitcairn. Yes, Pitcairn. But why an island for the leadership? For the colonies that made some sense, but she thought the leadership would not want to be so remote, but maybe she was letting her own frame of reference get into her way. These were not people who wanted to be able to stop off at the mall on the way home from a nine to five job. These were people who seriously thought they could get along just fine if the rest of humanity suddenly vanished from the planet.

They were also people who would take steps to see that the rest of mankind did vanish. But the reason for their actions remained a mystery. That gave her the uneasy feeling Silmara's team may be totally off target. The Hamartia had looked like a group that might want to take over the planet and return to a simple society. But maybe they had become desperate to find anything that suggested a motive even if not clear. Maybe she and the team had willingly read things into something that had absolutely no connection with the virus. No indication of a capability had come to light. If anything the philosophy of the group would seem to indicate exactly the opposite. But she had noticed the discussions were literate. The organizers could easily have produced the virus before establishing the colonies. The release seemed to be timed or connected to some kind of trigger which gave the organizers time. Someone could have worked for one of the major companies, developed the virus, planned the insertion and then gone on to form the colonies. All of this added up to the same thing. A plausible approach to how someone could have done what they were now trying to undo. She just didn't know what the smoking gun would look like. Maybe she wasn't in the right place yet on the portal, but as the main communications link among the sites, she thought it would be the most likely place to find such a smoking gun. And yet she did not see it, if indeed it was there.

She tabbed across several more of the discussion pages, still quickly scanning for anything that would give her hope of some importance she could rely on. Nothing appeared that caught her attention.

Kalindi tabbed back to BIRD1 and SEABREAM. The discussion had moved on to the need to get adequate sleep. *For what?* She wondered. *Why would they be discussing sleep across locations? Had they found people taking naps when they should have been tending the crops? She would not have thought attention to the amount of sleep would have been a major concern for people off the grid.*

She wondered *where are these colonies? The names deliberately hid that information.* But she doubted anyone would find this portal given the obscurity of the password. She decided to join the conversation between BIRD1 and SEABREAM and see what hints she might get about their location.

Kalindi pulled down the drop down menu and found a name: MOUNTAIN LION. She went back to the conversation screen and typed in MOUNTAIN LION in the same font as BIRD1 and SEABREAM. Then she typed in, 'We are well rested'.

The almost immediate response from BIRD1 came as: 'Is there some problem?'

Kalindi typed in MOUNTAIN LION – 'No. Everything is good.'

SEABREAM responded, 'Why are you joining now?'

Kalindi knew she made a mistake, what could she say? MOUNTAIN LION – 'Between things.'

BIRD1 responded: 'Looks like breach. Alert everyone.'

Then the site went down. Kalindi looked at the blank screen

thinking, she had blown the whole thing. *The Hamartia now knew someone had gotten into the communications level who wasn't authorized. The word will spread quickly. Or would it? Do they have another communications level to the site or some other means of communicating? The last word was alert everyone. How would they do that? Would they be able to communicate without that website?* The more she thought about it she realized that the response of intrusion was an indicator that they were doing something they did not want the outside world to know about. If that were the case they probably had some kind of backup system for communications.

She knew what she had to do now, although she dreaded it. She called Silmara.

"Hi. Have something I need to report to you." Kalindi started the conversation, waited to see if Silmara responded, which she did not. Kalindi always hated it when Silmara was silent. She couldn't read the silence and that made it worse. "I entered the communications level of the suspected Hamartia website. I confirmed there were approximately thirty-two communications sites."

"Go on."

"The sites have non-descriptive names, like BIRD1, so it is impossible to tell where they are."

"Are you sure they are different locations and not individuals?" Silmara asked.

Kalindi hadn't considered this question, "No. Not enough information. I observed the dialog between various sites, most of which was about crops and operational activities, which seemed normal for such a group."

"So what is the reason for this call?" Silmara heard the tension in her voice. She had never been able to keep bad news from her."

"I entered one discussion to see if I could learn more about where they were. Those in the dialog almost immediately determined I was an

368

intruder and shut down the site."

Silmara said nothing for at least thirty seconds. Then, "So those on the site now know someone is observing them? And upon discovering this, shut down the site?"

"Yes."

"Kalindi. You must find how they are now communicating or we will both be replaced."

Chapter Sixty-Four

Mimi, Walt and I drove to the police station that evening. With riots still going on throughout the city we weren't going to take the detectives out. Instead I thought we'd join Kareem and Pete in interrogating Alice, Sherice, Finch and Wilson. In that order.

"Why would you want to do that?" Kareem asked when I told him of my plan.

"I have to know what they know about the Hamartia." I responded.

"The who?" Kareem hadn't heard that name before from us.

"The people who we believe might be behind the Googlecar virus."

"So you think they're connected." Kareem seemed surprised.

"Limited evidence, but enough it makes sense." I confirmed.

"All right." Kareem went off to bring in Alice. Walt went to film through the observer window so it wouldn't distract Alice. Mimi joined me in the small room.

Alice came in, looking gaunt. Her LAPD orange jumpsuit hung on her. She'd lost weight since the city couldn't provide food for her or anyone. Just water. "Hi, Alice. Remember us?"

"Douche bags, the both of you."

"It's good to see you too. I have only one question."

Alice looked at me like the situation was a set up and she wasn't going to fall for it.

"How much did Hugh Aguirre pay you for your part in stealing the weapons?"

"Not enough." She replied.

Next Kareem brought in Sherice. "I only have one question for you." I began.

"I plead the fifth." Sherice replied.

"Since you were the key person in this whole deal, did Hugh Aguirre pay you more than he paid Alice to steal the missiles?"

Sherice, who was already pasty white lost even more color in her face. "I wasn't the key person. I told you it was Oliver. He did it. He was the key person."

"We know that's bullshit Alice. You were the inside person. You set it up. You opened the store room for Oliver. Jim took possession from Oliver to ship to the other cities. And Jim used the first one here in LA on the Googlecar repair facility. Just as he tried to level the phone exchange."

"No. Jim had nothing to do with it. Oliver's the one. Only Oliver."

"You can explain it all to us if you want to, Sherice. Alice already has. We have her side of the story and it doesn't match yours."

"She would never do that." But Sherice wasn't sure, that was evident.

"If you would like to read her transcript I can arrange that. Hunger does strange things to people." I noted for her.

"How did you find out about Aguirre?" Sherice must have replayed the conversation and just picked up on his name coming up.

"Mutual friend." I responded.

"He approached Alice first. Knew we were sisters. He had something on her... would send her to jail, so she didn't have a choice. You have to understand. She didn't have a choice."

"But the money was good." Mimi this time.

"Yes, very good. And he said no one would ever find out. All I had to do was not check them out and the inventory system would hide the whole thing."

"But somebody figured out what had been used to level the repair depots and traced it back to your company." Mimi continued the questioning.

"I don't know about that." She was relieved it was over. She seemed to disappear into the chair in which she sat.

"Jim Finch shipped the other weapons so he has the list of shooters." I noted.

"He shipped them to addresses, not sure he has the real names. They were probably fake."

"An assumption on your part." I continued.

Sherice shrugged agreement.

Kareem brought Jim Finch in next with his arm still in a cast. "I only have one question for you." I began.

"You broke my fucking arm." Finch protested.

"You're lucky I didn't run you over." Was my instant response.

"Your fucking car's too low. Couldn't have."

"We know Hugh Aguirre paid you to blow up the Googlecar repair depot here in LA, we caught you in the act of trying to blow up the phone exchange and we know you shipped the other weapons to the various shooters around the country. Now you can either give us the list of names and addresses, or we take you out into the street and tell the mob you're the reason they're starving to death." I gave it to him straight.

"Hey. I ain't responsible for that. Blow up shit, I can do that all day long, but shut down the Googlecars? That ain't me." Finch wasn't going to be intimidated by the crowd outside.

"But it is Hugh Aguirre. You were the warm-up act. Get everyone's attention to the Googlecars. Get everyone's attention to the fact someone wasn't happy with them and then wham! Shut them down and watch everyone starve. It's all linked, Jim. And you're the key figure in it all. You were the LA shooter. You shipped the weapons to the other shooters. You were caught in the act of trying to fire the weapon. You don't have a chance except to cooperate and give us the names and addresses."

Jim Finch weighed his options and didn't like them. "What's your question since you got this all figured out?"

"You're a curious guy. When Aguirre came to you with his plan, I'm sure you asked him why he was attacking the Googlecars. What did he tell you?" I set the stage.

I watched Finch play that conversation back in his memory. Then he looked at me. "He said he was going to save mankind from itself."

"And you bought his explanation. You were willing steal military grade weapons from the Federal Government, Knowing it was a Federal crime to start, to blow shit up, and join a cause even though you had absolutely no idea what the hell he was talking about." I tried to make it clear where this was going.

"Hell no. I knew what he meant." Jim pushed back.

"Then explain it to me." I challenged him.

Jim Finch looked around furtively before answering. "I can't. Aguirre offered me a lot of money. Said Sherice was a great fuck and she'd fuck my brains out. It was a perfect opportunity. What more could a guy want?"

"To know why." Mimi responded.

Jim Finch looked at her, "They never asked me that in the Army."

Kareem brought in Oliver Wilson who looked ill. He had trouble keeping his gaze fixed and seemed totally lethargic. "I have just one question for you." I began like with the others.

Oliver Wilson finally looked straight at me, but said nothing.

"We have the whole deal, Oliver. Everyone has given us what they knew of Hugh Aguirre approaching all of you, paying you a lot of money, fixing it so you'd get laid, but you got the fat sister. So obviously Aguirre didn't respect you. After all, you were only the messenger, picking up the weapons and delivering them to Finch. So you weren't all that important. He paid you less and stuck you with Alice, who's probably given you the clap because I'm sure you have no idea who else has been visiting. And you've committed a Federal crime, by stealing government weapons and transporting them across state lines. Not that…"

Oliver spoke. "I didn't transport them across state lines."

"So you would have us believe Finch shipped those weapons?" I asked.

"He did." No question.

"And you are going to give us proof that Finch shipped them not you." I wasn't sure what Wilson had, but it was clear he thought he had something on Finch.

Oliver Wilson showed a slight grin. "Got it all on tape. I passed the weapons to him in view of a security camera in the Staple Center parking lot. I installed the camera and system. Video is archived on August seventeenth. Two-forty-five am, camera D twenty-nine."

"So, Oliver, my question. Why were you willing to commit a Federal crime when you didn't even know why you were doing it?"

"You make a lot of assumptions." Oliver began but started coughing and couldn't continue until the coughing passed. "You think you know everything. But you don't. Aguirre hasn't even started yet."

Chapter Sixty-Five

Kalindi spent the whole night on the suspected Hamartia website looking for any indication of how they might continue to communicate with the Aguirre portal shut down. Out of frustration she finally called Dyllan.

"Kalindi? What do you need?"

"Help. I've done something terrible and I have to fix it tonight."

Dyllan looked at his other screen, "Just a minute." He muted the line. After a minute he came back on. "What can I do to help you?"

"You're working the app fix for the Googlecars."

"Yes, but Bomani is on with them too. So it is in good hands."

"I shut down the Aguirre portal."

Dyllan was confused, "Why? What happened?"

"I joined a dialog, trying to learn where they were. They figured out almost immediately I was not one of them and they shut the site down. Now we do not know how they are communicating."

"We didn't before I found the access code, so we are not in a much different place."

"But Silmara will discharge me unless I find out how they are communicating now. I must do it tonight. I have no choice."

"Just a minute." Dyllan went back to the other screen. "I'll be a while, Bomani. Just keep them running through the acceptance checklist."

"Thank you. I knew you would help me." Kalindi said relieved.

"Are you on the homepage?" Dyllan was already there.

"I can go there." Kalindi sounded unsure of what to do.

"Please do." Dyllan looked it over. He ran his cursor over a symbol in the upper left corner of his screen and clicked on it. A nodal diagram exploded into view. "I'm on the nodal diagram. Which one was the comms portal?"

"A fifty-seven." Kalindi responded.

Dyllan clicked on the node, the blank screen appeared. He clicked on the screen in each corner and in the center where the password box used to be. Nothing. He then clicked in the upper left corner and dragged the cursor to the lower right corner. The password screen appeared. He typed in 'Aguirre'. Nothing happened. He typed in 'Deng Lo Minh'. Nothing happened. He typed in 'Thyagaraj' and the screen changed. "Click upper left and drag to lower right. Password is Thyagaraj." Dyllan told Kalindi as he began to look around the site. "Once you're in, don't click on anything."

"Why?" Kalindi wanted to know.

"Intrusion detection software. You can look but if you click on anything the system will record the click, validate it against a list of authorized alias' and since you don't have one, it will alert the systems admin someone is in without proper authorization."

"Why didn't it pick us up coming in?"

"We had the password. They assume only authorized people will have the password so no need for a validity check at that level."

"So they'll pick me up if I even click on a tab?"

"Yes. We only get to look at this page." Dyllan spotted a note inserted into a posting. "What's stage nine?"

"I don't know." Kalindi responded.

"Right hand column about half way down. It reads, 'Stage nine completes at midnight.' Did you see anything that could refer to when you were in the Aguirre site? You said you read some of it."

"Nothing I remember. Do you think the Aguirre site was the day-to-day conversations between sites or colonies or whatever organization they have and this is their tactical site?"

"Let me finish reading. You do the same."

Dyllan and Kalindi read every word on the webpage. "I don't see anything more about it." Kalindi seemed ready to throw in the towel.

Dyllan continued to look at the page for anagrams or any kind of embedded code that would be visible without a decoding system. Then he got excited, "Look at the last line on the page, Read it backwards from right to left."

Kalindi did so and read it out loud, "Get ready for the New World Order. Do you think the two are related? Stage nine ends at Midnight, get ready for the new world order?"

"Since nothing else on this page seems related to either of those statements, it appears they were trying to hide the communication in plain sight where it would be easy for people in remote places to be able to read and understand without complicated code equipment."

"Do you think they know we're here?"

"I don't think so. You said they immediately shut down the Aguirre site when you tried to participate in the dialog. I would expect the same behavior if they discovered us here. In fact, I would expect they are on heightened alert, looking for anyone who might find a way of getting into this page."

"We need to inform Silmara."

"I'll let you do that. She does not need to know I was involved. This can be your discovery."

"But how did you know to try other passwords on a dead site?"

"The unexpected. I would have done that. You didn't say they changed the password on you. You said they took the site down. Going there it looks like a dead site. So most people would just leave. If you click the usual places you get nothing. You have to try something unconventional to get a dialog box. Most people would give up long before then."

"You are a true friend. Thank you."

"I am happy I might help you." Dyllan was already looking at his other site to see where Bomani was with the checklist on the app.

"Might I ask a question?" Kalindi asked shyly.

"Yes, anything." But Dyllan is distracted.

"Why did you not share with me the news of your discovery before the call yesterday?"

Dyllan heard in her voice that she was hurt he had not done so. "I am sorry. I discovered it just before the call and I got distracted with the Microsoft control system success."

"But you talked about the site first, even though you had good news about the control system. You knew the control system was your priority. Why did you discuss the site when you could have called and talked to me about it before you announced it?"

"Kalindi, listen to yourself. We are a team. If one of us succeeds we all succeed. Why is it important to you that you knew about something first? Why were you willing to delay discussing it with Silmara until you could claim to know all about it? That would delay our progress. It would result in possibly thousands or millions more people dying because of another day delay."

"You make me sound selfish." She sounded hurt again.

"No, I think you may not have had time to think through the implications of your hurt feelings. I do not think you would consciously prioritize yourself over your job, which is to find the perpetrators as quickly as possible. That is the only way we can be sure we will not have a tenth stage succeed, when we don't even know what the ninth stage is. The Hamartia may have already launched another virus or another attack of some sort on us, with a trigger of midnight. We have no information other than their cryptic message. Tomorrow we will bring the transport back up. Tomorrow the starvation will end. People will be able to obtain their medicines once again. Go to hospital, visit doctors, and see family and friends they have not seen for many weeks now. This will all happen because of you, Silmara, Bomani and all the others who are working to restore the world to the society we knew. Be proud you are part of the team. It is not necessary that you alone solve the mystery."

Kalindi was quiet for several moments. "You must think I am an awful person."

"On the contrary. I think you are a wonderful person. I enjoy talking with you, solving mysteries with you, exploring new places with you. We are much better together than either of us is alone. We complement each other in many different and unique ways. I want our collaboration to continue when this adventure is over. It is an adventure you know."

"I have not thought of it as such," came as a small shy voice.

"It is just the beginning, but you need to call Silmara now. Please."

Chapter Sixty-Six

I called Alistair at the Fox farm from the Tesla. Walt, Mimi and I were already on the road.

"Yes, yes. The Fox family is wonderful to us. I cannot tell you how relieved we are to be here."

"I need you to do something for me now." I didn't want it to sound so harsh, but we were running out of time and I needed him to help us.

"Of course." Alistair sounded flustered not knowing what I was about to ask.

"We're going back up to visit with Hugh Aguirre. It will go much smoother if you're with us. He knows and trusts you. We also don't want this visit to look like anything other than the last one, gathering information about people who are doing what he is doing."

"Why is it so important to go back up there?" Alistair sounded suspicious.

I wasn't sure if I could trust him with the truth so I gave him just enough so he would commit. "We've found indications Hugh may know more about recent events than he gave us cause to believe last time."

"And that would explain why he never showed us his video set up?"

"Probably more elaborate than would be needed to monitor

sitcoms." I affirmed.

"And he didn't want us asking more questions than we did."

"I need you to come up with us. Can you be ready in a couple of hours?" I asked as I looked at Walt who was filming the conversation.

"That means you're leaving now." Alistair noted.

"Just leaving the city as we speak."

Barton Fox insisted on giving us vegetables to eat in the car.

"You are so kind." Mimi responded.

"Alistair said you're hoping to find the person responsible. I got the news the transports will be by tonight to pick up our harvest. I assume you had something to do with that."

I shrugged.

"Whatever you did, we can't thank you enough."

"Just taking in Alistair's family is more thanks than I could ever want." I shook his hand and we departed the farm. Barton's son was operating a fork lift bringing crates of vegetables to the staging point for pickup. So the first phase of restoration had begun. Farm vehicles were operating normally. Something we hadn't thought about. I expected the emergency and governmental vehicles were probably operational as well. *Kareem and Pete won't need me anymore,* I thought.

As we drove to the mountains Alistair was silent, probably embarrassed about having to almost force me to help him and his family. So I decided to call Xian and see if he could help me come up with a plan of what to do.

"It's Desmond, Xian. We're on our way to the mountains for the confrontation. You've been on the calls. Any friendly advice?"

"More evidence. Diaoyu Dao have satellite dish. Much activity. Prepare something."

"You're telling me the deadline seems to have stimulated activity amongst those who shouldn't have reason to employ technology."

"Yes."

"What do you suggest I do when I get there?"

"Police?"

"No, it's the same as when we went up last time. Didn't want to tip our hand too early, so we can hopefully find out about the midnight deadline before we move on him. Besides, we'll need room in the car to bring him back with us."

"Harder. Better you take one officer. No matter. Interrogation difficult. Not want you know. Must overcome resistance. Difficult."

"I've been thinking about that. I agree. He won't want to tell me his plans, but I'll have to find a way to make him say something that will reveal what he's up to. No suggestions there?"

"No meet. Hard when no meet."

"Yes and I wasn't wildly successful getting him to say much last time. If I'd been more successful we probably wouldn't have needed to make this second trip."

"Arrest difficult. His house. Try escape, maybe. Find in woods difficult. He know, you not know."

"So I don't want to let him get out of the cabin. Got that. If he has any weapons that could be a bit of a problem as well since I don't have any." For the first time I regretted my aversion to weapons.

"No weapon?" Xian was amazed I'd go to arrest someone unarmed. "More difficult. How arrest?"

"I haven't figured that part out yet either. Any suggestions?" I didn't want to admit I was unprepared, but I was.

"You bigger?"

"About the same size, really."

"No advantage. May not violent." Does Xian know something or is this hopeful thinking?

"I hope not as a sitcom guy. I'd be more worried if it were your friend Deng. He was super violent as I remember."

"Question."

"Sure."

"He try kill you. You kill him?"

His question caught me completely off guard. I'd not thought I'd have any trouble with Hugh Aguirre. I had to rethink that. If I'd worked my whole life to change the world and someone showed up to stop me, I'd probably not be too happy. I knew I'd not let them stop me. So how was I going to stop Hugh Aguirre? "I don't know, Xian. As an actor I've killed my share of folks, but in reality I'd have trouble putting a pet down, that is if I had a pet, which I don't."

"Must decide."

"Thanks for helping me think this through. Talk soon." I felt totally unprepared mentally or physically for this coming encounter.

"Soon you return."

I sat quietly contemplating how I could get Hugh Aguirre to tell me what he was up to and then how to get him into the Tesla to bring him to justice. This whole confrontation was going to be much harder than I'd thought. At least I had some time now to work it through.

Mimi's cell rang. "Yes?"

After a moment of silence Mimi responded, "When did this happen, Silmara?"

She listened again then said, "Let me put you on speaker, Desmond is right here."

Silmara's slightly echoing voice filled the car. "Where are you?"

"On our way to the mountains." Mimi informed her.

"Alone or with law enforcement?"

"Alone." I responded. "We want to see if we can get Aguirre to talk about what's planned for tonight. We just arrest him, it may be too late by the time he talks."

"I don't agree with your strategy."

"We're half way there." I wasn't going back now. "Hopefully in a few hours we will be able to call you and let you know what we may have to do to stop their plot. It may take you a while."

"I will alert the proper people there to back you up." Came across strangely to me.

"Just make sure they don't come bursting through the door just as we're about to get him to talk."

"They will be instructed to wait for you to call them."

"I can live with that. What did you say to Mimi before we got on the line?"

"I have been relieved of responsibility for this assignment." Now I understand the strain in her voice.

I was amazed that whoever was in charge would make a change at this critical juncture, particularly since transport was up and the Googlecars would be back on line in the morning. "Why now?"

"It does not matter why. What you must know is I cannot help you now. The task force is being reconstituted and only law enforcement will be permitted on the team."

"So we're really on our own out here." *Just fucking great. Just like a bureaucracy to find a way to mess up something that was about to deliver results*, I thought.

Chapter Sixty-Seven

We drove the rest of the way up into the mountains in silence. We soon went off the main road over the dirt and grass road and arrived at the point we'd left the Tesla the last time. Alistair had been quiet the whole way up, but finally said something just before we parked. "I hope you don't mind me telling the Foxes why we are taking this trip."

I shook my head as I didn't want him to detect the uncertainty I felt on how to proceed.

The mile hike took longer than last time. It occurred to me since we'd not been eating Mimi and I were probably weaker than last time and Walt hung back with us. Alistair had had a few good meals at the Fox farm so he charged ahead and had to slow to wait for us a few times. About the third time Alistair finally asked, "Are you really up to this?"

"Yes." Was my full and complete answer. Alistair shook his head and walked slower so we could stay together. It wasn't long before we came into the glade where Hugh Aguirre lived. The log cabin stood brightly against the brown and green background of tall pine trees and the glittering gold of the photovoltaic solar panels. The lake between us and the cabin was calm, just as it had been the last time. Mirror-like. We waded through the tall grass, smelling the wildflowers on the air. I'd forgotten places like this exist. I needed to find time to get out of the city once in a while and reconnect with the beauty of nature. The fact I was paying attention to my surroundings and not thinking about the coming encounter was probably a good thing, but my thoughts quickly returned to Hugh Aguirre and how we were going to deal with him. I really didn't have a plan and that worried me.

By the time we arrived at the cabin the sun was already beginning to set behind the trees, casting long shadows across the lake and the solar array. He would have to go onto battery power soon, from the energy he stored during the day when the sun was on his array. A very complex system for someone who professed to not want to be dependent upon technology. Ironic, I thought.

Alistair knocked. I heard voices inside. Hugh had company or was communicating with someone elsewhere. It took a few moments for Hugh to answer the door. He had a concerned look when he opened the door and it quickly changed to one of annoyance particularly when he saw he was being filmed by Walt. "Oh, hello. Didn't think I'd be seeing you again so soon. I'm afraid this really isn't a very good time for me right now. Could I ask you, and I know this is a real inconvenience, but could I ask you to come back some other time? Tomorrow would be much better than today."

I stepped forward, "Actually no. We need to talk with you today and promise this won't take much of your time."

Hugh looked over his shoulder. I saw at least four men in the cabin with him and then recognized Deng Lo Minh. I looked for Raj Thyagaraj, but he wasn't visible from the door. Hugh stepped outside and closed the door behind him. "I can give you a few minutes but that's all. I have neighbors in and we are trying to finish a project we've been working on for quite some time."

"That's what we've come to talk with you about. You see we have the Googlecar repair depot bombers in custody. All of them. It's funny how people who are starving to death are willing to talk about all kinds of things."

Hugh glanced at me and then out over his private lake. I don't know what he was thinking, but he clearly wasn't pleased to learn of my news. He didn't respond so I continued. "I thought Jim Finch said it best when he told me you gave him a lot of money and arranged for Sherice Novak to fuck his brains out so he would not only take possession of the weapons, but ship them to those on your list and also personally use them here in LA."

Hugh Aguirre smiled a warped one-sided smile. "You liked that."

"And we visited with the Hamartia. Interesting how your last name happened to be the password to the communications portal."

Hugh looked at Alistair and then Mimi. I knew he was trying to decide what we were going to do about this little discussion we were having.

"And then we learned that stage nine was complete and the new world order begins at midnight tonight. You showed a lot of discipline, keeping the dialog on the humdrum daily stuff while you had your sites drilling for their new roles."

Hugh looked towards the setting sun. "Thank you for stopping by, but I must return to my guests now." Then he noticed that Walt was transmitting what he was filming and his expression hardened.

"If only it were that easy." I said, not in a threatening manner, but ensuring he knew we weren't simply going to leave.

"I'm afraid you're no longer welcome. Please leave, now." He looked right into the camera.

"You know I've always wanted to meet Deng Lo Minh and Mimi knows Raj Thyagaraj from 'Desperation'. I'm sure they'd be happy to chat with us for a few minutes."

"I'm afraid that's not possible."

I pushed past him, opened the door and proceeded to enter his cabin. "Gentlemen." I began in order to get their attention. Before I could say anything more I noticed the double doors to the communications suite were open. A large screen monitor and racks of electronics were visible. On the screen was a map of the world with pin lights showing locations. I assumed they were the locations of the Hamartia groups, poised to carry out whatever Hugh had arranged. "I'm afraid we're here to change your plans for tonight."

Hugh followed me in. "Don't pay any attention to this man. He's in no position to affect anything."

"I saw Raj Thyagaraj by the fireplace. So the big three were here with their other accomplices. I was sure I'd have time to take an inventory of names once I found a way to stop their plan. I expected the communications panel had to be the key, so I walked straight to it.

Once inside the alcove I quickly found wires and started pulling them from the racks, pushing the racks over and letting them crash on the floor. Like a madman, I started pulling wires from anything that was electronic. I looked up and the large screen blinked out. I disconnected wall outlets and made sure no two pieces of equipment remained connected. I also made sure it would be very difficult to reconnect anything.

When I was done I looked up and the six men, including Hugh, were simply staring at me. Walt was getting the whole thing. No one had moved to stop me, which told me this was not what I needed to do to prevent tonight.

Chapter Sixty-Eight

Hugh Aguirre looked at me as I walked towards him from his now useless communications node. "I'll send you a bill." He quipped.

"Didn't know they have postal service up here." I replied trying to figure out what I needed to do next to prevent Hugh's plot. I still didn't even know what the plan was.

"They don't. Nor do they have law enforcement or any other means of restricting the freedom of those of us who live here." Hugh responded to his guests more than me.

"I take it you all have homes nearby?" I asked everyone together, but no one responded to me.

"You've learned much about what I've been doing recently. If you remember, when you stopped by last time I said I didn't think you'd be interested in what I'd been doing. But I guess I must have been wrong. You've clearly done much more homework than I expected." Hugh noted watching my moves.

"And shared that information with the appropriate officials." Mimi responded.

Hugh looked at her, shaking his head, "You mean the LAPD?"

"Didn't know you were watching the show." I responded surprised.

"Not been much else worth watching recently." Hugh replied.

"Actually we've been working with the International Task Force. Silmara Cardoso and her team."

"Really? An actor?" Hugh clearly didn't believe me.

"Actors." Mimi corrected.

"Even more unbelievable." Hugh looked around at the others in the room. They were stoic, standing as if waiting for him to resolve this inconvenience.

"Transport came back on line last night, by the way."

"I don't think so. There's no way anyone could have defeated my virus." A man in the back of the room responded.

"Rehosted with the Microsoft control system that lost out to the Googlecar software. By the end of the day all autonomous cars will be operating normally." I informed him.

"Meet Jonas. He used to have a last name, but chose to give it up when he gave up modern society. Jonas was the original developer of the Googlecar control system. But Jonas thought all modern technology had the potential to change society in unexpected and not wholly desirable ways. So Jonas inserted a poison pill in the code that could be activated remotely if he ever believed it was needed."

"You used to be Gabriel von Horn. You don't look old enough to have been on the original team." I challenged, although I expected it was true.

"I'll be sixty-two my next birthday." Jonas responded.

"You obviously live right." Mimi interjected. Smiles from all of the men, including Hugh.

"We do." Hugh affirmed. "But as for tonight? Well, your valiant effort to dismantle my communications suite is an annoyance, but it doesn't preclude anything."

"If you can't launch from here, nothing will happen." I bluffed.

"I've already launched. Midnight is just when everything starts happening." Hugh responded. "This is like New Year's Eve. We're here to celebrate the beginning. It will roll around the earth at midnight, just like New Year's rolls around the earth when midnight arrives bringing in the New Year. And just like New Year's Eve, nothing can stop it."

Hugh seemed calm. I had to believe my rampage in his communications suite hadn't prevented him from executing his plan. But what could I do now?

Hugh turned to his compatriots. "Don't you think it ironic that transport would come back on line today, if he's not bluffing?"

Jonas responded, "The approach he mentioned could work. Particularly with the amount of time they've had to work it. There's no reason to believe he's not telling us the truth."

"I mean," Hugh began. "Just the irony that people who have survived all that has happened, those who have had faith that government would save them, are about to be crushed again. I think it's just so fitting that all their efforts, finally rewarded, should have been for nothing."

I waited hoping Hugh was going to give away the big secret, but he turned back to confront us. "Thank you for working so hard to make our triumph so final. I couldn't be happier for you."

I looked at Mimi, who was staring at Raj Thyagaraj, probably reliving her time with him. That would explain why she only seemed to be intermittently involved in the exchange that had just taken place. I needed to know what the big plot was. Somehow it was going to render the Googlecar restoration meaningless. But I still didn't have any clues as to what was going to happen at midnight.

"So at midnight civilization as we've known it will end." I said, thinking back to the interrogation techniques I'd used.

A big smile appeared on Hugh. "You don't know what happens at midnight, do you?" Hugh turned to the other men, "They don't know. Should we tell them and watch their reaction or keep them in the dark until they're in the dark?"

In the dark? I thought, Hugh must be talking about bringing down the electric grid. Of course. The Googlecars were all electric like the Tesla. That meant if the grid went down the Googlecars would stop again, because they couldn't recharge.

I started looking around the room. Hugh must have some means of communicating other than his big system. With all the careful planning we'd seen evidence of, he wouldn't leave himself without the ability to communicate if there were a catastrophic failure.

"There's nothing you can do, Desmond. It's over." Hugh taunted.

I spotted a laptop computer next to the back door. I instantly moved towards it. No one moved to stop me so I kept walking and bent down to pick it up. The computer had a satellite aircard. I was right, Hugh was still very much connected. Seeing what I'd discovered Hugh ran at me to recover his lone remaining communications device.

I caught the movement from the corner of my eye, but too late, Hugh tackled me and the computer flew from my hand. Hugh crawled over me to get at the laptop, but I grabbed him and wouldn't let him get to it.

"Damn you. Let go." Hugh wasn't very strong. I silently thanked Jake Goodbody for all his exercises I never thought important. But even though in much better shape, my lack of eating had me weak enough it wasn't the clear contest I'd have expected it to be.

Hugh almost got away, but I grabbed his waistband and held him back as he tried to crawl towards the computer. Hugh started kicking and hitting me to get me to release him, but I gathered my strength and pulled him back, sliding him across the rough wooden floor so he was behind me. I scrambled clear of him and crawled on hands and knees toward the computer.

Hugh grabbed my foot. I dragged him behind me and finally reached the laptop, picking it up and removing the aircard, which I crushed in my fist.

Hugh was back up on me, grabbing for the computer. We wrestled with it. I was finally able to pull it away from him, and get my leg up to push him away with my foot in his chest. Hugh seized my ankle and held on. I kicked at him with both feet now, but Hugh simply batted my other foot away. I put the laptop under my left arm, stood up and punched Hugh in the face with as much power as I could muster. Hugh let go, but came right back at me, swinging his fists as well.

I took aim and hit him square in the nose. Hugh was stunned, stepped back as blood began to gush from his now probably broken nose.

I moved to the fireplace and dropped the laptop into the fire, turning and standing guard over the now melting device.

"Why didn't you stop him?" Hugh asked the other men.

"We abhor violence." Deng Lo Minh responded.

"Really?" I responded, surprised. Noting Walt was getting this whole exchange.

"Our movies have always been means of discussing absurdity of violence by showing corrosive effects on human nature." Deng replied.

"Did you think we were glorifying violence?" Raj Thyagaraj interjected seemingly amazed.

"I think most people interpreted your movies as showing the end justifies the means."

"We do believe in macro, but not in micro." Deng replied. "Our efforts to change society, in macro, can justify whatever means necessary. We are talking survival of species. But in micro, nothing justifies killing a person."

Chapter Sixty-Nine

Silmara was unhappy. Not just because she had been reassigned, but with Mimi and myself for going it alone. She evidently forgot I was born in Texas. But anyhow, she decided she needed to help me because as an actor, she just didn't think I'd be able to pull off the role I'd accepted. She called Dyllan, who was now officially off the team with Mimi and me so she wasn't interfering. "Dyllan? It's Silmara. We need your help tonight. Can you call Bomani for me and ask him to do something?"

Dyllan evidently found this a curious request, "Something happen I need to know about?"

Silmara didn't know how to tell him, so she did the only thing she could, which was to just tell him. "I've been reassigned and the Task Force is being reconstituted. I'm afraid you're off the team."

"Why?"

"I have not been informed of the reasons why, and they are unimportant in any event. This change of situation may actually help us. Since I am no longer in charge, I cannot call Bomani and ask him to do anything. But since you are off the team you may."

Dyllan must have wondered what in the world was going on. "I understand. That mean Desmond and Mimi are off too?"

"Yes and they are on their way to arrest Aguirre, but they have not taken anyone to help, because they want to try to find out what the plan is for tonight before they arrest him."

"Why am I thinking this will not turn out well? But then again, Desmond has continued to surprise us throughout this whole event."

"Yes, he and Mimi have done much more than I would have ever imagined."

"So what do you want me to say to Bomani?"

"If he brings down the communications portal before midnight, it may thwart the plan, whatever it might be."

"How would you suggest he do that?"

A sudden thought popped into Silmara's mind. "A virus would be most fitting, I think."

Dyllan laughed, "It would, but where would Bomani find such a virus with so little time?"

Silmara had anticipated this question when she had the thought, "Leave that up to him. Bomani has many connections and some of them will be able to help us, I am sure."

"Good to know. Do you have friends like that too?"

"Bomani's friends are my friends."

"I'll keep that in mind the next time we work together."

"I truly hope you are right that we have such an opportunity. I would like to tell you how important you have been to the team, but you know already and you must call Bomani now to give him the time he will need."

"Just a personal question. What will happen to Kalindi?"

Silmara heard the concern in Dyllan's question. She knew she must not tell him the truth, but it would be hard to mislead him. "Kalindi and Bomani both have been reassigned as well. My superiors wish to have a clean start."

"A clean start? When everything will be decided tonight?" Dyllan sounded incredulous.

Silmara couldn't answer Dyllan's question. "Please call Bomani."

Chapter Seventy

Hugh Aguirre willingly, well… almost willingly, came down off his mountain with us. After the backup computer went into the fire the conversation ended. In fact Hugh's, guests all left without so much as a good-bye to return to their mountain homes. Hugh wasn't going to confirm or deny anything, but when I insisted, he came along.

"You know this is all an exercise in futility. The end will come and you will all die. You're not worthy of representing humankind on this planet."

"And you are?" Mimi was so ready to drop Hugh off at the LAPD. She had tried to talk with Raj Thyagaraj as he departed, but he shook his head and simply left. I think Raj hurt her feelings and she was taking it out on poor Hugh.

"Of course. I have only the noblest of intentions. I want mankind to flourish. But as long as we're dependent upon machines and continue to let our populations grow unabated and poison our mother planet we will only creep towards extinction."

"What gives you the right to select who lives and who dies?" I asked as we walked.

"You have self-selected. Those who have learned to live on nature's bounty will survive. Those who have chosen to worship the devil of technology shall follow that devil to the underworld."

"The flaw in your plan is mankind has responded to the challenges and threats nature has fostered with technology to extend our defenses and abilities. You and the Hamartia have threatened us and we have used those same technologies to defeat you the way we have pushed back Mother Nature."

"But you've abused your intelligence. You have pushed beyond what nature intended for mankind. Nature wishes to find a balance, an equilibrium. You have destroyed that balance. Mankind is killing the planet and consuming the abundance at rates that don't permit nature to restore the balance. Only by bringing down the number of people on the planet can we survive as a species."

"Alone and in the dark." I parroted his earlier brag.

"Better to live in the dark than to die horribly as our planet dies about us."

"Hugh, I hope you don't mind me calling you Hugh?" Mimi began. "Who made you God? Ever since God made Eve to be man's partner all important decisions have been made by discussing and coming to an agreement. When tyrants have tried to impose their will on the people, in every instance it has ended badly for the tyrant. People want a say in the important decisions about themselves, their families and yes their planet. Everyone gets a chance to vote on the outcome. When it comes to selecting who should survive. That's just not your decision."

"An interesting position, Mimi. I hope you don't mind me calling you Mimi. But the law of the jungle is only the strong survive. I'm strong because I'm independent of all of the technology that enables your pampered lives. Technology is responsible for your livelihood. Without technology you have no audience, no sponsors and no paychecks. You and Desmond are among the worst offenders of those who are raping our planet. You take, but you give back nothing. You consume, but you don't produce. You expect everyone to love you, but you give no love back in return. I know. I was like you before I made the choice. I was a taker, but now I'm expressing my love of mankind by enabling it to survive and restore the balance in nature and our planet. I'm giving back."

We reached the Tesla. I knew Alistair wouldn't be able to control Hugh if he chose to create a disturbance on the way back down. I didn't think he would try to escape, but Xian had warned me to be prepared. So I taped his hands behind his back and had him sit in front with me.

Chapter Seventy-One

Mimi, Walt and I picked up Kareem and Pete at the station. This was to be the final episode of the season. Kareem tapped on Mimi's window. She lowered it. "Yes officer? He had his speed in check. He was just following the car in front and must have been lulled. You know how hard it is to stay alert with all the Googlecars on the road."

"I've been told that's a problem, but since I don't own one of these I really wouldn't know."

"What can we do for you tonight?" Mimi continued.

"Thought you might like to visit with some friends of yours. They've been asking about you. Since we've been able to feed them again, Alice has gained back every pound she lost and probably one or two more."

"When's the sentencing?" I asked.

"Next week." Pete called over Kareem's shoulder.

"Why don't we visit with them once they know what the court's decided." I suggested. As entertaining as they'd been, I didn't think our audience wanted to revisit what had been the dominant news for what seemed months. I wanted the season finale to be something that might set up interest in next season, not just wrap up the last.

"I was hoping to get another ride when the Googlecars are on the roads. This ought to be fun." Kareem said as he and Pete got into their usual seats.

"Where to tonight?" I asked as usual.

"Brentwood. We have a strangulation victim. Rich. Pillar of the community type." Pete laid out the situation.

"Family dispute or did someone break in?" Mimi asked.

"If it was a break in, which episode would guide you tonight?" Pete was giving me a ration of shit.

I had to think for a moment, "Eighty-eight, The Case of the Last Breath."

"Who did it that time?" Kareem asked.

"The butler with the help of the driver, the upstairs server and the family dog."

"Really?" Pete answered in such a way it almost seemed he believed me.

"You'll have to watch to find out." Was my usual response.

I pulled out onto the city streets, working my way in between the steadily moving Googlecars with their passengers ignoring the world around. I knew Kareem and Pete wanted me to drive recklessly or something to see what the Googlecars did in reaction to my unpredictability. But on the city streets the drone of the cars moving hemmed me in so there was really nothing I could do to send the autonomous cars scrambling out of my way. I planned to come back on the 405, where I might be able to actually give them the ride they hoped for.

We drove on over to Brentwood, with more bantering about previous episodes and the few clues they had about the rich victim from Brentwood. As we pulled into the drive Mimi asked, "UCLA professor?"

"You know this address?" Kareem asked.

"No, but the banner in the upstairs window's a give-away." Mimi replied.

"Could be a kid." Pete suggested.

"What and display school spirit? Come on officer. A student would get arrested for that." Mimi was deadpan in her reply.

As usual, Walt climbed out the back first so he could film us getting out at the scene. We went to the door and found it open. Investigators were already combing the scene for clues. "I bet they're glad to be back on the scene, doing the real work of any investigation." I noted to Kareem who just nodded in reply.

Kareem went over to talk with the investigator in charge, Pete disappeared to walk around the property. Mimi and I headed upstairs to the bedroom where the body had been found. There she was, still in bed, naked and dead. She looked to be fifty-ish, black raven colored hair and still wearing her makeup. I looked closer at the pillow under her head. No makeup on the pillow. Mimi came over and looked over my shoulder as Walt filmed us. "What?"

"Do you see anything strange?"

Mimi looked more closely, wrinkled her nose and replied, "Her cologne is not my type."

Since she mentioned it, I wrinkled my nose as well, almost involuntarily. A stronger sniff and I knew why. I lifted the covers to reveal she had soiled herself, and not just a little. She'd been dead long enough that her sphincters had relaxed and let everything flow out.

Mimi covered her nose and looked away.

I stepped back to be beside her. "She wasn't killed here."

"Why do you think so?"

"The pillow. She didn't put up a fight here. If she had her makeup would have rubbed off on the pillow. My guess is she was strangled from behind, maybe here in the room, but she was laid out on the bed afterwards."

"And the semen? Mimi asked, referring to the report she had recently had intercourse. "You think that might have been afterwards?"

"Entirely possible." I responded, not really comfortable with the scene or the implications.

"You are talking about one sick bastard." Mimi replied.

I looked around the room. "Samantha." I was using her series name since we were filming this for the next broadcast. "Who is this set up to implicate?"

Mimi thought for a moment, "No visible forced entry, nothing missing, set up to look like consensual sex. That would mean either the jealous husband or her lover."

"Maybe that's what's bothering me. I sense a woman was involved here somewhere. Maybe it's the makeup. The fact someone was careful not to smudge it. A violent man wouldn't think twice about it. To kill her like this, a man would have had to be violent. To strangle her, particularly with her looking at him while he did it. And the covers. Pulled up like she'd been taking a nap. If a guy had been in bed with her, strangled her with her struggling, it wouldn't be neatly tucked in like that."

"Unless the strangler did her somewhere else and brought her here as you suggest."

I looked around the room more carefully than before, and closer at the Persian rug on the floor covering dark hand scraped hardwood. And then I saw what I was looking for. A clod of damp mud that had fallen from the sole of a hiking boot tread. I bent down and picked it up with my handkerchief. "Where are her clothes?"

Mimi found them laid across a chair at the foot of the bed.

"That's wrong." I said as I slipped on plastic gloves and bent down to pick up her shoe. An expensive black leather pump. A trace of mud in the etched name across the sole. "If they came here to make love her clothes would have been there." I pointed to a dresser next to the bed where she would have slipped under the covers.

Kareem came in, glanced around and approached Mimi and myself. "Find anything?"

I looked around once more to be sure of my hypothesis and nodded. "See if you can find the gardener. I suspect he lives in the apartment over the garage."

Kareem frowned. "The gardener? You want me to find the family dog while I'm at it?"

"Would help." I responded seriously.

I looked at the woman's clothing, finding traces of mud on her skirt, but not her blouse. By the time I completed my examination of the clothing, Kareem brought in a tall and thin man with a week old gray speckled growth on his face and salt and pepper hair. He was wearing hiking boots. They were muddy as would be expected.

"This is Josh Porter, Mrs. Brigham's gardener. He was where you said I'd find him."

"And the dog?" I asked?

"Pete's finding him."

I pointed to the chair. "Would you take a seat, Mister Porter?" I picked up his left boot and examined the tread. All clotted with mud. I picked up the right and found one tread empty. The piece I found slid in perfectly. "The gardener, in the garden with a hose." I suggested. "A crime of passion. An illicit love affair."

"What about the woman's touch?" Mimi asked.

"I suspect the maid helped him stage it."

"The maid?" Kareem asked, "Don't you think anyone other than domestic help kills rich folks?"

Evidently not buying my theory yet. "This has the marks of a jealous husband."

"Have you seen any signs of kids in this house?" I asked.

Kareem shook his head.

"Neither have I." I scanned the room once more to be sure. "My guess is if you read the will they have no blood heirs so they gave their estate to their faithful servants. If the husband fries, the gardener and the maid get everything."

"But you said a crime of passion, an illicit love affair." Kareem protested.

"It was a crime of passion. The gardener and the maid have been getting it on for a while. If you check his apartment you'll probably find her clothes there as well. They wanted to live in the big house rather than always be relegated to the garage. They lived in fear their relationship would be discovered and one or both might be discharged. They needed to move quickly. So they hatched a plan to do in the wife while the husband was out for his morning run. Only the wife came outside early with the dog, something she seldom did."

Pete brought in the family cocker spaniel. "You wanted the family dog?"

I looked at the dog's mouth, measuring the separation of the incisor teeth with my knuckle. I turned to the gardener and found bite marks in his right pant leg. I measured the distance of the holes and they matched the dog's mouth. Kareem looked down at me, "Any questions?" I asked.

"The gardener, in the garden with a hose. Even the dog confirms it." Kareem shook his head.

Chapter Seventy-Two

I got a message Silmara wanted to have a conference call the next morning at the usual time. Mimi woke and showered in time to actually look presentable, something she hadn't done for the last several calls when she was slowly starving to death. The call came in and the rest of the team showed up in their little windows.

"What's the occasion?" I asked.

"Final status." Silmara responded

"I thought you'd been relieved." Mimi was unsure of Silmara's intentions.

"As you know, I was relieved of my responsibility. However, thanks to all of you, my superiors did not have time to find a suitable replacement before Bomani and Dyllan brought the Googlecars back up. That made them hesitate just long enough for Desmond and Mimi to bring in Hugh Aguirre and for Bomani to shut down the Hamartia network."

"What happened there?" I wondered aloud. "Why were they unable to create the chaos they expected to?"

"We have friends who know how to do strange and wonderful things." Bomani began. "Following the lead of the Hamartia, we released a virus into the website that erased the code and shut it down completely."

"Wouldn't they have a backup communications channel outside the website?" Mimi asked.

"If you remember, because Kalindi was discovered on their primary communications channel, they shifted to their backup, which was still on the same infrastructure." Dyllan filled in that piece of information, and at the same time complimented Kalindi for doing what everyone thought was a disastrous thing at the time.

"But I would have thought the thirty or so affiliates would have some other means of launching their attack." I added.

"It appears to me, "Dyllan continued, "That Hugh Aguirre didn't trust his affiliates. While we will never know for sure, since we erased the whole site, I think all code needed to shut down society was embedded in password secured sections of the website. Each affiliate had codes to launch their particular elements, like a submarine captain on a missile carrying nuclear submarine. Hugh Aguirre controlled everything. He didn't want someone making a preemptory strike. He wanted the whole thing to come down at once. No going back. No ability to absorb one blow, figure out how to defend against it and make the larger attack meaningless."

"You're making some heavy duty assumptions there, Dyllan." I responded.

"I am. But having spent so much time on the website Aguirre created, I think I have a good grasp of the man's mindset."

"Since you have such a good insight to Aguirre's soul, why'd he want to bring down society?" Mimi inquired of Dyllan, apparently not sure she got the real reasons from Aguirre in his rant on the way down from his mountain.

"My guess?" Dyllan began. "Hugh Aguirre accomplished everything he could in Hollywood. He was done. No one was calling anymore. But having been center stage for so many years he could not sit on the sidelines and watch others do what he was so good at. And then he met Jonas. Suddenly he was presented with an opportunity to leave a much larger mark on mankind. And like any good director all the pieces needed to pull it off presented themselves to him when the time was right."

"Aguirre not alone." Xian reminded us he was on the line as well. "Deng and Thyagaraj egos not checked. Suggest impossible ... possible."

"What happened to them?" Bomani asked.

"Arrested as accomplices." Mimi responded.

"Investigators are combing their mountain homes." Kalindi added. "They have found very interesting details of the entire operation. Seems Aguirre was not completely trusted by his co-conspirators. Each had a similar communications center in their homes. Some evidence indicates they rotated homes for meetings to make their plans. They wanted to ensure there was no trail in the systems that would incriminate them if the plot was discovered or failed."

"But there was other evidence found?" Mimi asked.

"Yes. Both directors had files on their computers, notes of meetings and plans. Enough to indict them both."

"Then this is our last call." I noted for everyone. "The conspirators are in custody, the transport system is back up and operating, and what of the Hamartia?"

"Those who chose to stay have been taken into custody for questioning. We think the leaders all fled when the system went down. Those we arrested were probably the least involved in the larger plot. If they can satisfy us that is the case, they will be released." Silmara summarized for us.

"So until the next time." I raised my cup of coffee to them all.

"Next time will be." Xian assured us.

Chapter Seventy-Three

Around noon, Alistair arrived at my trailer. He came in without knocking, which was his way. I'd given up suggesting I might be in the middle of something embarrassing. I guess with Mimi's attitude towards me he saw little chance of something embarrassing going on in my trailer.

"Ola." He greeted me. Mimi was changing clothes in the bedroom.

"Como esta?" I replied.

"When you hear what Regina has in mind you'll understand my mood." Alistair sounded weary. Made me think Regina was playing hardball, or had simply given up hope of keeping us since we'd become too big for her cheapskate theory on talent management.

"Mimi will be right out. You want to do this here or are you hungry?"

Alistair smiled for the first time that day, "When have I ever not been hungry?"

Apparently having overheard the conversation, Mimi came out of the bedroom, wearing a clingy white dress I'd never seen before. She was still very thin, but looked great now that the glow I so loved had returned. I couldn't take my eyes off her as she crossed the room and kissed Alistair on the cheek. "The Ivy?" She asked.

I drove us to the restaurant in the Tesla. Even though the Googlecars were operating and more convenient, there was something about the Tesla I wasn't about to give up. Maybe I'd become Uncle Jim, flaunting the law prohibiting driving your own car. I thought the LAPD wouldn't stop me since they'd gained so much positive publicity from our show. But then again I could be wrong.

All heads at the Ivy turned to look at us as we pulled to the curb in front. As we got out of the car, people started applauding and then they stood up welcoming us. I nodded and waived to everyone, shook a few hands of people I knew and we soon disappeared into the back and our usual table.

As we took our seats I noted that Alison Andress was with Johnny Hollywood in the other room. She was deeply engaged in her discussion and evidently didn't see us come in. The waiter knew what we always had for lunch. He filled the water glasses and disappeared. So we went right to the discussion while our meal was being prepared.

"How bad is it?" I asked.

"Five." Alistair responded.

"Five million. That's what I made last season when they were planning to get rid of me." I noted, discouraged. I'd hoped that they would come up to something that would at least indicate they wanted to keep me, even if it was below market. But this contract wouldn't be market for the viewership we had now.

Mimi shook her head. "What's our alternative?"

Alistair took a sip of water and cleared his throat. Every time he did that it had always cost me a million dollars in the past. He leaned across the table so others would have a more difficult time hearing. "Not five million."

I was confused. "Then what are you talking about?"

"Five years. They want to give you a five year contract."

"What compensation level?" I asked suspiciously.

"Well, that's the hard part. You see they want to void the last year of Mimi's contract and give her a five year contract as well, starting next season."

"Big of them." Mimi wasn't impressed either.

Alistair was playing with us and I wasn't happy about it. "The number, Alistair."

"It's the same old story. They want to give you more than Mimi and I told them that wasn't acceptable. You're co-stars of this series and Mimi needs equal compensation. I really hit Regina as a woman studio head she had to be a leader in equal pay. That was a long conversation, let me assure you."

"You were negotiating with Regina?" I asked since she never came out of the fox hole until everything was done and she just had to bless it.

"I insisted and they gave in on that one point. About the only point I won, incidentally."

I shook my head, "You're really making it sound like there's no reason for us to listen to the rest of the offer, so why don't you just give us our alternatives and we'll tell you which one sounds more appealing?

Alistair frowned and sat back. "If that's what you both want, I can do that."

"Why do I hear this big but?" Mimi went after him also getting tired of the discussion.

"Regina signed off on fifty each."

"Fifty million?" Mimi asked him to confirm.

Alistair nodded.

"Per year for five years." I wanted to clarify.

Alistair nodded.

"Yeah, right. What are the other studios offering?" Mimi didn't believe him.

"You know I tried to get the other studios to commit to a number, but none would until Regina put a number on the table for you."

"So, you going to shop the deal for us now?" Mimi was tired of the back and forth.

"I have."

"And?" I asked to keep Mimi from walking out on Alistair.

"No one will match it. Next best deal was sixty for you thirty for Mimi and only three years."

Disgusted, Mimi pointed to the lady's room and excused herself.

"Champaign I think is in order. The richest contract ever for a weekly series." Alistair gloated.

"This mean you're going to join your partners with an autonomous Lamborghini and a trophy wife?" I couldn't help myself.

"My wife has me by the testicles. I make any attempt to replace her she gets everything. So all major purchases will be her idea." Alistair made me laugh.

The waiter appeared and opened the Champaign as Mimi returned to join us.

"To the contract of your dreams." Alistair proposed the toast. "So what about you two? You going to get back together?"

I glanced at Mimi who looked down.

"Negotiate an escape clause after every season." I didn't think I could do five with Mimi like this.

Pete and Kareem entered the Ivy looking for us.

"Hey guys. What's up?" I asked

Kareem handed me a summons.

"What's this?" I asked as I opened the document.

"We're seizing your car. It's illegal." Kareem responded.

"Come on, Guys. That's my living. Without that car my series will fold."

Kareem looked around to see who was listening, and since the Ivy is a tiny restaurant that was just about everyone. "Look, I'm sure we can work a deal. You may have to ride with us rather than the other way around. Maybe we can even let you drive when you're filming. I don't think the Chief will have a lot of heartburn over that. But a judge called the Chief and said he wouldn't tolerate us letting you just flaunt the law like you are. So we have to do something."

"Who's the judge? I'll talk with him." Alistair to the rescue.

"Masciarelli. You know the judge who's running for US Senate?" Pete filled in the blanks. I'd become a pawn in an election. That was absolutely the last thing I wanted. And the Chief and the Mayor weren't going to alienate someone who might be the next US Senator.

"Can we get the Mayor and the Chief together for a conversation and work this out?"

"I'm sure of it." Kareem wanted me to know he was on my side. "And you know what? I'll even call the Googlecar for you to take you home. You can charge the department for your transportation home. Gesture of good will."

I felt empty. Not as bad as the morning I'd come home and Mimi was gone, but empty nonetheless.

Chapter Seventy-Four

The Googlecar dropped Alistair at his house first and then took Mimi and me to the studio. After dropping Alistair, Mimi wanted to talk about the contract offer. "What Alistair didn't say was whether their plan is to keep the reality format or return to scripted episodes." She began. "If we're doing reality that takes a lot more from us to ensure a good story."

"We can ask for producer credits." I suggested.

"Writer credits too." Mimi mused. "And I want a piece of the residuals. If this is going to be my whole life for the next five years I need some back end incentive."

I was surprised Mimi apparently wasn't overwhelmed by the offer Regina made. One year was double what I'd made in my whole career. It was probably three times what she'd made. And yet that wasn't enough. I tried to understand what was driving her unhappiness. "I think we have a little time before we have to respond. Why don't you let it sit for a bit? Sleep on it. See how it feels in the morning?"

She wouldn't look at me, instead she looked out at the traffic and passing familiar buildings on our way to the studio. We'd been passing this way for nearly a decade on our way to work. I'd long ago stopped looking at the buildings. It was all just background. Familiar sights I recognized but took no notice of, even when things changed. It was a metaphor for my life. Everything had become just background, as I rushed through the day. I never slowed down to look at the familiar sights as I was now that Mimi wouldn't engage me. And somehow, what was probably most important to me, having someone I loved and who loved me too, had passed me by and was now out of reach, even though she sat right next to me.

The Googlecar dropped us at the entrance to the studio and went on to pick up the next passenger. Mimi walked slowly so I adjusted my usual more rapid pace to walk alongside her.

"Why did you tell Alistair to negotiate an out clause at the end of each season?" Now I knew what was bothering her. Why she wanted residuals. Between my yearly out clause and the seizure of the Tesla, Mimi wasn't sure there'd be more than one year to the contract. Still, fifty million would carry her a long way.

"This past year has been hard for me." I started. "I'm not sure I'm ready for even one more, let alone five where I see you every day but we aren't together."

"I know I'm not." Mimi responded firmly. I was surprised by her being even more adamant about not being ready for another five years. I heard contradictory things and wasn't sure what she was trying to tell me.

The mystery remained as we reached the door to my trailer and I could hear voices inside. Who was in my trailer? I opened the door and familiar faces I'd seen on the monitor, but never in person turned to smile at me and Mimi.

"Hello Silmara. I just saw you. Apparently you weren't in Rio."

"No, I was at LAX waiting for Bomani's flight from Cairo."

I was confused. Bomani had been on the call. Bomani stepped forward, "I sent a tape she could play during the call. I was on, but from the flight. We were delayed out of New York."

As I stepped into the trailer, the familiar faces were translated into three dimensional people, shorter or taller than I'd imagined, heavier or skinnier than I'd pictured in my mind's eye, except for Xian, who I had

420

met while on location in China. I shook hands and hugged each and every one.

"Why have you all come to LA?" I asked still overwhelmed they were all here together at last.

"Your President is making a special award to you and Mimi tonight at 7pm. We are your escorts as we are also receiving recognition for our combined efforts at the United Nations tomorrow."

"I don't know about all of you, but I'm here to meet Kalindi in person." Dyllan added, holding hands with Kalindi, who was beaming at his side.

"Where will you live?" Mimi asked the obvious question.

"We rented an apartment in Culver City sight unseen. Saw Culver City in your episodes and it appeals to both of us. So we're going to start there and see where life takes us." Kalindi responded for both of them.

"What about you two?" Dyllan asked, knowing our history.

"Live happily ever after." Xian answered for us.

"I wish that were my fate, but no." I responded. "The studio has made a generous offer to extend our show. We each have to make our individual decisions so we'll see."

Mimi took my arm and came up next to me. "The best is yet to come. Stay tuned."

I looked at her unsure of what she was saying.

"Alison and I had a little chat in the ladies room at the Ivy. She said you took her to the hospital and stayed with her through her appendectomy. You only came home when her parents arrived the next morning."

"Does the truth change anything?" I asked, still unsure of where I stood with her and what she wanted.

"It changes everything." She kissed me, and then we kissed each other like we used to.

About the Author

dhtreichler toured the global garden spots as a defense contractor executive for fifteen years. His assignments covered intelligence, training and battlefield systems integrating state of the art technology to keep Americans safe. During this time he authored seven novels exploring the role of increasingly sophisticated technology in transforming our lives and how men and women establish relationships in a mediated world.

Keep up with all of dhtreichler's latest work and essays at www.dhtreichler.com and www.GlobalVinoSnob.com

Also by dhtreichler

Hope

The Great American Cat Novel

My Life as a Frog (Novella)

Emergence

Barely Human

The Ghost in the Machine: a novel

Life After

Lucifer

The End Game

I Believe in You

Succession

Rik's

The Illustrated Bearmas Reader – Ralph's Ordeals

The First Bearmas

www.ingramcontent.com/pod-product-compliance
Lightning Source LLC
LaVergne TN
LVHW091212080426
835509LV00009B/954